Waterloo and the Campaign of 1815

Waterloo and the Campaign of 1815
Quatre Bras, Ligny, Waterloo, Wavre and the Allied Invasion of France

George Robert Gleig

*Waterloo and the
Campaign of 1815
Quatre Bras, Ligny, Waterloo, Wavre
and the Allied Invasion of France
by George Robert Gleig*

First published under the titles
Story of the Battle of Waterloo

Leonaur is an imprint
of Oakpast Ltd

Copyright in this form © 2009 Oakpast Ltd

ISBN: 978-1-84677-772-1 (hardcover)
ISBN: 978-1-84677-771-4 (softcover)

http://www.leonaur.com

Publisher's Notes

In the interests of authenticity, the spellings, grammar and place names used have been retained from the original editions.

The opinions of the authors represent a view of events in which he was a participant related from his own perspective, as such the text is relevant as an historical document.

The views expressed in this book are not necessarily those of the publisher.

Contents

Preface	7
State of Europe consequent on the Peace of Paris	9
Escape of Napoleon from Elba	17
Arrival of Napoleon in Paris, and its immediate Consequences	28
Distribution of the hostile Armies early in June	37
State of Brussels and the Netherlands in the early Summer of 1815	49
Continued Preparations on both sides	56
Rumours of coming Events—Commencement of Hostilities	64
Concentration of the English and Prussian Armies at Quatre Bras and Ligny	77
Battle of Quatre Bras	86
Battle of Quatre Bras—continued	97
Battle of Ligny	104
Battle of Ligny—continued	117
The Night after the Battle	130
Movement on Mont St. Jean	139
State of Feeling where the War was not	147
Movements of the French on the 17th of June	156
Operations of Retreat, and Pursuit to Wavre	165

The Position of Waterloo	174
French Position	186
Last preparations—First Shots	194
Attack and Defence of Hougoumont	202
Advance of the French Centre and Left—Flight of Bylandt's Belgian Brigade	211
Attack and Defence of the British Left Centre	224
Cavalry Operations	234
Second Attack on Hougomont—Advance of the French Cavalry	242
Renewed Attack of Cavalry	252
Continuance of the Battle—Capture of La Haye Sainte	261
Advance of the Prussians—Attack from La Haye-Sainte	269
Attack of the Imperial Guard	278
Close of the Battle—Bivouac of the British Army	287
State of Feeling and Condition of things in the Rear	298
Battle of Wavre	307
Renewal of the Battle—Retreat of Grouchy	315
Advance of the English Army	323
Entrance into France—Abdication of Napoleon	332
Advance upon Paris	345
Occupation of Paris	356

Preface

I shall be very glad if the following attempt to describe the great military operations of 1815, and to connect them in some sort with the state of public and private feeling as it then operated both in this country and at the seat of war, shall prove acceptable to the class of readers for whom it is intended.

My object has not been to enter into controversy with anyone. I believe that I have read most of the published accounts of the Waterloo Campaign which have appeared both here and on the Continent, and I know that I have always had before me, while writing, the twelve volumes of Colonel Gurwood's invaluable work. If, therefore, my views shall in some respects differ from those which others have taken, I am not without hope that they will prove, upon investigation, to be at least as accurate.

I have not applied to many of the minor actors in the great game for information respecting its details. Captain Siborne, in his valuable work, has saved all who may be curious in these matters, a great deal of trouble; and if I shall seem somewhat to have overlooked the advantages which he offers to me, I trust that he will not on that account consider that I think lightly of what he has done. His *History* will always stand upon its own merits; and his plans are invaluable.

But I confess that my recollections of war lead me somewhat to undervalue—perhaps in a measure to distrust—the stories told in perfect good faith by parties who happen to be the heroes of them. Modern battles are not won by feats of individual heroism; indeed, many gallant deeds achieved embarrass more than they facilitate the accomplishment of the general's plans. I have, therefore, endeavoured as much as possible to avoid entering into minute narrations of these things—except where simple facts were to be stated; and I hope that this course will prove satisfactory to my readers.

Finally, I have to throw myself on the indulgence of the public on account of errors, which, though I have not been able to detect them, may abound in my narrative; of whatever nature these be, they are certainly not wilful; for I have left no means that were accessible to me unexplored, in order to guard against them. But a work would not be human which was free from such; and mine must take its chance.

CHAPTER 1

State of Europe consequent on the Peace of Paris

On the 4th of April, 1814, Napoleon Bonaparte descended from the throne of France. The deed of abdication—at first personal, though subsequently so altered as to include the family of the fallen Emperor—was signed at Fontainebleau; whereupon the victor in a hundred fights, bidding farewell to the wreck of his guards, proceeded to establish himself in the island of Elba, which had been assigned to him in the twofold capacity of a principality and a prison. Thus—after much suffering, and long years of alternate triumph and defeat—the purposes of the revolution of 1789 seemed to be accomplished. France, having passed through the various stages of anarchy, republicanism, the Consulate, and the Empire, sought refuge from dismemberment in submission to her ancient rulers, while her people, guarding their personal liberties by wise enactments against the encroachments of kingly power, were received once more—or seemed to be—with hearty good will into the bosom of the great European family.

Throughout the whole course of the war of liberation, the conduct of the Allied Sovereigns had been magnanimous in the extreme; their manner of conducting the negotiations which led to the peace of 1814 well sustained their character for moderation. Territorial France was indeed reduced within the limits which circumscribed her in 1792; but from everything like interference with the management of her internal affairs the Allies religiously abstained. Louis XVIII. was permitted to enter with his subjects into whatever political compact might seem expedient to both parties.

The constitution which he established was neither dictated by foreign influence nor sustained by foreign intrigue. Of the charter by which it was confirmed, he was himself the author. His court, his army, the municipal institutions of the country—the affairs of the church—the administration of the laws—were all left to his own adjustment; because from the spirit of the proclamation which they issued when first entering France the invaders refused to be diverted. They had proclaimed to the world, by the document in question, that their war was not with France, but with Napoleon; and now that success had enabled them to set that individual aside, there existed no further grounds of hostility towards any one.

However, while care was taken to abstain from all appearance of dictation in regard to the form of government which the French people might prefer, the public choice was no sooner made known than the Allied Sovereigns acquiesced in it; and the better to demonstrate their confidence in the good faith of the nation, they entered into negotiations for the surrender of the fortresses, and made arrangements for returning as soon as possible to their respective countries.

But though an excellent spirit swayed them in their dealings with France, there were not wanting, among the Allies themselves, many and urgent causes of disunion. The result of twenty years of war was to leave, in 1814, not one European nation precisely the same, in regard either to its political influence or its territorial importance that it had been in 1792. Austria and Prussia had both suffered dismemberment, and had gathered themselves up again more than once. Belgium and Holland, after being absorbed in the French empire, now stood apart, the former without any ostensible head at all. The States of the Confederation of the Rhine might be freed from the tyranny of their protector, but they neither knew themselves, nor were others prepared to tell them, into what new arrangement they should enter.

Italy was in confusion; and the relations of Russia towards her neighbours on every side were the reverse of satisfactory. Hence, though they saw the propriety of evacuating without delay, the territories of a people whom they desired to conciliate, the crowned heads made no haste to reduce their armies to a peace establishment, but kept them up till the result of the conferences should become known, at which it was proposed to settle, in an amicable manner, the balance of power in Europe.

In obedience to the dictates of this generous policy, the several posts which had been occupied in and around Paris were, on the 2nd of June, given over by the Allied troops to the National Guard. By-and-by the Emperors of Austria and Russia, with the King of Prussia, took their departure; and Louis XVIII. proceeded to assemble the states of his kingdom, and to make a public declaration of the principles upon which France was henceforth to be governed.

The part which the restored monarch was thus suddenly called upon to play proved to be one of extraordinary difficulty. Two extreme factions, of very unequal strength, divided, at this time, public opinion between them. On the one hand were the Republicans, numerous, resolute, and free of speech, who demanded the constitution of 1791, and would be satisfied with nothing less—on the other the Absolutists, composed chiefly of *émigrés* and the ancient *noblesse* of the south, clamoured for a return to ancient Usages.

The Count d'Artois, and to a certain extent Talleyrand himself, stood forward as the heads of this latter party; the former, to the surprise of the rest of Europe, found an able supporter in the Emperor Alexander of Russia. But the King refused to put himself into the hands of either. When the Republicans made a tender of the throne on the conditions which to themselves appeared expedient, Louis XVIII. declined to entertain their proposal. He told them that the throne was his by the same right which had secured it to his ancestors; and that whatever concessions he might be disposed to make to the popular will, he should make of his own accord as an act of grace, and not in the terms of a bargain.

When the Absolutists urged him to govern without the aid of a parliament, he refused to make so rash an experiment. The result was the Charter of the 4th June, 1814, of which, though, it contained in abundance the elements of a rational freedom, both the manner of giving, and the spirit of the gift itself, were peculiarly unsuited to the genius of the French people. As a necessary consequence the work, however well designed, failed to effect its purpose; and events were precipitated of which the more immediate causes may be stated in few words.

It was impossible for the King of France, circumstanced as he was, to satisfy any section of any one of the parties into which the nation was divided. He could not, either, in policy or in justice, yield to the demands of the Royalists; and his refusal to throw the country in a flame by wresting their estates from existing holders, lost for him, in a great measure, the confidence of that somewhat unreasonable body. In like manner the bulk of the church's property was gone beyond the reach of recovery; and his endeavour to compensate for the loss of their possessions, by heaping honours upon the clergy of the Church of Rome, and upon them alone, while it served but in part to conciliate the priesthood, gave great umbrage to the rest of his subjects.

France was not, in the beginning of the present century any more than at the close of the last, remarkable for her attachment to the religious principle, and the revival in her streets and churches of the pomp and parade of the Roman Catholic worship especially offended her. A similar effect was produced by the issuing of an ordinance which forbade the prosecution of men's ordinary callings on the Lord's day. This arrangement, however just, because founded on a divine command, was treated by the French people as a grievance, and its supposed authors were covered with alternate ridicule and abuse. And when in addition to this an order came out, that the troops should march to church and be present at divine service, public indignation burst forth with a cry which was quite appalling.

It was at this unhappy moment that the King and his advisers set about what they considered to be a reform of the military institutions of the country. The army was greatly reduced in numbers; and of the men still nominally retained on the muster-rolls of regiments, not fewer than one hundred thousand were sent home on furlough. In the room of the Imperial Guard—which was wholly disbanded—came a body of Swiss, and a *garde-du-corps*, dressed in red, and recruited from La Vendée. The tricolour-flag likewise, under which so much glory mixed with many reverses had been acquired, made way for the ancient standard of the Bourbons; and the very numbers of the regiments as well as the titles of officers of rank were changed. French soldiers heard no more of their generals of division and of brigade, but found themselves under the orders of lieutenant-generals and *maréchals-du camp*.

All these arrangements were exceedingly unwise; and their folly stood the more prominently forward, that while in themselves they did not deserve a moment's consideration, the nation, and especially the army, regarded them as premeditated insults, especially when it was observed that they all bore and were intended to bear upon the events of by-gone times. For example, the King dated the first of his ordinances, the decree which granted the Charter, and officially settled the government, in the nineteenth year of his reign—thus ostentatiously treating the entire space of the Republic and the Empire as a blank. In the same spirit, while he continued in their situations almost all the civil functionaries that served under the Empire, he never spoke of the Empire itself except as the Usurpation.

As to the military classes, his jealousy of them was shown by the requirement that no officer reduced to half-pay should reside in Paris, unless he could show that his natural home was there. And the numbers reduced to half-pay were very great. It would have been strange had the parties thus dealt with failed to take offence; and it was peculiarly unfortunate for the government that the manners of the court—especially of the female portion of it—went far to increase this feeling. Finally, when the bones of certain Chouan and Vendean chiefs were exhumed at the public expense, that they might be buried with great honour in consecrated ground; when a solemn funeral service was performed for the soul of Marie Antoinette in the cathedral of Notre Dame; and a monument was erected on the shores of Quiberon Bay to the Royalists who fell there fighting against France; a cry arose that time was about to be rolled back, and that not only the family but the prejudices of the ancient regime were all to be forced upon France.

In such a state of things, and amid the feelings of discontent which were produced by it, no sentiment of loyalty to the throne, or respect for the constitution, could strike root. Indeed, the constitution itself operated as little else than a perpetual eyesore to the great body of the people. By fixing the money-qualification at a rate unnecessarily high, the King gave the right of vote to not more than 800,000 persons; while his establishment of a body of hereditary legislators, in a country which could not understand their value, weakened instead of giving strength to the principle which it was meant to sustain.

The truth is, that France, unripe in 1814 for self-government at all, was especially averse to institutions which, however excellent in themselves, had been borrowed, or were supposed to be, from England. Indeed France, though weary of war, was still mad upon the subject of military glory. People met in coffeehouses, or stood at the corners of streets, to discuss past events and speculate on the future, and such speculations gradually took a tone which was not very favourable to the maintenance of quiet. This was especially the case when a host of disbanded soldiers began to pass to and fro among them, and declaim about tarnished honour.

In particular, the loss of Flanders and the abandonment of the Rhenish frontier furnished fruitful topics of complaint; while recent disasters were all referred to the treachery of individuals, not to the superior valour of the invaders, or the inability of France, to avert them. It was reiterated, moreover, that the Bourbons had been forced upon a reluctant nation by foreign bayonets, and that the glory and the grandeur of Franco were the price at which a hateful family had purchased back the privilege of occupying a throne which was not sustained by the love of the people. Accordingly, the summer of 1814 was yet young when plots and conspiracies began to be concocted, which grew continually more formidable, and spread their ramifications before the beginning of winter into circles which enjoyed, or seemed to enjoy, the confidence of the prince whom they sought opportunity to betray.

Meanwhile Napoleon, from his island principality, watched the progress of opinion in France with a keen eye. As no restriction seems to have been imposed on his correspondence, he received daily tidings of the proceedings of his friends, and the blunders of his enemies; and began, ere long, to make arrangements for a design of which posterity must forever be at loss whether to admire the most, its exceeding boldness or the marvellous success which attended it. Nor will other causes of wonder be wanting, in the entire absence of suspicion from those whom duty and interest alike ought to, have stirred to exceeding watchfulness.

How a secret which appears to have been confided to many hundred persons in all parts of the world should have escaped the vigilance of the French police, it is very difficult to conceive. And our astonishment is increased when we remember that the government of France, by the exercise of an unwise economy, had afforded to the exile plausible grounds on which to complain of a breach in the treaty that bound him to a state of quietude. Nevertheless, it is certain, that while Napoleon's correspondence with Paris grew continually more voluminous, and a recurrence to the glories of the Empire began to enter largely into men's topics of daily conversation; while songs were sung in the streets, of which it was difficult to mistake the meaning; and at the house of the ex-Emperor's sister *soirees* were held, of the right of admission to which a violet worn in the dress constituted the symbol, neither the King nor his ministers entertained, or seemed to entertain, the slightest apprehension that a counter-revolution was meditated. And the sense of security which they experienced being imparted, as was natural, to the Allies, all things went on throughout Europe as if the peace of Paris were to be eternal. But the passage of a few months sufficed to dissipate the illusion.

Chapter 2

Escape of Napoleon from Elba

The Congress of Vienna, which ought to have assembled in July, 1814, did not meet till the month of September. It gave little promise from the outset of much unanimity of sentiment; for on two subjects, preliminary to all others, the representatives of the Great Powers stood apart. First, the question of relative rank was mooted; and so uniform is human nature in all circles, and so full of weaknesses under every variety of circumstances, that about an arrangement of mere etiquette the statesmen to whose care the welfare of Europe was committed had well nigh separated in anger. Happily, the Emperor Alexander took of this knotty point a more rational view than his colleagues. He proposed that the ministers of the various countries should have precedence in the alphabetical order of the courts which they represented, and did not refuse to gratify the pride of Austria and the vanity of France, by placing the Russian signature under both of them on the list.

This obstacle being removed another presented itself, which threatened for a while far more serious consequences, and which was not surmounted at last without leaving the seeds of after disunion behind. The Northern Powers, as they were called, contended, that forasmuch as Europe had been delivered through their exertions and the strenuous co-operation of England and of Austria, in them, conjointly with Austria and England, was vested the right to dispose of the territories won from France, without any reference to France herself or to other powers of Europe.

Perhaps there might be strict justice in this demand, but there was neither generosity nor political wisdom; and it was instantly protested against by the representative of France. Lord Castlereagh did not hesitate to view the subject in the same light with Talleyrand, and by-and-by Prince Metternich professed a similar opinion; whereupon a protracted and somewhat warm correspondence ensued, which ended, however, in the abandonment of the claim. The result was that the right of France and of Spain to vote upon the question was recognized equally with those of Austria, England, Prussia, and Russia; and Portugal, Sweden, and the Pope himself being subsequently added. the council of partition, so to speak, became full.

No great difficulty was experienced in settling the affairs of the Netherlands, or in doing justice, as it was called, to Hanover, Sweden, Lombardy, and Savoy. A junction of Belgium with the Seven United Provinces made up the kingdom of the Netherlands, of which the crown was bestowed upon Frederick William of Holland; while Hanover was compensated on one side for the territory which she gave to Prussia on another; and Sweden yielded to Denmark a portion of her soil, on condition that Norway should be permanently annexed to her. We have nothing to do, in the present narrative, with the consequences of this latter paction. Sweden might be satisfied with it, but Norway was not and she offered as much resistance as her weakness would permit, though without avail.

In like manner Austria took possession of the plains of Lombardy, amid the loud but vain murmurs of the inhabitants; and the ancient Republic of Genoa, after protesting against the wrong, became an integral portion of the kingdom of Savoy. Not so easily dealt with were the claims of Prussia and Russia. The former, referring to some arrangements in 1813, to which Prussia and Austria were parties, insisted upon extending her sway over the whole of Saxony. The King of Saxony, it was said, by adhering to the French alliance, and putting himself out of the pale of German society, had forfeited all right to be dealt with as a sovereign prince, and Prussia, as the state which had suffered most in the cause of public liberty, was entitled to annex his kingdom to her own. In like manner Russia, having expelled the French from Poland, insisted that the sovereignty of the whole country had devolved upon her, and refused to relinquish a single province of it.

Now, though it might be true that the King of Saxony delayed too long in joining the Northern Alliance, it was equally certain that the passing over of his troops during the battle of Leipsic had operated an important diversion in their favour; and his personal character being much and deservedly respected, there was a strong reluctance everywhere, except with Russia and Prussia, to crush him. Besides, Austria had no desire to find herself closed in, upon the right and left, with two such empires as Russia and Prussia, after these changes, would become. She therefore refused to sanction the proposed arrangements, and found both in France and England a ready concurrence with her views; on the other hand, Russia and Prussia remained obstinate.

The former halted her armies in Poland, and spoke of leading a portion of them into Moravia if necessary; the latter, so far from reducing, increased the numbers of her regulars, and declined to send her *Landwehr* to their homes. As a necessary consequence, Austria, England, and France entered into a separate alliance, and agreeing each to keep on foot a force of 150,000 men, made dispositions for quartering them upon lines whence they might be able to move with the greatest facility, to meet and repress the threatened danger.

With whatever secrecy the negotiations for this counter-alliance might have been conducted, knowledge of the truth gradually got abroad, and the tone of the two Northern Powers was lowered. Neither made any secret of the ill humour with which she was affected; indeed, the Emperor of Russia expressed himself in terms which, however justified by the event, had no tendency at the moment to allay the irritation which prevailed on all sides. He spoke, wherever he went, of the unfitness of the elder branch of the Bourbons to reign; and foretold, that ere many years passed, they would be superseded by the house of Orleans.

In the same spirit he took under his special protection the only relic of the Napoleonic crowned heads which had survived the fall of their creator. Murat, King of Naples, whose existence was a continued eyesore to the Emperor of Austria and King of France, he pronounced to be a legitimate member of the Holy Alliance; and though rumours were rife of the evil designs of that personage, and the increase to the strength of his army which daily went on, gave to them a strong show of reason, Alexander refused to sanction any measure which should seem to aim at his over throw.

All this while the situation of Murat himself was as equivocal as it was unsafe. A vain man, and jealous, perhaps naturally so, of his rights, he endeavoured to command from the fears of his neighbours the respect which would have been best secured by conciliating their good will. He recruited his army to an extent out of all proportion to his wants; and caused suspicions of his integrity to be entertained, which in some sort led to their own confirmation. It was rumoured in Vienna, for example, that he was in correspondence with Napoleon, and intended to make himself master of the whole of Italy south of the Po; and the encroachments which he had begun to make upon the Papal States gave to the report every semblance of probability.

Without a moment's hesitation, therefore, Austria proposed to dethrone him, and to remove Napoleon to a more distant place of exile than that to which he had been sent. But Alexander of Russia would not listen to either suggestion. There was no proof of Murat's treachery—his own personal honour was pledged in regard to the undisturbed residence of Napoleon where he was; and thus the march of the force which Austria had equipped for an Italian campaign was suspended; and the exile of Elba continued to mature at his leisure the gigantic project which was well nigh ripe for execution.

Such was the state of feeling at the Congress of Vienna, and such the attitude of mutual distrust assumed by the representatives of the powers there assembled, when an event befell which turned the attention of all into a new channel. On the 7th of March, 1815, during the progress of a grand ball at the house of Prince Metternich, tidings arrived that Napoleon had escaped from Elba.

The consternation excited in the minds of the few to whom this fact was communicated could be equalled only by their astonishment. At first there appeared to be an inclination to question the truth of the report; but when the evidence on which it rested came to be weighed, conviction of its truth entered into every mind, and the effect produced was as wonderful as it was instantaneous. In a moment all the grounds of difference which, up to that hour, seemed to threaten the most serious consequences, were forgotten. Russia withdrew her claim upon the whole of the Grand Duchy of Warsaw, Prussia consented to leave to Saxony a mutilated independence, Austria thought no more of guarding her Moravian frontier, and the Germanic Confederation, as yet but partially organized, drew together like an institution of ancient standing.

There was but one thought, one voice, among the powers thus forced into a renewed alliance. They were again banded together for the defence of Europe—their common enemy was in the field, whom it was their common duty to put down; and, to accomplish this purpose, they agreed with one consent that their best energies should immediately be directed.

For a day, and only for a day, the councils of the Allies were distracted by their ignorance in regard to the point on the Continent to which Napoleon might have betaken himself. At first it was imagined, and not without apparent reason, that his landing would be effected in Naples, where Joachim Murat had for some time past been making preparations for war. In this case Austria felt that on her would devolve the necessity of striking the first blow; and she was both ready and willing to do so. But when the lapse of four-and-twenty hours brought the truth of the ease to light, the necessity of a more cautious, though not less energetic plan of operations, became apparent.

On the 9th it was known that Napoleon had thrown himself on shore near Frejus, in the Gulf of St. Juan; that he had taken the road for Paris through the mountains of Gap; that the garrison of Grenoble, including the regiment of Colonel Labedoyère, had joined him; and that he was marching in triumph on Lyons. All this pointed to a bolder policy than the invasion of Italy. It showed that he had thrown for no less a stake than the sovereignty of France; and the eagerness with which the French troops gathered round his standard foretold that the game was in his favour. Once more, therefore, France—or, at least, her ruler—must be put without the pale of European society; and the Allies lost no time in proclaiming to the world that they were prepared so to deal with the occasion.

At the first meeting which was held for the purpose of formally deliberating on the course which under existing circumstances it might be expedient to pursue, Prince Metternich spoke out in a tone becoming the position of the power which he represented. Napoleon had given out, during his advance upon Grenoble, that his return to France was sanctioned and would be supported by Austria: it was expedient that the world should be undeceived in regard to this matter, and that Austria should at once clear herself from suspicions to which the nature of the family tie that subsisted between the House of Hapsburg and the intruder could not fail of giving some kind of plausibility. Accordingly, on the 12th of March, Prince Metternich proposed to his colleagues a series of resolutions, which they immediately adopted, and of which the publication left no room for doubt in regard to the policy on which they were prepared to act. The resolutions in question stated:

> that Napoleon Bonaparte, in quitting the island of Elba, and disembarking in France at the head of an armed force, had openly rendered himself the disturber of the public peace; that as such he could no longer claim the protection of any treaty or law; that the Powers who had signed the treaty of Paris felt themselves in an especial manner

called upon to declare, in the face of Europe, in what light they viewed that attempt; that they were resolved at all hazards to carry into effect the whole provisions of the treaty of Paris; and were prepared to support the King of France with all their forces, in the event of such assistance being necessary.

These resolutions, which had been previously seen and approved by Talleyrand, were accepted with acclamation by the representatives of the other powers; and a paper appeared the same day imbodying them, to which the signatures of Metternich, Talleyrand, Wellington, Hardenberg, Nesselrode, and Löwenhielm were appended.

Having dispatched this energetic and decisive proclamation to Paris, and directed the messenger who conveyed it to circulate copies at every town and village through which he passed, the members of the Congress proceeded to arrange their plan of operations. It was agreed that the Russian army now in Poland, to the number of 280,000 men, should be held in readiness to march upon the Upper Rhine at a moment's notice; Austria was to raise her army in Italy to 150,000 and with 100,000 more to reinforce the army of Bavaria; Prussia was to move with 150,000 men upon the Lower Rhine; and England, with as many more,—partly native, partly foreign troops in her pay— was to occupy the Netherlands.

All the other Gorman states were in like manner to furnish their contingents, and Spain and Portugal to arm. Thus it was calculated that, within six months at the latest, France, as the occasion required, could be invaded by 600,000 men, who, advancing from different sides, would all be able to unite under the walls of Paris, and at the point of the bayonet win again, as they had done before, peace for Europe.

While the Allies are thus adjusting their differences, and making preparations to meet the coming storm, it may not be amiss if we trace with a rapid hand the progress of the events which rendered such preparations immediately necessary.

When by the treaty of Fontainebleau the island of Elba was

assigned as the future residence of the deposed French Emperor, one minister of the Allied Powers, and only one, protested against it. Lord Castlereagh warned the parties who were consenting to this arrangement that they were laying up for themselves, and for Europe at large, the elements of future disturbance; and it is now well known that the exile scarce touched the shores of his now principality ere he began to provide the means of verifying this prediction.

As if it had been the purpose, likewise, of his too generous foes to tempt him into a second struggle for power, they left him in the command of an ample revenue, and placed at his disposal an armed force, inconsiderable, no doubt, in point of numbers, but quite sufficient, circumstanced as both he and they were, to form a nucleus round which a greater might gather.

No care was taken, moreover, to interrupt, or even to impede, his communications with the Continent. A solitary English brig of war had it in charge to cruise round about the island; but no instructions were given to the commander to stop or examine any vessel which might put into Porto Ferrajo, or to see that Napoleon himself was not on board when it should put to sea again. The strangest delusion, in short, to which statesmen ever gave themselves up, seems to have come like a cloud over the minds of potentates and their ministers in 1814; for if they did not believe, they certainly acted as if they believed, that the most restless spirit which the world had ever seen was become suddenly in love with retirement.

It would be an old story to tell how Napoleon took advantage of the unaccountable fatuity of his late enemies. It would be to repeat what is familiar to every reader of history, were we to say how eagerly his partisans throughout the Continent cooperated with him. In the hearts of the great body of the soldiers of France, as well of those discharged as of such as continued to serve, his image was still embalmed—and care was taken that there should be mixed up with the memories of the past, strong hope in regard to the future. Beranger tuned his harp to good purpose in a cause which he had formerly denounced.

Various soubriquets—the sure tokens of a soldier's love—were bestowed upon the exile. All spoke of "*Père la Violette*" and the "*Petit Caporal*" with the flush of excitement on their cheeks, and whispered one to another that they should see him again at their head. It has already been explained with what apparent industry the powers that were laboured to give force and consistency to these sentiments; and that they did not work in vain, the progress of less than twelve months gave proof.

All this while Murat, dissatisfied both with his position and prospects, maintained through trusty agents frequent and confidential intercourse with the exile. The latter does not appear to have built much upon the exertions of his ancient subaltern; for he knew the worth of the man, and dealt with him accordingly. But while he declined to trust himself in Naples, he offered no objection to the diversion which Murat proposed to effect in his favour by engaging in war with Austria. Hence the eagerness of the intrusive King to increase the numbers of an army already too large for his resources; of which, but for the ill humour of Alexander with the Alliance, he would have reaped, long before he did, the fruits and hence also the state of preparation in which Austria stood, to deal with his folly when it should display itself.

While Murat played with a danger which was destined to crush him, Napoleon preserved, in all his intercourse with the agents of the Allied Powers, the utmost show of moderation. He complained, as it was natural that he should, of the refusal of the French Government to pay the stipend which had been awarded to him; and appealed for redress to the crowned heads under whose guarantee the Treaty of Fontainebleau had been effected. But he cautiously abstained from everything like the language of threatening, and seemed to deplore the faults which the Bourbons were committing, only because of the evils which they threatened to bring upon France.

Meanwhile, however, neither he nor his agents were idle. Hundreds of tricolored cockades were secretly scattered among the French soldiers. By twos and threes deserters from the French ranks—men of tried courage and inured to war—came over to him; and being received into his guard soon raised the numbers of his little army to twelve hundred. He did not desire more. The winter of 1814 was passed. The spring of 1815 came in, with better hopes for him than ever; and he was too bold a politician to let them pass unimproved.

His favourite sister Pauline, bringing other ladies in her train, paid him a visit. There was much hospitality with great apparent politeness, at the palace; and much talk was held concerning the improvements which he meditated both in the form and size of his own residence and in the harbour and town.

His guards also he frequently reviewed, and seemed to take as much pleasure in the exercise as if he had been passing a whole army before him. So passed the beginning of February, 1815, and on the 26th a grand entertainment was given at the palace. Sir Neil Campbell, the English resident in Elba, was not there, for he had gone in the only cruiser that observed the coast to Leghorn; but the representatives of Austria and Russia were present, and marked attention was paid to them.

Napoleon walked through the several halls, saluting his guests; and then, leaving the ladies to do the rest, went about his own business. His guards, to the number of 1100, had been directed to parade near the quay at three in the afternoon. They stood under arms till half-past four, when Napoleon joined them; and he and they were all on board of ship by seven o'clock the same evening. For this facility likewise of troubling Europe the Allies had left him, that he retained at his disposal a flotilla more than sufficient to transport his troops to the Continent whenever the desire of doing so should become strong with him.

How he bore himself during that brief voyage—commanding the respect of his followers by the calmness and self-possession of his manner—is a matter of history, he felt from the moment that his foot pressed the deck that "the die was cast;" and when, on baffling winds arising, and the little fleet making imperfect way, it was proposed to put back to Porto Ferrajo and await a more favourable opportunity, he scouted the idea—"Officers and soldiers of my Guard," he said, "we are going to France;" and the shout of enthusiasm with which the announcement was greeted, told how well he understood his followers.

They went to France. They saw a French frigate at a distance, but it neared them not, and they passed. Napoleon himself answered the hail from a French brig, which sought to be informed how it fared with the exile of Elba; and finally he and all his people made good their landing on the beach of the Gulf of St. Juan, just as the topmasts of the vessels from which they had descended were descried from the quarter-deck of a British sloop-of-war. So close was the run of this extraordinary man's fortune at the commencement of the last act in his public life, and so resolute the spirit which urged him to enter upon it, and to go through with it successfully.

CHAPTER 3

Arrival of Napoleon in Paris, and its immediate Consequences

Into the minute details of Napoleon's progress from Frejus to Paris it is not necessary to enter. Not one arm was raised to oppose him,—not a shot was fired either upon him or upon his followers. Wherever he presented himself the troops, sometimes headed by their leaders, sometimes deserting them, gathered round his standard. The peasantry, in like manner, not only exhibited no signs of hostility, but supplied his retinue with abundance of provisions, and wished them God speed. It was to little purpose that the Princes of the House of Bourbon put themselves at the head of corps, and marched out to give him battle. The soldiers refused to act against a chief whose name sounded in their ears like a watch-word; and though they abstained from making prisoners of their generals, the latter scarcely quitted them to return to Paris ere they passed over to the enemy. At length Ney's treason, and the defection of the army of reserve, which, under the Duke de Berri and Marshal Oudinot, had been assembled at Essonne and Fontainebleau, put an end to all hope; and Louis XVIII., after an uneasy reign of ten months, bade *adieu* to the courtiers who still remained faithful to him, and fled towards Lille.

It was on the evening of the 19th of March that the King of France set out from Paris. The same day Napoleon reached Fontainebleau, well nigh unattended; for he travelled with such rapidity that his guard could not keep pace with him; and it affords one of the strongest proofs of the disposition of the nation towards him that his equipage met with no interruption. Here, at an early hour in the morning of the 20th, tidings of the flight of the King were conveyed to him; nevertheless he delayed his onward journey till two in the afternoon, and did not reach the Tuileries till nine at night. Possibly he may have made his entrance into the capital under cover of darkness through some apprehension of its effect upon the populace had they witnessed it; for he well knew that with a majority of the Parisians he was not a favourite.

But if any such consideration throw a shadow over his thoughts, the anxiety produced by it must have been dispelled by the enthusiastic reception which awaited him. The whole inner court of the Carrousel, from the triumphal arch to the great staircase, was filled with a crowd of officers and soldiers, to whom the fact of his coming had been communicated; and these, dragging him from the carriage, bore him aloft upon their shoulders with shouts of joy, and amid a blaze of torch-light. Never in all history has such a reception been recorded. No wonder that it thrilled through the heart even of the leader of the grand army to Moscow—no wonder that it caused tears of transport to rain from the eyes of the excitable warriors who played a part in it;

Napoleon had regained the throne of France without difficulty. He has left the avowal on record, that the days which saw him pushing for the noble prize, and the night which testified to its acquisition, were the happiest of his life. But with the morning of the 21st came time for reflection, and the necessity of looking the real nature of his position in the face. It was the reverse of satisfactory. The sceptre which he grasped must be retained with the strong hand against the whole of Europe, and the war, which he felt to be imminent, entered upon with very inadequate means; for, though the army was with him, it had been reduced during the previous year to somewhere about 150,000 men; and the arsenals, emptied both of cannon and of small arms, offered no direct facilities for recruiting it. Neither were the political circumstances by which he was surrounded much more encouraging.

Almost all the able men whom he invited in the first instance to take office under his government declined to do so. Some, feeling that they had enacted the traitor's part often enough, were ashamed to be seen any more in public life; others, distrusting the stability of the new order of things, preferred lying by to watch the event; and when at length he did prevail on Cambacérès, Caulaincourt, Maret, and Carnot to serve him, it was by dint of compromises, the nature and extent of which proved that his confidence in his own fortune was shaken.

The same disinclination for office which perplexed Napoleon in the arrangement of his government in Paris operated to deter men of respectability and station from accepting, under him, commissions in the provinces. To the first burst of enthusiasm there appeared to succeed an almost universal distrust; and in several places, particularly in Guienne, Provence, Languedoc, and about Bordeaux, bands of Bourbon Royalists took up arms. Indeed, partly through the force of the Allied proclamation, which was circulated with great industry among the inhabitants of the eastern departments—partly because, when the crisis came, the least contented with the government of the Bourbons shrank from facing it—the tumultuous joy which seemed to welcome the adventurer on his first appearance in France died out almost as suddenly as it had arisen.

Moreover, the spirit of faction was as busy as it usually is, when nations are either in a state of transition, or have become loosened from the wholesome restraints of all authority; for the Republicans, feeling that they had come once more into the ascendant, played the Emperor's game only so far as they imagined that his success would lead to their own ultimate triumph.

Perhaps the genius of Napoleon never displayed itself so conspicuously as in his mode of meeting and overcoming these difficulties. He won individuals to himself by the charms of an address which was irresistible when he chose to exert it, and quieted public bodies by professing to place abstract questions in abeyance till there should be an opportunity of discussing them fully. Moreover, while his speeches and letters breathed nothing but the desire of peace, he turned vigorously to preparations for war. Generals whom he could trust were marched against the insurgents of the south, with orders to suppress the revolt by every means, and at any expense of pledges as well as of blood.

Workmen were hired by thousands, and employed in the fabrication of arms. All discharged and pensioned soldiers were invited to return to their standards, and the re-enrolment of the National Guard enabled him, by a stroke of the pen, to dispose of 200 battalions, numbering in all 112,000 men, for the defence of the fortresses. Besides those, the registered seamen in the various ports of France were regimented, clothed, and equipped, to the number of 30,000; and wherever horses could be found fit for the service either of the artillery or the cavalry or the train, they were impressed without scruple, and their owners recompensed by bills on the treasury.

It is well known that one of Napoleon's first measures after his return to the Tuileries was to address to the crowned heads of Europe a sort of circular, in which he avowed his anxious desire to remain at peace, and endeavoured to convince them that France, not his own will, had placed him where he sat. It is equally well known that he received no answer to this appeal, and that he never really expected to receive one; but the proceeding was politic, because it furnished him with an argument in the appeals which he made to French patriotism and vanity.

Hence, at the celebrated meeting of the Champ de Mai, he was able to connect his own fate and that of the nation plausibly together; and the result of the meeting undoubtedly was, to allay for the moment the strife of parties, and to concentrate and attract public attention and public anxiety to the issues of the struggle which all felt to be impending. Neither can it be denied, that though there might be less enthusiasm in the nation than stirred it in 1792, enough was called up materially to strengthen his hands, and to give him hope, in the event of victory at the outset, of ultimate triumph; and so his efforts were redoubled, not merely to organize forces for present use, but to prepare against that future on which he could not fail to reckon.

When Napoleon arrived in Paris on the 21st of March, he had but the remains of the Bourbon army to depend upon. On the 1st of June he had arrayed, for purposes of defence, not fewer than 559,000 men under arms. He so distributed his depôts and reserves, moreover, as to satisfy himself that by the first of October this force would be raised to 800,000; and made still further arrangements, with the view of guarding the empire, ere long, with not far short of two millions and a half of soldiers.

These were marvellous exploits to be performed in the space of three short months, of which one was almost wholly spent in passing from Elba to Paris; and yet they stood not alone. In the, sixty days that preceded the 1st of June, 1815, Napoleon suppressed a formidable rebellion, organized an efficient government, established or confirmed a representative constitution, and put party spirit to sleep. He replenished an exhausted treasury, filled the arsenals with munitions of war, and gave back to the troops the *prestige* of invincibility, which is with all people, and especially with the French, the best guarantee of victory. He was the admiration of Europe at the moment, though it both feared and hated him; and his deeds are still spoken of with the respect which they deserve.

The time which Napoleon thus vigorously improved was not wasted by the Allies. They had chosen their ground in the meeting of Congress which put forth the declaration of the 13th of March, and they expressed, and indeed experienced, the greatest desire to enter upon it. But a serious hindrance to this was presented by the want of money. The Continental Princes had men enough under arms to render victory certain; but armed bodies cannot be moved, especially to a distance from their own homes, without a large expenditure of money; and in money they were all miserably poor. It was felt by the English Government and people that this was not a time to higgle for hard bargains.

Accordingly after the war taxes had been re-imposed, and

a new loan negotiated, not less than 11,000,000*l.* sterling were distributed as subsidies among the continental powers; of which Austria received 1,796,220*l.*; Russia, 3,241,919*l.*; Prussia, 2,382,823*l.*; while Hanover, Spain, Portugal, Sweden, Italy, the Netherlands, and the smaller German States divided the residue among them.

Thus furnished with the sinews of war, the Allies began, early in April, to put their columns in motion. Austria found, indeed, for a brief space, occupation nearer home, for Murat seized the opportunity to rush into hostilities, and on the Austrian troops devolved the duty of expelling him from Italy; but Russia, Prussia, and the States of the Germanic Confederation drew at once towards the French frontier, and England prepared to co-operate with them. A few words will suffice to explain whence it came about that on Prussia and England the brunt of the gathering storm might be expected to fall.

Though by the peace of Paris, France seemed to be effectually bound against extending herself beyond the limits which were therein assigned to her, it was not unknown to the allied cabinets that she was exceedingly dissatisfied with the arrangement; and it was more than suspected that both in Flanders and among the people of the Prussian Rhenish provinces a strong Gallican spirit prevailed. Under those circumstances, and as a measure of mere precaution, Prussia had undertaken to occupy for a while her newly-acquired possessions with a corps of 30,000 men, while England placed in garrison among the frontier fortresses of the Netherlands about 10,000 or 12,000.

Upon these latter, as a sort of nucleus, the King of the Netherlands proceeded to form regiments of his own, and the supreme command of the whole was assumed by the present King of Holland, then His Royal Highness the Prince of Orange. No sooner was the return of Napoleon made known, however, than the representatives of the Great Powers renewed, in formal terms, the treaty of Chaumont, by which England and Prussia had alike agreed to employ 150,000 men in the common cause; and it was further arranged that these forces should assemble on the Lower Rhine or in the Netherlands, as being the points whence, whether for offensive or defensive purposes, the war might be expected to open. Accordingly, Prussia put in motion one division after another till she had reinforced Kleist's corps to the extent of 116,000 men; while England sent over to Ostend and the adjacent harbours every man and horse which the home government could be persuaded to regard as disposable.

There could be little hesitation, either at Berlin or in London, regarding the officers on whom the supreme command over each of those armies should be conferred. The Duke of Wellington, at that time England's representative at the Congress, was requested to proceed, as soon as the state of business in Vienna would permit, to the Low Countries; while Field-Marshal Prince Blücher put all competitors out of the field by arraying himself in his war attire, and claiming, as a sort of right, that which his sovereign freely conceded to him.

The Duke set out on the 29th of March, and travelling with such speed as to overtake and pass his own messenger, arrived on the 4th of April in Brussels. Prince Blücher reached his own headquarters about a fortnight later. But both then and previously the best understanding prevailed among the chiefs of the allied armies, which, though in communication, were wholly distinct, and so continued to the close of this memorable campaign.

The Duke of Wellington, with prophetic eye, appears early to have foreseen that under the arrangements which ensued upon the treaty of Paris, the peace of Europe could not long be preserved. While filling the place of English Ambassador at Paris he was no unobservant spectator of events as they passed around him; and so early as the month of September, 1814, sketched out a plan for the defence of the frontier of the Netherlands, which had for its object the repulse of any attempt from France to recover by a sudden inroad her sovereignty over the Flemish provinces.

It was very imperfectly acted upon, as were other hints which he threw out in regard to the wisdom of strengthening the alliance with the Peninsula, and thus having a corps of good Portuguese troops available for any emergency. As soon as the landing of Napoleon was made known, he wrote from Vienna to Lord Castlereagh, urging him to reinforce the army in the Netherlands as much as he could, particularly in cavalry and artillery. The advice, to what causes owing does not appear, seems to have been but little regarded, and hence his letter of the 6th of April,—the second, which he addressed from Brussels to the English government,—describes in just but not very flattering terms the state of military preparation in which he found his command.

The troops of the Netherlands which were to serve under his orders could not be otherwise than inefficient. They were to a great extent raw levies, and of the Belgian portion of, them the spirit was not supposed to be good; of the British infantry regiments by far the larger proportion were composed of second battalions, the *débris* of Lord Lynedoch's corps constituting the chief portion of the force. For it must not be forgotten, that after the conclusion of the Peninsular war England had still America upon her hands; and that from the ports of France and of Ireland the flower of that army which had delivered Spain was shipped off on ill-arranged and worse commanded expeditions to the other side of the Atlantic. Hence, when the emergency arose in Europe, England was not, or her government assumed that she was not, in a condition to bring a fitting array into the field.

"It appears to me," writes the Duke of Wellington, "that you have not taken a clear view of your situation, that you do not think war certain, and that a great effort must be made if it is hoped that it shall be short. You have not called out the militia, nor announced such an intention in your message to Parliament, by which measure your troops of the line in Ireland or elsewhere might become disposable; and how we are to make out 150,000 men, or even the 60,000 of the defensive part of the treaty of Chaumont, appears not to have been considered. If you could let me have 40,000 good British infantry, besides those you insist upon having in garrisons, the proportion settled by treaty that you are to furnish of cavalry, that is to say, the eighth of 150,000, including in both the old German Legion, and 150 pieces of British field-artillery fully horsed, I should be satisfied, and take my chance for the rest, and engage that we would play our part in the game; but as it is, we are in a bad way."

At the time when the Duke was thus expressing himself to a member of the government at home, he was encouraging General Kleist, the officer in command of the Prussian corps on the Meuse, to assume a more advanced position, so as to cover Brussels, and render its seizure by a *coup-de-main* impossible. He describes himself in this communication as being able, after providing for the garrisons of Mons, Tournay, Ypres, Ostend, Nieuport, and Antwerp, to bring 23,000 good British and Hanoverian troops into the field, of which 5000 should be cavalry; and to support them with 20,000 Dutch and Belgian soldiers, of which 2000 should be horse.

He opened the campaign, nearly two months afterwards, with scarcely 30,000 of these same good British and Hanoverian troops; and fought and won the battle of Waterloo with 18,000 British infantry instead of 40,000, and not quite 8000 horse. So imperfectly were his suggestions acted upon by the home authorities, and so unvarying continued to be the operation of the principle which throughout the whole course of the war in the Peninsula had crippled him for want of men and means, while every town in Great Britain and Ireland swarmed with soldiers eager to gather laurels under his guidance.

CHAPTER 4

Distribution of the hostile Armies early in June

Days and weeks passed on, amid anxious preparations on both sides. The forces of the allies, though enormous in the aggregate, were too widely dispersed to admit of prompt and decisive operations. The Russians had an arduous march to perform from Saxon Poland to the further borders of Germany. The Austrians, entangled in hostilities with Murat, were unable to accomplish more than the occupation of the most important posts between Basle and Manheim. Bavaria, Wurtemberg, and Baden mustered indeed among them eighty thousand men, with which they took post upon the Upper Rhine, but it was never contemplated that they should advance beyond it till the Austrians should have joined them.

Meanwhile these various movements of concentration must be covered and protected, and it devolved upon the troops on the Lower Rhine and in the Netherlands to do so. For the latter constituted, in fact, the outposts of a great army; which, having the quarters of its several corps much divided, and all of them remote from an intended field of operation, requires time to bring its strength to bear, and to render certain the results of combinations which no human exertions can precipitate.

Moreover, as it is the duty of the outposts of an army, while they are very vigilant, to preserve as long as possible a purely defensive attitude, so it was the obvious business of the armies of which Wellington and Blücher were at the head not to take, except under some pressing and unlooked for emergency, the initiative in active hostilities. A forward movement on their part, even if successful, could hardly render more sure than it was the ultimate triumph of the allies.

Defeat, or even disaster incurred in such circumstances, might, and probably would, do unspeakable damage to the cause. And this wise policy, dictated by every principle of the art in which Wellington and Blücher were not learners, the peculiar nature of the ground occupied by the enemy, as well as by their own troops, rendered absolutely indispensable.

The amount of force with which the allies proposed to operate from different parts against France may be estimated at 600,000 men. To resist these Napoleon had under arms in the beginning of June 559,000., of which 250,000 were at this time complete in all the equipments of cavalry, infantry, and artillery. The remainder, made up of regimental depôts, national guards, marines. coast-guard veterans, and organized pensioners, though very useful for defensive purposes, could not easily be moved.

Out of the disposable troops of the line, reinforced by a portion of the *national guard élite*, were formed seven *corps d'armée*, four corps of reserve cavalry, four corps of observation, and an army of the west or of La Vendée. The army of the north—or grand army— to be directed by the Emperor in person, was composed of five of these *corps d'armée* (the 1st, 2nd, 3rd, 4th, and 6th), the whole of the reserve cavalry, and the Imperial' Guard. It mustered about 120,000 men, and was distributed in the following order:—

The 1st corps, commanded by Count d'Erlon, had its headquarters at Lille; the 2nd, of which Count Reille was at the head, occupied cantonments in the environs of Valenciennes; the 3rd, under Count Vandamme, lay in and about Mézières; the 4th, under Count Girard, in the neighbourhood of Metz; the 6th, of which Count Lobau was put in charge, had its headquarters in Laon. The whole of the reserve cavalry—namely, four corps— were cantoned, under Marshal Grouchy, between the Aisne and the Sambre; while the Imperial Guard abode in Paris.

The 5th *corps d'armée*, under the command of Count Rapp, formed the basis of what was intended to grow into the army of the Rhine. It consisted of 36,000 men, and, having its headquarters in Strasburg, occupied the principal posts along that portion of the frontier between Landau and Hagenau; it communicated by its left with the 4th corps about Metz, by its right with the 1st corps of observation. The 1st corps of observation, called likewise the army of the Jura, was under the command of Lieutenant-General Lecourbe.

It was weak in point of numbers, not exceeding 4,500 men, though strenuous efforts were making to raise it to 18,000; and stretching from Altkirch, the headquarters, along the line between Huningen and Befort, it felt with its left towards the 5th corps, and with its right towards the 7th.

This latter, having the Duke of Albufera at its head, formed the basis of the army of the Alps. It held the passes along the Italian frontier, had strong posts at Grenoble and Chambery, communicated on its left with the 1st corps of observation, and covered the approach to Lyons. Intended to be raised as soon as possible to 40,000 men, it consisted, at the period of which we are now speaking, of 15,000 only; but as formidable works were already begun on the heights which overlook Lyons, hopes were entertained that in case of attack, it would be competent to maintain that place till a blow should be struck with effect in another quarter.

Of the three remaining corps of observation, one (the 2nd,) commanded by Marshal Bruno, had its headquarters at Marseilles, and occupying Toulon and Antibes, watched the frontier of the Maritime Alps. Another (the 3rd), under Count Decaen, observed from his headquarters at Perpignan the line of the Eastern Pyrenees; while the 4th, called the army of the Gironde, or Western Pyrenees, had its headquarters at Bordeaux, and was commanded by Lieutenant General Clausel. All these, it is worthy of remark, were the mere skeletons of corps, to reinforce which time and great exertions would be required.

And finally, the army of La Vendée, of which General Lamarque was at the head, absorbed 17,000 good troops, and found ample occupation—at least for awhile—in restoring tranquillity to the disturbed provinces.

Finally, the care of the fortresses, of the coasts, and the magazines, was committed to the national guard and the miscellaneous levies, to which the title of "*Armée Extraordinaire*" had been given; and a line of redoubts being marked out and begun, so as to render Paris more capable of resisting an attack than in the previous campaigns, Napoleon may be pardoned if he looked round upon the results of two months' exertions with complacency, not unmixed with confidence.

Though the minute details of these several arrangements might not be made manifest to the allies, enough was seen or known to satisfy them that in the north the cloud would probably burst. There was every reason to believe, likewise, that having gained sufficient time to organize a fine army, and to bring it to a head, Napoleon would seize the first convenient opportunity of commencing hostilities. For whatever further preparations might on his side be in progress, it was certain that they could not be matured so as to anticipate the arrival of the allied columns on the French frontier, and against the weight of numbers—operating on different points, but all bearing towards a centre—he could not hope to make head.

His policy, therefore, was to take the initiative; and by a sudden attack upon the English and Prussian armies to force his way to Brussels. This was clear enough; nevertheless, as more than one avenue of approach lay open to him, and that the nature of his position behind the strong fortresses which cover the north of France left him at liberty to select which he might prefer, it was equally clear that by the Prussians or English decisive steps could not be taken till surmise should have been changed into certainty, and the exact time not less than the manner of his offensive operations should have been fully discovered. A few words will explain as well the positions of the allied armies as the important objects for which their commanders found it necessary to provide.

In the second week of June the Duke of Wellington had under his orders a numerical force of 105,950 men, with 196 guns; of these, 82,062 were infantry, 14,482 cavalry, 8,166 artillery, and the remainder engineers, sappers, miners, wagon-train, and staff corps. This army, strong upon paper, and formidable enough when looked at from a distance, was, owing to its composition and the inexperience of the major portion of the troops, scarcely, in all parts at least, to be depended upon. Of the infantry 23,543 were British, and 3,301 soldiers of the Old German Legion.

There could be no doubt in regard to them; for though most of the English regiments were second battalions, of which perhaps two-thirds had never served a campaign, the remainder were veterans trained in the school of the Peninsula—and their spirit was largely infused into the ranks of their younger comrades. And the German legionaries had always been among the elite of the Peninsular army. But the rest, made up of Hanoverian militia, of Brunswickers, men of Nassau, and Dutch Belgians, as they were all without experience, imperfectly drilled, and strangers to the English and to one another, their pliability as well as their power of endurance had yet to be tested; and the hopes of their commander in regard to them could not be very high. For they were not, like the Portuguese, willing to be taught, and ready to postpone considerations of national vanity to the common good.

On the contrary, each nation claimed—and not perhaps unnaturally—the right of serving under its own generals and its own staff; and all showed such a disinclination to be closely mixed up with the British, that the plan, though suggested on the Duke's first arrival in Brussels, was neither pressed nor acted upon. The consequence was that the advantages to be derived from mere numbers were seriously lessened, through the impossibility of organizing the raw levies by distributing them in brigades, divisions, and even in *corps d'armée*, with troops better disciplined than themselves.

And when it is further considered that the tactics of each na-

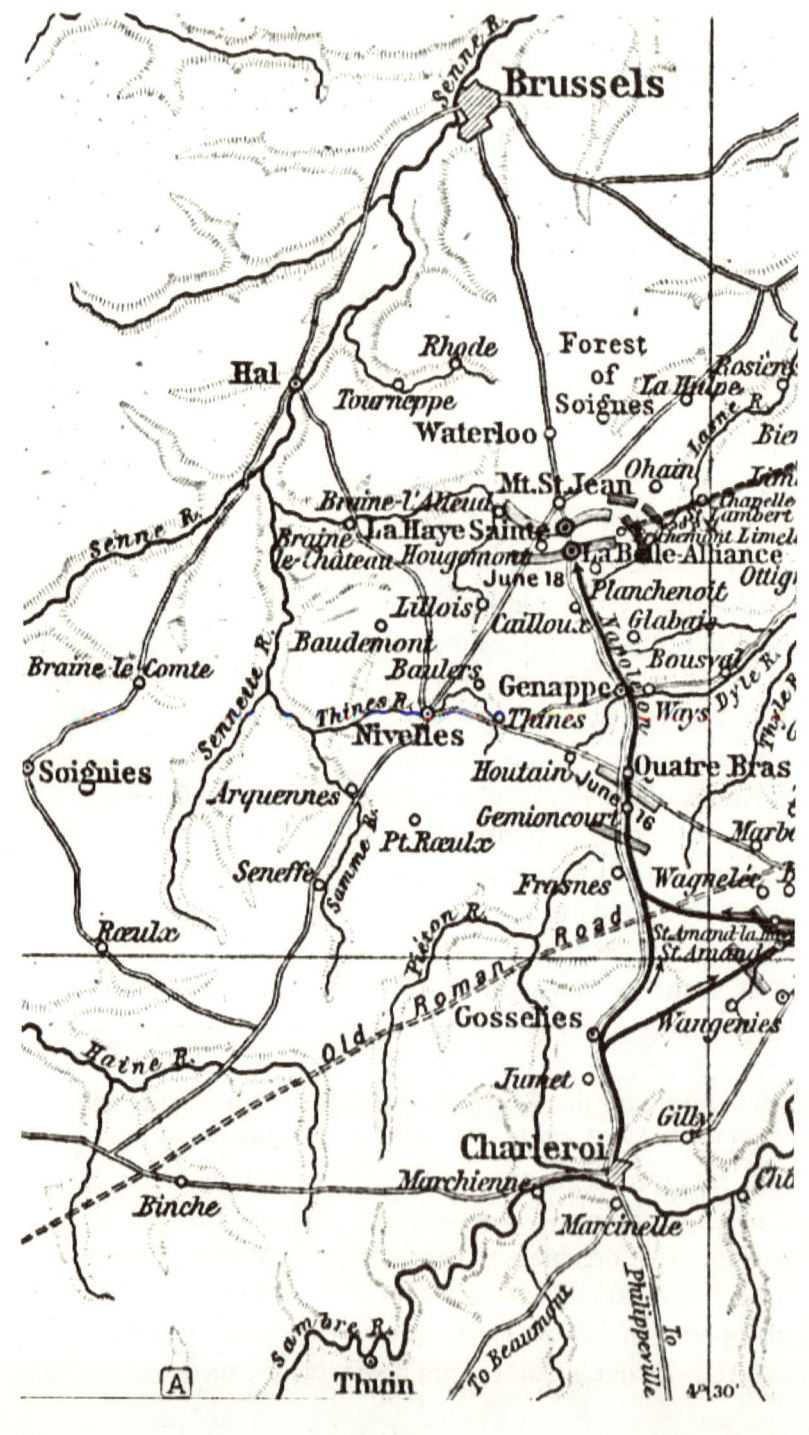

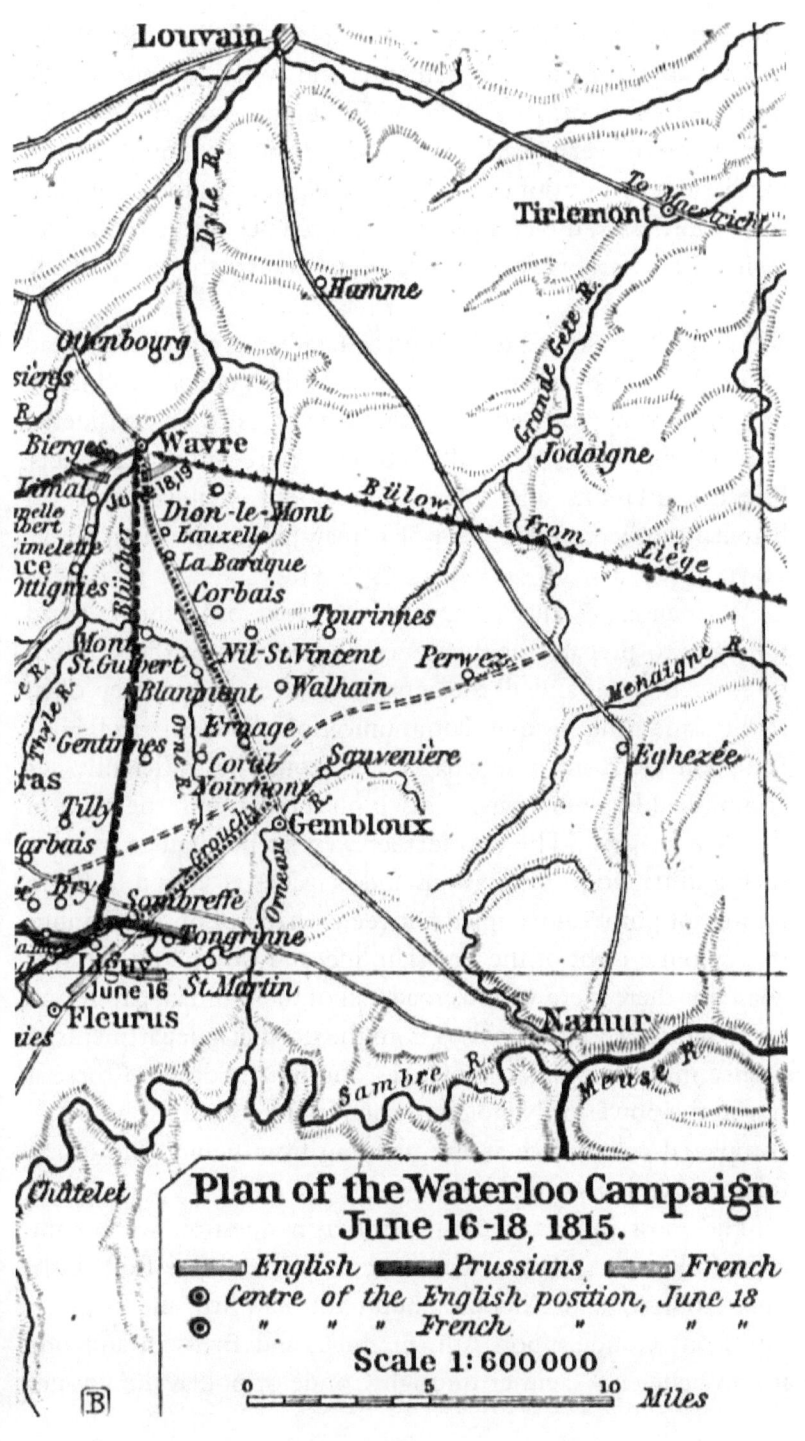

tion differed materially from those of all the rest, the difficulty of making anything out of so heterogeneous a mass cannot well be overrated. In a word, the Duke of Wellington was assumed to be at the head of very nearly one hundred and six thousand men; but besides that out of these there were garrisons to be supplied to the fortresses, the composition and temper of the remainder were such as in a very great degree to destroy the unity of the whole.

Hence he deserved to be regarded, rather as the chosen head of a collection of allied armies, than as the general-in-chief of one great army; for that army along deserves to be considered one, which is ready and willing to take, in regard to regiments, brigades, divisions, and their commanders, whatever order of battle the officer at the head of it may judge expedient to lay down.

With an army thus composed, the Duke of Wellington had not only to prepare for the general operations of the war, but to cover Brussels and all the approaches to it, and to keep open at the same time his own communications with England, Holland, and Germany. The latter object could be sufficiently accomplished by connecting himself on the left with the right of the Prussian army. The two former were to be attained only by such a distribution of divisions and brigades as should leave no important point unoccupied between Charleroi on the Sambre, the. extreme right of the Prussian line, and Ostend on the seacoast; for there were various roads, all of them broad, paved, and open, which led in those days from the northern departments of France into the Belgian provinces; and by any or all of these it was in the power of Napoleon, when his preparations should be completed, to advance at any moment from behind the strong fortresses which screened him.

The most important of the roads in question were—one from Lisle, upon Menin, Courtray, and Ghent; one from Lisle, upon Tournay and Ghent, or upon Tournay, Ath, and Brussels; one from Condé, upon Ath, Enghien, and Brussels; and one from Valenciennes, either through Condé or not, as the invader might prefer, upon Mons and Brussels. They all passed through a country level, and destitute of natural defences, and could communicate by a multitude of cross-roads, the whole of which were passable in winter to infantry, and in summer to artillery and cavalry likewise.

It was necessary that the Duke of Wellington should occupy his defensive position in such a manner as might enable him, after providing for the security of his military communications with England, Holland, and Germany, to assemble, when the proper time came, the largest disposable force that could be brought together. It was equally necessary that, in effecting this concentration, he should not expose to risk any of the objects which, under the treaty of peace and by the acts of the Congress of Vienna, had been intrusted to his care. His first proceeding, therefore, after arriving at Brussels in the beginning of April, was to give orders for the strengthening of the posts on the frontiers, by the construction of new works at Ostend, Nieuport, Ypres, Menin, Courtray, Oudenarde, Tournay, Ath, Mons, Charleroi, and Namur.

It is true that there were already field-works on the sites of most of the ruined fortifications, by which these towns used in former times to be covered, and the Prince of Orange, at the Duke's suggestion, had already begun to clear out the old ditches, and to make arrangements for inundating the country, should the necessity for so stern a measure arise. But the field-works were still incomplete, and the ditches to a great extent filled up; and though the means of inundation were in a state of considerable forwardness, still the mischief done by covering the whole face of a country with water is too serious to be lightly resorted to. The Duke, therefore, directed that not only the troops, but as many of the peasantry as could be spared from the labours of the field, should be employed upon the construction of these works; and large numbers coming in, the operation proceeded apace.

This done, he proceeded to organize and distribute, as advantageously as circumstances would allow, the troops under his immediate command. The infantry was divided into two *corps d'armée* and a reserve. The first corps consisted of four divisions, the first and third British, and the second and fourth Dutch-Belgian. Major-General Cooke commanded the first British division; Lieutenant-General Sir Charles Alton the second; the second Dutch-Belgian division was commanded by Lieutenant-General de Perponcher; the third by Lieutenant-General Baron Chasse; and his Royal Highness the Prince of Orange was at the head of the whole. The distribution of this corps was as follows:—

De Perponcher's division, forming the extreme left, had its headquarters at Nivelles, on the high road from Brussels to Binche, and communicated with the right of the Prussian army through Hautain-le-Val, Genappe, Quatre Bras, and Frasne. On the right, but more in advance towards Mons, lay Chassé's division, occupying principally Rœulx and the villages between Rœulx and Binche. Next came Alten's, with its headquarters at Soignies, and its strength disseminated in the villages between Mons, Rœulx, Braine-le-Comte, and Enghien; and further to the right still, with its headquarters at Enghien, lay Cooke's division.

The Second corps, of which Lord Hill was in command, comprised in like manner two British and two Dutch-Belgian divisions. The Second British, Lieutenant-General Sir Henry Clinton's division, communicated by its left with that of Alton; its headquarters were at Ath on the Dender, observing the high road from Condé to Brussels, and one brigade stationed in Sens, kept open the communication between Ath and the fortress of Mons. The Fourth division, under Lieutenant-General Sir Charles Colville, still further to the right, was divided between Renaix and Oudenarde, and detached a brigade (the Sixth Hanoverian) to garrison Nieuport on the coast.

Finally, the First Dutch-Belgian division, with the Colonial division—or, as it was then called, the Indian brigade—occupied cantonments along the line of the high-road from Grammont to Ghent, or was scattered amid the villages a little more retired between this great road and Alost. Lieutenant-General Stedman was at the head of the former of these divisions, Lieutenant-General Baron Anthing commanded the latter.

Besides these corps, there was a reserve of infantry consisting of the Fifth British division, under Lieutenant-General Sir Thomas Picton; the Sixth, under Lieutenant-General Sir Lowry Cole; the Duke of Brunswick's contingent; the Hanoverian corps, under Lieutenant-General Van der Decken; and the Nassau regiment, containing three battalions, which worked together in brigade, under the command of General Van Kruse. Of these, the Fifth and Sixth divisions, with the Brunswickers, were quartered for the most part in and around Brussels; Van Kruse's Nassau brigade lay between Brussels and Louvain; while the remainder, including one British brigade, the Thirteenth veteran and Second garrison battalions, were distributed in garrisons among Antwerp, Ostend, Nieuport, Ypres, Tournay, and Mons.

Meanwhile the cavalry, divided into fourteen brigades, of which seven were composed of British and horsemen of the old German Legion, extended all the way from Ninhove on the right, to the vicinity of Binche on the left. The English and Germans occupied Ninhove itself, Grammont, and all the villages on the Dender. The Dutch-Belgians lay above Rœulx, and between Roeulx and Mons, and on the south of Mons, in the direction of Maubeuge and Beaumont, and towards Binche. The Brunswick cavalry was dispersed chiefly in the vicinity of Brussels; and the whole were under the command of Lieutenant-General the Earl of Uxbridge, now Field-Marshal the Marquis of Anglesey.

While the Duke of Wellington's mixed force thus covered most of the great approaches to Brussels, without losing its hold upon Holland and England, the Prussian army, composed of the people of one nation, well appointed, well drilled, and accustomed to a system of its own, took up the line on the left, and kept open the door between Belgium and Germany. It numbered in all about 117,000 men, of whom nearly 12,000 were cavalry, with 312 guns; and being divided into four corps, of which the headquarters were respectively at Charleroi, Namur,

Ciney, and Liège, was under the control and guidance of Field-Marshal Prince Blücher.

Its object, in reference to the enemy, was to guard the high-road which leads by the valley of the Sambre to Charleroi, and to watch the course of the Meuse, as far as it seemed probable that a force operating from the north of France upon Brussels would operate by that line. With this view it touched the left of the British alignment, with a brigade posted in the vicinity of Fontaine l'Evêque, and had posts as far in advance of the Sambre as Lobbes, Thuin, Gerpannes, Fosses, and Soissoie. In observation of the Meuse, in like manner, it occupied in strength Profondeville, Bouvignes, Diuant, Rochefort, and Marche, while Marshal Prince Blücher's headquarters were at Namur.

From this brief description it will be seen that the position of the Prussian army was considerably more compact than that of the allies. Its commander had less to do, fewer objects to divide his care; and was therefore enabled to post his men, rather with a view to their speedy concentration, than to provide against attack on various assailable points. Twelve hours, it was calculated, would suffice to assemble each of the four Prussian corps at its own headquarters; and four-and-twenty well used, would bring them together anywhere along the extent of their line.

The Duke of Wellington could not possibly accomplish this. Nevertheless, so wisely had he disposed his corps, keeping a strong reserve in hand, that not one point in all his line was opened to be forced ere he should be able to support it with numbers capable of holding their ground till the rest of the army should have time to form and co-operate with them. And that he did thus wield his masses, through lines of communication so direct, that in six hours from the issuing of his orders the whole were in motion—events of which it is the business of the present narrative to give some account fully prove.

CHAPTER 5

State of Brussels and the Netherlands in the early Summer of 1815

One very natural result of the peace of 1814 was to excite in the breasts of our countrymen and countrywomen an ardent desire to travel. Shut up, with a brief interval, more than a quarter of a century within the limits of the British Isles, their curiosity to become acquainted with the manners of continental nations had grown into a craving, and they hastened to indulge it, as soon as the ports of France were open to them, by flocking to the farther shores of the Channel. Paris was of course the great point of attraction; and it soon became crowded with very miscellaneous company. A few, and but a few, wandered further—into Germany and Italy; and some, especially those who had relatives attached to the army, passed into Flanders.

No sooner was the landing of Napoleon made public, than France, Italy, and Germany gave back their visitors. From Paris, especially, people fled as from an infected city; and happy was he who found himself first on the deck of the packet-boat which was to carry him from Calais to Dover. Even Belgium itself seemed for awhile to be left to the enjoyment of its native population, and the care of the troops that were appointed to guard it.

There was nothing to be wondered at in this. Men remembered how it had fared with the travellers of 1802, whom Napoleon, contrary to the faith of nations, detained twelve long years in captivity; and, believing that he might possess the power, as no one doubted that he had the will, to play the same barbarous game over again, they judged it expedient to escape while the roads were open, and fled accordingly. In process of time, however, the exaggeration of alarm which emptied Paris and filled London began to subside.

The conviction gradually gained ground that hostilities would not be renewed under exactly the same circumstances which marked the commencement of war in 1803. It was seen that, though he might command France, Napoleon's influence extended little farther; and that the chances were at least as much against him now as they had been in his favour on a former occasion. Accordingly many, whose tastes for foreign travel were as yet imperfectly gratified, took courage to go abroad again.

But as the voice of prudence continued to make itself heard, they cast about for the means of combining safety with amusement; and resolved, while breathing a continental atmosphere, not to lose their hold, so to speak, upon England. Hence Belgium became the great resort of these seekers after pleasure. They landed at Ostend; passed thence to Malines, Ghent, Antwerp, and Brussels; and took up their temporary residence in one or other of these cities, according as each presented to them points of attraction more enticing than the rest.

During the spring and early summer of 1815 Brussels was thronged with visitors. As fresh troops arrived, and they came in as fast as the Governments which combined to form an army for the Duke of Wellington could equip them, fresh families, some of them wealthy and of good repute, arrived in their train. Many officers brought their wives, and some their very children along with them; under the impression that war, though inevitable, was distant; and that it would be aggressive on their parts, not defensive.

The same belief seemed to actuate noblemen and gentlemen who had no official connection with the army. The Duke and Duchess of Richmond, the Duke and Duchess of Buccleugh, Lady Caroline Lamb, and many other persons of distinction, hired houses or apartments according as one or the other might be had; and, throwing open their saloons, rendered the second capital of the Netherlands a scene of continual hospitality and pleasant bustle.

Meanwhile Louis XVIII. had established his court at Ghent, though far from crowded, it was in the highest degree respectable, as well for the rank as for the talents of its members; and being reserved and very formal, it agreed admirably with the character of a city which, in all its architectural arrangements, if not in the order of its society, may be considered as belonging rather to the middle ages than to our own times.

Thus the din and bustle of military preparations were strangely intermingled with the pomp of fallen royalty and the gayeties of fashionable life; for the intercourse between Ghent and Brussels was constant, and the condition of society in one of these cities made itself felt in the other, while both exercised a marked influence over the manners of the camp.

While the larger towns were thus enlivened by the presence of princes, courtiers, officers of rank, and their families, there was not a village or hamlet between Binche and the sea-coast, but swarmed with armed men. Every *chateau*, farmhouse, and labourer's cottage, afforded accommodation to a greater or smaller number of soldiers—whose horses, if they happened to belong to the cavalry or artillery, filled the stables and choked up the cowsheds.

On what terms the Belgians lived with the soldiers of their own nation, and with the levies which came from Hanover, Brunswick, and Nassau, no very accurate record has been preserved; but between them and the British troops the best understanding prevailed. Portions, indeed, of the Duke's army seem to have made themselves perfectly at home among the Flemings. It is recorded of the Highland Regiments in particular, that so completely had they become domesticated with the people on whom they were billeted, that it was no unusual thing to find a kilted warrior rocking the cradle while the mother of the little Fleming, which slept under its mountain of feathers, was abroad on her household affairs. Indeed the feelings of the great body of the Belgians were at this time decidedly against the French.

The remembrance was too recent of the sufferings which they had endured, the ruin of their trade, and the unsparing exercise of the law of conscription over their families, not to excite, in a commercial and naturally unwarlike people, abhorrence of their old masters; and though there can no longer be a doubt that their unceremonious junction to Holland displeased them—even that connection appeared in their eyes less odious than a reunion with France. Hence no sooner was the fact of Napoleon's return made known, than they manifested their hostility to him and to his system in every way which was consistent with their personal security. Comparatively few took up arms.

They had little taste for military show—none for the business of war; but they covered the usurper and his Myrmydons with execrations, and shouted all manner of cries in their streets to the glory of the English, their protectors. The consequence was that as regiment after regiment arrived from England, the inhabitants of the rich country through which they passed ministered liberally to their wants, while the owners of the houses among whom they were scattered received them freely, and gave them the treatment of brothers.

Brussels, from the beginning of April to the middle of June, was the scene of great and untiring festivity. Dinners, *soirées*, balls, theatrical amusements, concerts—in which Catalani, then in her prime, played a prominent part—caused the streets of that beautiful and picturesque city to echo with sounds of gladness; while the fields and meadows around were alive all day long with military parades and reviews. There was not a grove or wood within six miles of the place but afforded shelter, as the summer advanced, to frequent encampments. The troops lay, for the most part, in quarters, or were distributed through the villages as they arrived; but the artillery, with the wagons and tumbrils belonging to it, was parked—and pickets slept, and sentries kept guard beside them.

Moreover, the whole line of road from the sea-coast to the capital was kept in a state of constant bustle. Travellers hurrying to the focus of gayety passed, at every stage, corps of infantry or cavalry, or guns on the march—and were enchanted as darkness set in, with the spectacle, to them as new as it was striking, of bivouacs by the wayside such as Teniers delighted to represent. Nor were they more delighted than astonished to find that among the gayest of the gay in all the festive scenes to which they were introduced, the Duke and the principal officers of his army took the lead.

They did not know—what to his followers in the Peninsula was a matter, already well understood—that the Duke of Wellington never felt more thoroughly unembarrassed than when cares under which other men would have sunk demanded his attention; and that the mind which was found able to arrange plans for the preservation of Europe, could, while it worked, enter with perfect freedom and even zest, into every scheme of fun or enjoyment which might be proposed to it. Yet so it was. He who, at his own table, or as the guest of one or other of the leading fashionables of Brussels, was over the keenest promoter of that polished mirth which more than all others he seemed heartily to enjoy, suffered no point, however minute, to escape his notice, to which it behooved the commander of a great army to pay attention, while, at the same time, he conducted and brought to a favourable conclusion political and financial negotiations, which, but for the skill and firmness displayed in his management, might have ended disastrously.

The Duke was not over and above well pleased with the constitution of the force of which he was at the head. He had little reason to be so: for, independently of the mixture of nations which composed it, there was a melancholy deficiency of almost all that renders an army effective—such as guns, horses, drivers, and even of intelligence in the general staff. In regard to cannon, his Grace, in a letter to Lord Bathurst, bearing date 21st of April, 1815, says—

I have received a letter from Lord Mulgrave, of the 15th,

from which I see, that, after doing all he can for us, we shall have only 84 pieces of artillery equipped (now only 72), instead of 150, for which I asked, including German artillery to the amount of 30 pieces, leaving 42 as the number which the British artillery can supply.

His complaint in reference to horses is, that though authorized to purchase them in the country, he had stayed the proceeding, because he had no drivers to take charge of them.

"I conclude," he continues, "that in consequence of the reduction, they can no more furnish drivers than they can horses; and that being the case, I beg leave to point out to your Lordship, that as the drivers of the country cannot be depended upon, and as, at all events, I have not time to form them, I have no other means of providing for this absolutely necessary service, than to take soldiers from the British infantry to perform it, and that very badly. If you will look at our returns you will see how little able we are to afford a soldier to take care of each pair of horses we require."

Of the staff, it is not worthwhile to say more, than that, with some noble exceptions—particularly among the generals commanding corps, divisions, and brigades—it was by far too numerous, without being remarkable for its efficiency. His Grace naturally desired to have about him men whom the war in the Peninsula had educated, and whom he knew; but there was an influence at home, which in great measure thwarted him. He remonstrated, but to no purpose; and at last, on the 29th of April, wrote to Sir Henry Torrens, then military secretary, thus:—

I had desired Lord Fitzroy to write to Lieutenant-Colonel Grant, of the 11th Regiment, to beg him to come out, with the intention of employing him at the head of the Intelligence department; and Lieutenant-Colonel Scovell at the head of the department of Military Communications. It is quite impossible for me to superintend the details of the duties of these departments myself, having already more to arrange than I am equal to; and I cannot intrust them to the young gentlemen on the staff of this army. Indeed, I must say, I do not know how to employ them.

Nevertheless, that self-confidence—which, when it does not degenerate into self-sufficiency, is perhaps one of the surest tokens of a great military genius—never forsook him. While his private and confidential letters were describing his troops as "not what they ought to be to enable us to maintain our military character in Europe," and his demi-official dispatches were pressing for succours of every kind, the tone of his communications with Prince Blücher and with the allies in general was full of hope. Indeed it would appear, from a dispatch to the Earl of Clancarty—on whom, upon his departure, the duty of representing England in the Congress had devolved—that so early as the 10th of April he was meditating a speedy commencement of operations, and that he looked to the first of May as a convenient season for marching 270,000 men across the frontier.

He had then heard of Napoleon's proposed assembly of the Champ de Mai. He was desirous of anticipating its probable effect upon the minds of the French people; and knowing that there was civil war in La Vendée, he felt that there would be little wisdom in looking on till it should be suppressed. And though subsequent and better intelligence induced him, it is true, to abandon this project, the fact still remains upon record, that so far from adhering to a defensive policy through choice, he was forced into it, contrary to his wishes, by the weight of circumstances. But the season was approaching which was destined to put an end to all doubt as to when, how, and where hostilities should begin.

CHAPTER 6

Continued Preparations on both sides

On the 17th of April, Field-Marshal Prince Blücher assumed the command of the Prussian army. He lost no time in announcing his arrival to the Duke of Wellington, who replied to his communication with characteristic frankness; and it was by-and-by arranged that the two marshals should mutually visit one another, and look at the troops of which they were respectively at the head. Several reviews were the consequence, particularly a grand gathering of British and Hanoverian cavalry near Ninhove, as a sort of pendant to a previous exhibition of Prussian horse and foot at Hannut; and a general plan for mutual support in the hour of need was arranged.

Yet all the subjects discussed between these illustrious friends were not agreeable. A corps of Saxons, 14,000 strong, which was intended to reinforce the army of the Netherlands, Blücher, through some misapprehension of his instructions, detained on its march: he conceived that they had been sent to swell his own numbers; and either because he entertained some distrust of their fidelity, or that the exigencies of the service required it, he gave orders that they should be distributed among the different divisions of his army.

The Saxons refused to be separated, and applied, first through their commanding officer, and afterwards through their King, to be received into the army of the Duke of Wellington. But though his Grace would have been glad of such a fine body of men, and might have found them trustworthy had they passed under his command in the first instance, it was not in his nature to treat with mutineers. He therefore refused to entertain the application, and left them to be dealt with as Prince Blücher should judge expedient. The consequence was that after a little angry discussion, the Saxons were disarmed, and passed back by detachments, under escorts of Prussian troops, into their own country.

It was the end of April, and rumours of an approaching crisis grew daily more rife, though a strict vigilance was exercised on the French frontier, and the triple line of fortresses behind which they lay enabled the enemy to concentrate their columns in perfect security, the Duke of Wellington's sources of information never wholly failed him; and he received through various channels reports, more or less accurate, of all that was going on about Napoleon's person. That the Duke gave to these a full measure of regard seems now to be universally admitted.

He exhibited no symptoms of impatience, it is true—neither did he throw Belgium into a ferment by marching troops backwards and forwards, and assuming day by day some fresh position—but he quietly put his chiefs of corps upon their guard, and kept a steady eye upon every road or avenue by which his own outposts might be approached. It may be worthwhile to exhibit to the general reader a specimen of the forethought and calmness of this great man; and the following memorandum, extracted from Colonel Gurwood's *Dispatches*, affords the means of so doing. On the 30th of April, little more than three weeks subsequently to his arrival in Brussels, he thus explains to the Prince of Orange, the Earl of Uxbridge, and Lord Hill, his views of the allied position:—

> 1. Having received reports that the Imperial Guard had moved from Paris upon Beauvais, and a report having been for some days prevalent in the country that Bonaparte was about to visit the northern frontier, I deem it expedient to concentrate the cantonments of the troops with a view to their early junction in case this country should be attacked; for which concentration the Quarter-

master-General now sends orders.

2. In this ease the enemy's line of attack will be either between the Lys and the Scheldt, or between the Sambre and the Scheldt, or by both lines.

3. In the first case, I should wish the troops of the 4th division to take up the bridges on the Scheldt, near Avelghem, and with the regiment of cavalry at Courtrai to fall back upon Audenarde, which post they are to occupy, and to inundate the country in the neighbourhood.

4. The garrison of Ghent are to inundate the country in the neighbourhood likewise; and that point is to be held at all events.

5. The cavalry in observation between Menin and Furnes are to fall back upon Ostend; those between Menin and Tournay upon Tournay, and then to join their regiments.

6. The 1st, 2nd, and 3rd divisions of infantry are to be collected at the headquarters of the divisions, and the cavalry at the headquarters of their several brigades, and the whole to be in readiness to march at a moment's notice.

7. The troops of the Netherlands to be collected at Soignies and Nivelles.

8. In case the attack should be made between the Sambre and the Scheldt, I propose to collect the British and Hanoverians at and in the neighbourhood of Enghien, and the army of the Low Countries at and in the neighbourhood of Soignies and Braine-le-Comte.

9. In this case, the 2nd and 3rd divisions will collect at their respective headquarters, and gradually fall back towards Enghien with the cavalry of Colonel Arentschildt's and the Hanoverian brigade.

10. The garrisons of Mons and Tournay will stand fast; but that of Ath will be withdrawn, with the 2nd division, if the works should not have been sufficiently advanced to render the place tenable against a *coup de main*.

11. General Sir W. Ponsonby's, Sir J. Vandeleur's, and Sir H. Vivian's brigades of cavalry will march upon Hal.

12. The troops of the Low Countries will collect upon Soignies and Braine-le-Comte.

13. The troops of the 4th division, and the 2nd Hussars, after taking up the bridge at Avelghem, will fall back upon Audenarde, and there wait for further orders.

14. In case of the attack being directed by both lines supposed, the troops of the 4th division and 2nd hussars, and the garrison of Ghent, will act as directed in Nos. 3 and 4 of this Memorandum; and the 2nd and 3rd divisions, and the cavalry, and the troops of the Low Countries, as directed in Nos. 8, 9, 10, 11, and 12.

The preceding document shows that the Duke of Wellington was always jealous of his own right. He anticipated that Napoleon's attack, whether made by single or double line, would fall upon that flank; and to the last moment he retained that opinion. His reasons for doing so we cannot presume to give; but they may possibly have been of this sort:—He knew, that of the various roads which conducted from the French frontier to Brussels, those which ran through the valley of the Sambre and the Meuse were by far the least practicable.

The enemy, indeed, had previously broken them up, as a measure apparently of defence against the allies; whereas the *chaussées* from Valenciennes through Nevers, from Condé through Ath and Enghien, and from Lisle through Tournay, were all of them excellent. It is probable, likewise, that, being himself aware of the exceeding importance of keeping open and safe his communications between England and Holland, he conceived that they would be struck at, and that the same process which interrupted them might force Louis XVIII. and his court to flee from Ghent.

Perhaps, too, it may have occurred to him, that armies, and especially allied armies, stretching over a large extent of country, are necessarily more vulnerable, if attacked on one of their extreme flanks, than if approached by the centre. In the latter case, the assailant may succeed in dividing them for a moment; but this very success will bring him into a position of twofold danger; for, unless he utterly destroy one before the other can arrive to its support, his partial victory must place him at once between two fires.

Moreover, by seeking to pierce the centre, he enables both wings to collect, either upon their advanced line, or upon a second line in the rear, with far greater rapidity, as well as with more certainty, than they could have done had they been taken in flank. In the one case, the most remote corps in either has but the length of its own line to traverse; in the other, the extreme left will not have had time to communicate with the extreme right, far less to strengthen it, ere the latter will have been doubled up, and the roads which It was protecting be laid bare.

Accordingly, to the latest moment, the Duke of Wellington kept his eye steadily upon the approaches by the valleys of the Scheldt and the Dender to Ghent and Brussels, while at the same time he observed with sufficient attention the progress of events elsewhere. For example, we find him, on the 9th of May, writing to Lord Hill, to the Prussian general in command at Charleroi, and to Sir Henry Hardinage, at that time employed as English commissioner at Prince Blücher's headquarters, about movements on the side of the enemy which seem to have escaped all observation except his own. The dispatch addressed to the latter ran thus:—

> There appears no doubt that the enemy's forces are collected at Maubeuge and Valenciennes—principally at the former. The communication was put an end to yesterday, and it was said Bonaparte was at Condé. I was told at Ghent that he was to leave Paris this day. I have written to the general officer commanding the Prussian troops at Charleroi; and I will keep him informed of all that I hear.

With these documents before us—and they constitute but a small portion of those which Colonel Gurwood's invaluable publication has given to the world—it seems incredible that there should exist in any nation individuals so absurd as to contend that the Duke of Wellington was at any moment thrown off his guard. His views of the method by which the campaign ought to have been opened may have differed from those of his illustrious opponent, and the right or the wrong in regard to such men's opinions must always continue a moot point; but that the Duke was prepared for every emergency, the whole tenor of his correspondence proves; and the issue of the struggle has surely not left in doubt the wisdom of his preparations to meet it.

So passed the residue of April and the whole of May. The season was one of continued preparation on both sides, and of a watchfulness which, though little noticed by the casual observer, never relaxed itself. A chain of cavalry outposts covered, on the side of the allies, all the approaches from France. On the side of France, bodies of gendarmerie, mixed with pickets of hussars, impeded as much as possible the intercourse of the peasantry, and did their best to stop a more open communication between persons of greater weight; and they were alike vigilant and active.

But as money, and that passion for double-dealing which seems to have been characteristic of almost all the leading men of the French Revolution, worked out ways and means for defeating the precautionary arrangements of Napoleon, so Flanders swarmed with persons who accounted it an honour and a privilege to report progress regularly to the leader of the French army, and to keep him aware, as far as their means of doing so would allow, of all that might be going on within the lines of the allies. Hence the Duke of Wellington, as has already been stated, never lacked intelligence, more or less accurate, of the enemy's designs and preparations.

Hence Napoleon, in like manner, was well acquainted with the positions of the different corps, both of the British and the Prussian armies; and if he deceived himself respecting the temper which prevailed in some of them, the blame may be shared, probably in equal proportions, between him and his informants.

On the 20th of May the Duke of Wellington addressed, from his headquarters at Brussels, a letter of congratulation to Prince

Metternich on the success of the Austrian operations against Murat. On the 2nd of June he wrote to Prince Schwartzenberg, urging an immediate advance from the Upper Rhine. In this latter communication, he describes himself as ready, and Marshal Blücher as eager, to begin the fray—while he gives his reasons why it would be imprudent in either to do so till the Russians and Austrians were in the field.

But the Duke was not the only actor in this great drama, who felt that the moment for drawing the curtain had arrived. Tidings of fresh movements, and of preparations hurried forward on an enormous scale, came in daily from France. It was clear that Napoleon would not wait to be attacked. It was equally evident that, crediting the reports of those who described the French party in the Low Countries as being both numerous and influential, the first blow would fall heavily in this direction.

Again were orders issued to have all things in a state of preparation. Blücher was kept conversant with events as they befell, or were anticipated. Particular directions were given to regard the fortresses as in a state of siege "*le moment que l'ennemie mettra le pied sur le territoire des Pays Bas,*" and particular instructions laid down as to the manner of dealing with each of them. Finally, the whole face of the country between Brussels and the frontier was reconnoitred; and officers of engineers wore employed to make sketches of such positions as seemed to offer peculiar facilities for the display of troops in order of battle. Among others, the field of Waterloo was mapped and laid down by Captain Pringle and Colonel Wells so early as the 8th of June, and the plan which these officers had made being given to the Duke during the retrogressive movement of the 17th, his Grace on that day, while his army was retiring, filled in with his own hand the places which the several brigades and regiments were to occupy.

Thus, in every way, and to the utmost extent which circumstances would admit of, the energies of the allied chiefs were taxed to provide against the future. No point was left unguarded; no opening given through which the communications of the armies with Holland, England, Germany, and with each other, might be broken, or their depôts and magazines exposed. Brussels was covered; Ghent, Nieuport, and Ostend were placed in comparative security; the line of the Meuse was observed from Namur to Maestricht; and the roads from Philippeville and Beaumont through Charleroi and Gosselies were protected by a double line, first, of Prussians extending from Thuin to Chatelet, and in rear of them by a division of the Prince of Orange's corps at Nivelles and Genappe.

CHAPTER 7

Rumours of coming Events—Commencement of Hostilities

There were present at the headquarters of the Duke of Wellington and Prince Blücher respectively, officers commissioned on either side to act as media of communication between the two chiefs. Lieutenant Colonel Sir Henry Hardinge (now [at time of writing] Lieutenant General Lord Viscount Hardinge) held this honourable post on the part of the English; General Baron Müffling was the accredited agent from Prince Blücher to the Duke of Wellington. The duties of these officers were as much diplomatic as military. They were intrusted with discretionary powers to negotiate such arrangements as the exigencies of the moment might render necessary; and it was their business to detail in conversation or otherwise the wishes of their respective chiefs to the generals to whom they were attached.

It would appear, likewise, that the commanders of corps and brigades in the Prussian army had been instructed, in the event of any movement on the part of the enemy, to report the same immediately to General Müffling for the information of the Duke of Wellington. These facts the historian is bound to keep in view while describing the great event that gave its character to the year 1815; because on the last of these an important question turns, which, were we without the light thus afforded to guide us in its examination, would be involved in impenetrable mystery.

On the 12th of June Lieutenant Colonel von Wessel, of the 1st Hussars, King's German Legion, reported to Sir Hussey Vivian from his outposts in front of Tournay, that the enemy were assembling in force. On the following day Vivian repaired to the outposts in person; and found that the cavalry which used to face our people had been withdrawn, and that their place was supplied by mounted custom-house officers.

With these he opened a communication; and they informed him, without hesitation, that hostilities were about to commence, and that if the Allied army delayed to enter France, the French would take the initiative by penetrating into Belgium. Vivian, as in duty bound, lost no time in informing Lord Hill and the Earl of Uxbridge of what had befallen; and these officers, in their turn, communicated the tidings to the Duke of Wellington. But his Grace did not, therefore, feel that the time was come for effecting any decided change in the disposition of his corps; and the Allied troops continued, in consequence, to occupy their cantonments as heretofore.

It was now manifest to all who saw beyond the surface of things, that the storm was about to break. The proceedings on the occasion of the famous Champ-de-Mai had long been communicated to the Allied generals. It was not concealed that the several corps of the army of the North had drawn nearer to one another; and the march of the Guard and the departure of Napoleon from Paris were openly discussed. Still the exact time or line by which the enemy would advance was a mystery; and till these should be cleared up, no counter-movement on the part either of the Prussians or the English could be made, except at a disadvantage. Accordingly, so late as the 15th of June all things went on at, Brussels as if no enemy had been within a hundred miles of the city.

There were the same rounds of morning calls and evening parties as heretofore. Friends met and greeted one another in the park, with scarcely an allusion to what the morrow might bring forth; and the Duke himself sat down to dinner at three o'clock—ignorant that a shot had been fired, or a French column put in motion. It was then that the Prince of Orange, coming in from the outposts to share his Grace's hospitality, made him aware for the first time, that the Prussians had been attacked at Thuin; and the following memorandum was, in consequence, drawn up and dispatched without a moment's delay:—

Bruxelles, 15th June, 1815.

General Dornberg's brigade of cavalry and the Cumberland Hussars to march this night upon Vilvorde, and to bivouac on the high road near to that town.

The Earl of Uxbridge will be pleased to collect the cavalry this night at Ninhove, leaving the 2nd Hussars looking out between the Scheldt and the Lys.

The 1st division of infantry to collect the night at Ath and places adjacent, and to be in readiness to move at a moment's notice.

The 3rd division to collect this night at Braine-le-Comte, and to be in readiness to move at the shortest notice.

The 4th division to be collected this night at Grammont, with the exception of the troops beyond the Scheldt, which are to be moved to Audenarde.

The 5th division, the 81st regiment, and the Hanoverian brigade of the 6th division to be in readiness to march from Brussels at a moment's notice.

The Duke of Brunswick's corps to collect this night on the high road between Brussels and Vilvorde.

The Nassau troops to collect at daylight tomorrow morning on the Louvain road, and. to be in readiness to move at a moment's notice.

The Hanoverian brigade to collect this night at Hal, and to be in readiness at daylight tomorrow morning to move towards Brussels; and to halt on the high road between Alost and Assche for further orders.

The Prince of Orange is requested to collect at Nivelles the 2nd and 3rd divisions of the army of the Low Countries; and should that point have been attacked this day, to move the 3rd division of British infantry upon Nivelles as soon as collected.

This movement is not to take place until it is quite certain that the enemy's attack is upon the right of the Prussian army, and the left of the British army.

Lord Hill will be so good as to order Prince Frederick of Orange to occupy Audenarde with 500 men, and to collect the 1st division of the army of the Low Countries and the Indian brigade at Sotteghem so as to be ready to march in the morning at daylight.

The reserve artillery to be in readiness to move at daylight.

Wellington.

The above orders were issued at four or five o'clock in the afternoon of the 15th. The couriers that took them were not long gone when Baron Müffling arrived with a confirmation of the Prince of Orange's statement; and gave a much more circumstantial and detailed narration of the events which had befallen. The Duke received this supplementary and grave intelligence with perfect coolness. There was to be a grand ball that night at the Duchess of Richmond's, to which the commander-in-chief, the headquarters' staff, and many officers, some of them from distant divisions, had been invited.

It was suggested to the Duke that the Duchess should be advised to postpone her entertainment. He rejected the counsel with a good-humoured joke, observing, that it would never do to disappoint a lady of her Grace's merits; and thus, as his habit was, wrapped up the most important political considerations in an apparent regard to the punctilios of civilized life.

The Duke knew that Brussels and Belgium generally would take the alarm soon enough; and he was too prudent to precipitate the event. He thereupon dressed himself, caused his immediate followers to dress in like manner, and without making an effort to stop any one even from the outposts, repaired at the appointed hour to the Duchess's apartments.

He did not go, however, without in the first place putting all things in a train, as became the leader of an army in his situation.

Whatever doubts he might have heretofore entertained regarding the nature of the movement which the enemy were making had been removed. He saw that the attack on the Prussian right was a real one; and though he still experienced a jealousy of his own right, he hastened to meet the assailant on the ground which himself had chosen. The following memorandum will best explain his manner of effecting this important end:—

> Bruxelles, After Orders, 15th of June, 10 o'clock at night.
> The 3rd division of Infantry to continue its movement from Braine-le-Comte upon Nivelles.
> The 1st division to move from Enghien upon Braine-le-Comte.
> The 2nd and 4th divisions to move from Ath and Grammont, also from Audenarde, and to continue their movements upon Enghien.
> The cavalry to continue its movements from Ninhove upon Enghien.
> The above movements to take place with as little delay as possible.

While the Duke of Wellington is thus preparing to meet the danger with which he is menaced, yet sustaining the spirits of his troops and giving confidence to his Allies by bearing himself to the last like one who knew not what danger was, it may not be amiss if we throw a rapid glance over the proceedings of the enemy, so as to connect these, and the operations of the Prussians arising out of them, with the crises in the affairs of the army of Flanders at which we have arrived.

The grand military spectacle of the Champ-de-Mai being accomplished, Napoleon, in pursuance of the promise which he then gave, proceeded to bring his strength to bear upon the northern frontier. The 4th corps, of which General Girard was at the head, quitted on the 6th of June its cantonments about Metz, Longwy, and Thionville, and marched upon Philippeville. It reached its appointed place of concentration on the 14th, and entered at once into communication with the 6th corps under Count Lobau, the 1st under Count d'Erlon, the 2nd under Count Reille, and the 3rd under Lieutenant General Count Vandamme.

All these had removed from their respective stations at Laon, Lisle, Valenciennes, and Mézières, in sufficient time to arrive on the 13th at Maubeuge and Avesne, and with the four corps of reserve cavalry, which were concentrated on the Upper Sambre, constituted an army to which, both for its composition and its numbers, the world has never seen anything superior. For in addition to the magnificent troops of the line—the infantry, cavalry, and artillery, of which France had just cause to be proud—the Imperial Guard, which defiled out of Paris on the 8th, marched on the 13th into its bivouac. And finally, Napoleon himself, travelling with his accustomed celerity, compassed between the 12th and the evening of the 13th, the space which divided the capital from his army; and at an early hour in the morning of the 14th put forth the celebrated Order of the Day, of which the subjoined is a translation:—

> Soldiers!—This is the day—the anniversary of Marengo and of Friedland—which twice decided the fate of Europe. Then, as after Austerlitz, as after Wagram, we were too generous. We believed in the protestations and oaths of princes whom we left on their thrones. Now, however, leagued together, they aim at the independence and the most sacred rights of France. They have commenced the most unjust of aggressions. Let us then march to meet them. Are they and we no longer the same men?
> Soldiers!—At Jena, against these same Prussians, who are now so arrogant, you were one to three, and at Montmirail one to six.
> Let those among you who have been captives to the English, describe the nature of their prison-ships, and the frightful miseries they endured.
> The Saxons, the Belgians, the Hanoverians, the soldiers of the Confederation of the Rhine, lament that they are compelled to use their arms in the cause of princes—the

enemies of justice and of the rights of all nations. They know that this coalition is insatiable. After having devoured twelve millions of Poles, one million of Saxons, and six millions of Belgians, it now wishes to devour the states of the second rank in Germany.

Madmen!—One moment of prosperity has bewildered them. The oppression and the humiliation of the French people are beyond their power. If they enter France, they will there find their grave.

Soldiers!—We have forced marches to make, battles to fight, dangers to encounter; but with firmness, victory will be ours. The rights, the honour, and the happiness of the country will be recovered.

To every Frenchman who has a heart, the moment is now arrived to conquer or to die.

Napoleon.

Meanwhile the Prussians were neither blind to the preparations which the enemy were making, nor regardless of them. General von Zieten, who commanded the 1st *Corps d'armée,* and communicated by his right with the extreme left of the British army, saw from his outposts in front of Thuin and Lobbes the fires of the French bivouac. These had suddenly gleamed up from behind a range of slight acclivities, which pass from Solre-sur-Sambre, by Beaumont, as far as Philippeville, and led at once to the conclusion that on the right of the Sambre, so as to threaten the road to Charleroi, a strong force was assembled. Zieten lost no time in communicating the result of his observations to Marshal Blücher and to the Duke of Wellington.

Had he been equally alert in making the latter aware of the attack which was not long afterwards made upon his own position, the battle of Ligny might have either not been fought at all, or would have terminated less disastrously to his countrymen; but by a strange fatality he overlooked the necessity of doing this, and some precious hours were in consequence lost, and many valuable lives sacrificed.

General Zieten, and indeed the Prussians of all ranks, were

perfectly prepared for any event that might occur. So early as the 2nd of May, the commander of the 1st Corps had given particular instructions to the officers at the head of his brigades concerning the course which, in case of an attack, it behooved them to follow. They were to maintain themselves in Lobbes, Thuin, and the villages adjacent, as long as possible; to fall back fighting upon Marchienne, Charleroi, and Chatelet,—to defend the passages of the Sambre and the Picton; and last of all, if overpowered, to break down the bridges, and retire upon a new position, of which Gosselies should be one pivot and Fleurus another.

In strict agreement with the purport of these instructions were the orders which Blücher at ten o'clock on the night of the 14th dispatched to Generals Bülow, Pirch, and Thielmann, of whom each was at the head of a corps. The First was directed to march without delay from Liège to Hannut; the Second to move from Namur upon Sombref; the Third to fall back from Ciney to Namur; and the whole to unite, as soon as ulterior directions should reach them, in rear of Fleurus. Thus General Thielmann's corps became a screen for the other three, which, protected by it, were to concentrate and form; after which, either with or without the English, Blücher expressed himself ready to give battle.

The dawn of the 15th was just beginning to break, when Napoleon, who had slept the previous night in Beaumont, appeared with his brother Jerome at a balcony, and was seen anxiously to examine the state of the weather. This was to him a matter of vital importance, because it affected to a great extent the efficiency of his cavalry, to which, in the rich heavy plains of Belgium, he mainly trusted for separating the Prussians from the English and enabling him to beat them in detail. There was nothing unfavourable in the aspect of the heavens.

Some clouds floated over the face of the sky, but they could not be said to threaten a storm; and Napoleon, as if satisfied with the results of his observations, withdrew. In less than an hour afterwards, that is to say, about half-past three, or a little earlier, the whole of the French army was in motion, and in various columns directed its march upon Marchienne, Charleroi, and Chatelet.

As soon as the enemy's light troops crossed the frontier they became engaged with the Prussian pickets. The latter could not of course keep their ground, but fell back skirmishing, and all the open country between Binche and the Sambre was abandoned. The village of Lobbes and the little town of Thuin presented, however, more defensible features, and of these the French did not gain possession till after a severe struggle.

Upon this General Zieten withdrew into Charleroi with his 2nd brigade, and prepared to hold the bridges to the last extremity. Meanwhile his 1st brigade fell back, by Marchionne-au-Pont, upon Gilly—the 3rd and 4th marching direct towards Fleurus. At the former of these places the 1st brigade made a resolute stand, though numbers at length prevailed; and at the latter it took up a good position, and was permitted for an hour or two to rest. Charleroi became henceforth the object of the enemy's movements, and it was furiously assailed by General Pajol's light cavalry in the first instance, and next by the Imperial Guard, which occupied ground that ought to have been taken by Vandamme's corps, but which the latter, through some mismanagement, never received orders to seize.

The fighting at Charleroi was severe, but the result could not be doubtful. About eleven o'clock the French were, in possession of the town; and the bridges, both there and at Marchienne, higher up the stream, fell into their hands; being but partially injured, they were immediately restored.

That General Zieten bore himself throughout this trying day like a gallant soldier, and fully discharged the duty which, in this respect, he owed to his country, admits of no doubt. He did not give up an inch of ground so long as it could be maintained; and by the obstinacy of his resistance to immense odds not only retarded the advance of the enemy, but gave time to Blücher, with three out of the four corps which he had put in motion, to assemble. But for the negligence which hindered him from communicating with Brussels, as well as with Hannut, it is impossible to account. It does not appear that he entertained the smallest doubt, from the beginning, in regard to the nature and extent of the danger which threatened. At five o'clock in the morning he saw that the whole French army was in his front. At ten he was warmly engaged with the Imperial Guard about Charleroi, and could not have failed, had he thought at all, to perceive that it was quite as necessary to inform the Duke of Wellington of the circumstance, as to make it known to Prince Blücher.

Neither was there any reason, in the local situations of the headquarters of the two marshals, why the one should have been kept in ignorance of what was communicated to the other. Brussels is not further removed from Charleroi than Hannut. Both may be about thirty English miles distant from that town; and the road to the former was, in 1815, at least as passable as the road to the latter. Had General Zieten, therefore, as soon as he satisfied himself concerning the real state of the case, dispatched an *aide-de-camp* or a well-mounted orderly to Baron Müffling, tidings of Napoleon's advance would have reached the Duke of Wellington by ten o'clock in the morning at the latest.

This, however, he failed to do; and the consequence was, that orders which might have been issued to the English divisions at ten in the morning, were not dispatched till ten at night—a loss of time which wholly incapacitated the Allies from coming up as they otherwise would have done, *en masse,* to support the Prussians, and which, but for the sagacity and marvellous energy of their leader, must have left the Prussians on the 16th to sustain, single handed, the whole weight of the enemy's forces.

The French, though checked at every favourable position, were everywhere successful. They had carried all the advanced stations of the Prussians, and were in command of the great road which leads by Charleroi to Brussels. It became from henceforth their business to push this advantage to the uttermost, and to cut off, if possible, all communication between the Duke of Wellington and Prince Blücher. With this view Napoleon put two *corps d'armée* under the orders of Marshal Ney, who joined him at seven o'clock on this eventful evening, and directed him to press forward by the great *chaussée*, and to sweep before him whatever troops he might find cantoned on the way to Brussels. Meanwhile he himself, with the bulk of the army, took the road to Fleurus. It was his design, as it was evidently his interest, to throw back the Prussian right.

Could he but succeed in rolling it on towards Namur, his game might be played with good prospect of success, for he confidently anticipated that Ney, reinforced by a reserve corps of heavy cavalry, would be able to hold the English in check till the Prussians should have been disposed of. But Napoleon did not calculate either on the obstinacy of Blücher, or on the untiring energy of the British soldiers, and the fertile genius of their chief. He waged war as he had been accustomed to do against Melas in Italy, and the Duke of Brunswick at Jena; and the event proved that neither Blücher nor Wellington were to be foiled with such weapons.

The main body of the French army did not advance that night beyond Fleurus. Zieten and his corps were, indeed, in position about that place, and so well had they contested the ground intermediate between it and the bridges over the Sambre, that daylight was wanting to the enemy—had there been animal vigour enough left—to carry them through a struggle for its possession. Ney, however, pushed on. He passed through Gosselies, keeping a regiment of lancers in his front, and met with no resistance till he began to touch Frasne, when his cavalry was received with such a heavy fire of grape and musketry that it recoiled. A few words will explain whence this proceeded.

It has been stated elsewhere that the extreme left of the Duke of Wellington's line composed of the 2nd Dutch-Belgian division under General de Perponcher, rested upon the high road between Charleroi and Brussels; the 2nd brigade of this division, of which Prince Bernhard of Saxe Weimar was in command, comprised the three battalions of the 2nd regiment of Nassau, two battalions of the regiment of Orange-Nassau, and a Dutch battery of horse-artillery. Of these, the second battalion of the regiment of Nassau, with the Dutch guns, lay at Frasne and Villers Peruin.

They had heard from an early hour the sound of firing; but having long been accustomed to the noise of the Prussian practice, and no messenger coming in to warn them that work more serious was in progress, they naturally concluded that things remained as heretofore, and that there could be no particular demand upon their vigilance. By-and-by some wounded Prussian soldiers dragged themselves towards their cantonments, and then the truth came out. Major Van Normann, who commanded the battalion, beat to arms forthwith.

He threw out a picket in front of Frasne—chose ground for the main body of his infantry and of his guns in its roar—and, after informing General Porponcher of the state of affairs, lay upon his arms. He was attacked late in the afternoon, and his pickets driven in; but on the line and the battery which it protected, the enemy's horse made no impression. By-and-by a division of Reille's infantry assailed him—the lancers threatening at the same time—and he was forced to fall back, though in good order, upon the wood of Bossu. This, a covert of some extent, lay upon the right of the hamlet of Quatre Bras, into which place Prince Bernhard had thrown the main body of his brigade, and it afforded excellent cover to Major Van Normann's battalion.

He filled it in force; and such was the attitude assumed, both by him and the remainder of the brigade, that the enemy, after one or two attempts to overwhelm them, withdrew. That night the advance of Ney's force slept in Frasne and in the fields adjacent. Reille, with two divisions and a strong body of artillery, occupied Gosselies. Girard, with one division, was at Heppignies, in communication with the main army in front of Fleurus; while d'Erlon, whose corps was likewise under Ney's orders, bivouacked in and around Marchienne-au-Pont. Thus, after eighteen hours of constant marching and fighting, the French found themselves about fifteen miles in advance of their position of the 14th, having driven back, but not destroyed, one of the four corps of which the Prussian army was composed, and barely touched, without seriously engaging, two brigades of the Anglo-Belgian army.

CHAPTER 8

Concentration of the English and Prussian Armies at Quatre Bras and Ligny

The night between the 15th and 16th of June was an anxious and fatiguing one to thousands. The Prussians were in full march from Ciney, Namur, and Huy. Bülow's corps, likewise, which lay at Liège, had been sent for; but by some mistake on the part of the messenger the dispatch never reached its destination, and Bülow failed in consequence to take his prescribed part in the operations. Meanwhile the French, overcome with fatigue, lay, in marvellously loose order, over the whole face of the country from the Sambre to Fleurus.

The heads of their columns had indeed been pushed within three English miles of the Prussian point of concentration; but the rear straggled in a very unaccountable manner. Napoleon himself slept at Charleroi, a great deal too far in the rear, more especially as he kept with him the Guards, as well as the whole of Lobau's corps—for his own fate and the fate of Europe hung at that moment in the balance. He had struck a bold, perhaps a rash blow. He was seeking that which was scarcely to be obtained except by a fortunate accident, and the loss of which was morally certain, unless the search were followed up energetically.

He might not know—probably he did not—the exact position which Blücher had determined to take up; but the line of the Prussian fires showed him where their troops lay, and his own he ought to have concentrated within half cannon-shot of them. Instead of this he permitted brigades, divisions, and corps to establish themselves for the night wherever darkness overtook them, so that to renew the battle with any sure prospect of success on the first dawn of the morning was impossible.

Of the breathing space thus allowed them the allied generals made good use. The 1st Prussian Corps, that of Zieten, weakened by a loss of about 1200 men, Blücher placed in a position which he had well reconnoitred above the village of Ligny. The 2nd Corps, of which General Pirch was at the head, bivouacked between Onoz and Mazy, about six miles off. It had marched that day from Namur. The 3rd, or General Thielmann's corps, from Ciney, scarcely halted to rest in Namur, but moved on all night, and made strenuous endeavours to close. Bülow, as has already been stated, took things more easily, for though he had been warned to pass from Liège to Hannut, he was not made aware that there was need of haste; and Liège being full sixty English miles from Ligny, there was little chance of his arriving in time for a battle.

Still Blücher calculated on being able, about noon on the 16th at the furthest, to bring together, if not interrupted, 80,000 good troops; and Napoleon certainly did not act as if he had desired to interrupt him. Blücher, therefore, felt tolerably secure, for he knew enough of the character of the Duke of Wellington to be aware that on his Grace's part no exertions to co-operate with him effectually would be wanting. But Blücher either did not know, or amid the anxieties of his own situation forgot, that the Duke had been left too much in the dark concerning the events that were in progress.

It has been stated already that the first tidings communicated to the Duke of the attack by the French on General Zieten's outposts were carried to him about three o'clock in the afternoon of the 15th, by the Prince of Orange. His Royal Highness evidently did not know whether the attack was a real or a feigned one, for he described the enemy as having occupied and subsequently abandoned Binche; and the Duke had too much respect for the genius of Napoleon to risk, on such uncertain tidings, a movement that might prove to be a false one. He, therefore, contented himself by directing the various divisions of his army to assemble at their respective alarm-posts. But no sooner was General Müffling introduced as the bearer of intelligence that could he relied upon than he put the whole of the troops in motion.

All the corps lying to the left of Nivelles were directed to march on that point; they were to proceed, too, independently, under cover of the fortresses which the Duke's provident care had thrown up; and they did so without sustaining the slightest molestation. Moreover, so quietly was the operation planned and carried into effect, now that all fears of attack by the Mons road were removed, that in Brussels itself only a few vague rumours broke in upon the sense of security which, up to that moment, had pervaded all circles.

There was no interruption to the common business of life; people bought and sold, went and came, as heretofore; and in the evening the notes of a well-arranged military band proclaimed where the Duchess of Richmond held her revels. Little guessed the majority of the fair and the brave who met that night under her Grace's auspices, that before another sun should have risen and set, the dance of life would by many be ended.

The reserve of the Anglo-Belgian army, consisting of the 5th and 6th English divisions, under Sir Thomas Picton and Sir Lowry Cole, of the Brunswick division, under the Duke of Brunswick, and the contingent of the Duke of Nassau, under General Kruse, occupied quarters in and around Brussels. One brigade, indeed, the 7th, composed of the 2nd battalions 25th, 37th, and 78th regiments, of the 13th Veteran battalion, a foreign battalion of the same description of force, and the 2nd garrison battalion—in all 3233 men—had been sent to garrison the various fortresses from Mons to Ostend.

But the remainder, with its artillery, amounting in all to nine batteries, filled the town, or occupied the villages and hamlets adjacent to it, General Kruse's Nassau brigade stretching off along the road to Louvain. Among these troops were three Highland Regiments, the 42nd, 79th, and 92nd, which we stop to particularize—not because they surpassed their comrades in gallantry, but simply on account of a circumstance, unimportant in itself, which seems to connect them more than other corps with the transactions of this memorable night.

The Duchess of Richmond, of whose ball so much notice has been taken, was the sister of the late and last Duke of Gordon. The Duke was Colonel of the 92nd regiment, which, because it had been raised upon his estates, was called the Gordon Highlanders; and the Duchess of Richmond, being proud of her brother and of her country, made arrangements for exhibiting to her guests that night a perfect specimen of the Highland fling.

With this view she caused a selection to be made from among the non-commissioned officers of the above-mentioned corps, not only desiring such to be chosen as were most skilled in the mysteries of that national dance, but making a particular request that all should be, in point of personal appearance, excellent specimens of their race. The wishes of the high-born dame were carefully attended to. Preceded by their pipers, a little body of Highlanders marched that night into her Grace's hall, of whom it is not too much to assert, that Scotland could furnish nothing superior to them; and the admirable nature of their performance in reel, Strathspey, and sword dance, is still remembered by the fast-diminishing few who survive to speak of it.

They also, like the ladies who beheld them and admired, were little aware of the brief interval which should elapse ere the instruments which then stirred then in the game would cheer them to the battle. Indeed there were but few in that bright assembly who guessed that danger was near; and they who knew it best, including the Duke and the officers of his personal staff, were in their manner the most entirely unembarrassed.

It had been hinted to the generals of division and brigade, that, one by one, as the night drew on, they should take their leave. Orders likewise had been issued to the troops in and around Brussels to hold themselves in readiness to march at a moment's notice; and the consequence was, that without exactly anticipating the actual course of events, men packed their knapsacks, and officers arranged their baggage, ere they lay down. By and by general after general withdrew from the Duchess's party—some on the plea that their commands were far away—others, because duty or private business called them. The Duke remained till a late hour, and returned thanks after supper for the health of the Prince Regent, which was proposed by the Prince of Orange. He soon afterwards retired, and the company broke up.

There might have been one hour's quiet in the streets of Brussels. The rattle of carriages was over. Light after light had been extinguished in chamber and in hall, and sleep seemed to have established its dominion over the city, when a bugle-call, heard first in the Place d'Armes, on the summit of the Montagne du Parc, and taken up and echoed back through various quarters of the town, roused all classes of people in a moment.

From every window in the place heads were protruded, and a thousand voices desired to be informed if anything was the matter; for though they put the idea from them, few had lain down that night altogether free from uneasiness, and now the bugle's warning note seemed to speak to their excited imaginations of an enemy at the gates. Anxious, therefore, and shrill were the voices which demanded to be informed of the cause of this interruption to their repose.

But there was little need to answer them in words: the bugle call was soon followed by the rolling of drums and the screaming of bagpipes. By-and-by regiments were seen, by the dim light of the stars, to muster in park, square, street, and alley—horses neighed—guns rumbled over the causeways—drivers shouted—and overall was heard, from time to time, the short quick word of command, which soldiers best love to hear, and obey with the greatest promptitude. The reserve, in short, was getting under arms, each brigade at its appointed alarm-post; and by-and-by, one after another, as they were ready, they marched off in the direction of the forest of Soignies.

Many and heart-rending were the partings which occurred

at two o'clock in the morning of the 16th of June, 1815. As has already been stated, Brussels swarmed at that time with visitors not of the military order; and the wives and families of British soldiers of all ranks made up no inconsiderable part of its population. They hoard the bugle sound, and saw their husbands, and fathers, and brothers hurry to their stations with feelings such as they had never experienced till then.

They had heard often enough of mustering for the conflict, and read, when the carnage was over, long lists of killed and wounded; but on former occasions the scene had been at a distance from them, and even if individually interested in the result they had no opportunity of realizing its horrors. Now they were upon the spot, clinging to the necks of those dearest to them, and knowing only this—that a battle was impending. It was piteous to see and agonizing to listen to the wild tokens of their alarm.

Many a woman, cast in a more delicate mould than for the most part gives her shape to the private soldier's wife, refused to be parted from her husband or her brother, and marched with him. One in particular—a bride of two months—threw herself on horseback, and rode on the flank of the regiment; and yet she was a fair, fragile girl, who, under any other circumstances, would have shrunk with horror from such an undertaking. That was a night never to be forgotten by such as witnessed the strange occurrences which marked its progress. All thought, all feeling seemed, among the non-combatants, to merge and lose themselves in the single idea of a battle at hand; and where no nobler impulse urged to acts of self-sacrifice, terror appeared to deprive them of their senses.

The dawn was just breaking when the leading regiments of the reserve filed out of the park at Brussels, and took the road to Quatre Bras. It was at this point that the Duke had directed the several columns of his army to concentrate, and towards this same point he himself proceeded about seven or eight o'clock. He was in the highest possible spirits, as were the whole of the brilliant staff which surrounded him, and while he rode along, regiments and brigades cheered him as he passed. The Prince of Orange had quitted the ball-room about the same time with the Duke, but he made straight for the front. He reached Nivelles at six; and finding that General Perponcher had gone onto the outposts, and that a smart skirmish prevailed there, he put the troops which occupied the town, the 2nd brigade of Perponcher's division, in movement, and closed them up to support the 1st brigade. The occasion which rendered the operation necessary was this:—

There was a good deal of blackness in the advance of the French throughout the early part of the morning of the 16th of June. The fact is, that neither was Ney acquainted with the troops which had been put under his orders, nor had time been afforded to the force of which he was in command to know him. He arrived at Charleroi in the midst of the operations of the 10th, destitute of baggage, and having just purchased two horses, on which he was able to mount himself and his first *aide-de-camp*. He knew nothing of Napoleon's plans—of the strength of the force that was opposed to him, or of the nature of the country on which he was suddenly called to exhibit his capabilities of manoeuvring troops in the presence of an enemy.

The orders under which he acted seem, moreover, to have been as confused, as the disposition of his corps was loose and imperfectly defined. Having remained with Napoleon till two o'clock in the morning, he proceeded, without taking rest, to Gosselies, where he communicated with Count Reille; and by employing his first *aide-de-camp*, Colonel Heymes, to muster, in some sense, the several regiments, he obtained an imperfect knowledge both of the number and quality of the officers and soldiers of Reille's corps, of which he had been put in charge. Beyond this, however, he could not go. D'Erlon's corps lay still at Marchiennes-au-Pont with the 3rd corps of heavy cavalry under Kellerman; and though Lefebvre-Desnouettes' light cavalry of the Guard, which had been provisionally promised, was nearer at hand, he could not, in consequence of a desire from Napoleon to the contrary, make use of it.

It is not, therefore, to be wondered at, if, instead of pressing Prince Bernhard of Saxe Weimer at early dawn, he stood for some hours on the defensive. Indeed it was Prince Bernhard who, without waiting to be attacked, renewed hostilities as soon as there was light; and both General Perponcher and the Prince of Orange, finding him so committed, brought up all the reinforcements at their disposal, and gained ground, in spite of a sharp resistance, till they arrived within a mile of the village of Frasne.

About eight in the morning the Duke of Wellington quitted Brussels. About eleven, or a little later, he reached Quatre Bras; whence he closely reconnoitred the enemy's position, and satisfied himself that there was no immediate danger from the side of Frasne. This done, and having left directions with the Prince of Orange as to the points of halt for such corps as might arrive in his absence, he galloped off to communicate in person with Field-Marshal Prince Blücher.

The latter had, with exceeding diligence and activity, gathered three out of his four corps into position. lie occupied a chain of elevations, rather than heights, which, extending from Bry on the right, embraced Sombref in the centre, and terminated at Tongrines. The advantage of this position was, that it covered the high road from Namur to Nivelles and Quatre Bras, at the points where the roads from Charleroi and Thuin fall in with it. It had likewise in its front the rivulet of Ligny, into which a smaller stream, after winding through a ravine, falls; with several villages, especially St. Amand and Ligny itself, standing forward as outposts, at the foot of the slope. Its disadvantages were, that it offered no security to the right; in other words, to that flank by which the communications with the English were to be kept open; and that the villages in advance were too far removed from the line to permit of their being reinforced, in case of need, except at great hazard.

There, however, Blücher had drawn up his army; and when the Duke of Wellington joined him, he explained the dispositions of the several corps with much apparent complacency.

The Duke is said to have expressed, with characteristic good-breeding, yet firmness, his disapproval of Prince Blücher's arrangements:

> "Everyman," (such is the substance of the words which the Duke is said to have spoken,) "knows his own people best; but I can only say that, with a British army, I should not occupy this ground as you do."

Blücher, however, represented that his countrymen liked to see the enemy before they engaged him; and adhered to the opinion that St. Amand and Ligny were the keys of his position. And the Duke was at once too wise and too much under the influence of a right feeling to press his point.

It was the Duke's desire to co-operate with Prince Blücher actively rather than passively. He saw that against the latter the main strength of the French army would be carried, and he proposed to advance as soon as he should have concentrated force enough, upon Frasne and Gosselies, and to fall upon the enemy's rear. But this, which would have been both a practicable and a judicious movement, had his Grace received intimation of the French attack in good time, was now well nigh impossible.

It was idle to expect that Napoleon would delay his onward movement long enough to permit the concentration at Quatre Bras of such a force as would authorize an aggressive operation; and a project, admirable in itself, was at once abandoned. and an arrangement made, that by the Namur road the Allies should support one another. It is said that the Duke, as he cantered back to his own ground, turned to a staff officer deeply in his confidence, and said:

> Now mark my words: the Prussians will make a gallant fight; for they are capital troops, and well commanded; but they will be beaten. I defy any army not to be beaten placed as they are, if the force that attacks be such as I suppose the French under Bonaparte are.

Chapter 9

Battle of Quatre Bras

The outposts of the Anglo-Belgian army held their ground in front of Frasne, almost without firing a shot, from seven in the morning till two in the afternoon. The Prince of Orange, who commanded them, saw, indeed, that the enemy's force was accumulating from hour to hour; and cast many an anxious look behind, for the support which he knew to be on its march. But none arrived; and he therefore made the best dispositions which circumstances would admit of, to impede the progress of an onset which might momentarily be expected. His object was to retain possession of the Quatre Bras—in other words of the point where the four roads to Namur, Nivelles, Charleroi, and Brussels cross; and with this view he took up a position in front of the village, and as near to Frasne as was consistent with a due regard for his own safety.

Two guns, with a howitzer, were planted upon the Charleroi road; another gun, with a howitzer, a little to the right of it; and three more guns on the Namur road. This disposition exhausted General Perponcher's divisional horse artillery, and left but six guns and two howitzers of the foot artillery disposable. Four of these, with the howitzers, were disposed in a second line, immediately in advance of Quatre Bras.

The remaining two were thrown out, so as to give support to the Prince's first line of infantry; and finally, he made arrangements, in case of being forced back from the immediate vicinity of Frasne, to occupy in strength the farm of Gemioncourt, and the inclosures of Piermont, both to his left of the Charleroi road, and the wood of Bossu on the right; and to keep his ground there to the last extremity. The whole strength of the corps which he thus arranged in order of battle was 6832 infantry, with 16 pieces of cannon.

While the Prince of Orange was thus putting himself in an attitude of defence, Ney, to whom on the previous day Napoleon had given the command of two infantry, with an equal number of cavalry corps, seems, by some mismanagement or another, to have been paralysed. One corps, that of Reille, was tolerably well in hand, and Pire's light cavalry were manageable; but D'Erlon was far in the rear; and Kellermann's horsemen seemed, by orders from a higher quarter, to be kept irresolute. D'Erlon's corps, indeed, never succeeded in getting into line; and even of Reille's four divisions one was unexpectedly withdrawn.

Ney complains bitterly of these things, in a letter dated at Paris so early as the 26th of June, 1815; and the substance of the charge against his Imperial Master is fully borne out by the testimony of his opponents. The fact appears to be, that Napoleon finding a stouter resistance from the Prussians than he had anticipated, arrested the march of D'Erlon's corps from Marchienne to Quatre Bras, and turned it towards St. Amand. Neither this force nor General Girard's division, in like manner abstracted from Ney's corps, arrived in time to do any good service against Blücher: but both were withdrawn from the service to which they had been allotted, and so, to use the expressive words of the brave, but unfortunate soldier, whom Napoleon did not scruple twice to sacrifice;

> Twenty-five or thirty thousand men were, I may say, paralysed; and were idly paraded, during the whole of the battle, from the right to the left, and from the left to the right, without firing a shot.

At two o'clock in the day, or a little earlier. Ney counted upon being immediately joined by D'Erlon and Kellermann. He had communicated with both generals more than once, and satisfied them of what he believed to be Napoleon's intentions.

Indeed, his last orders required, that without further delay they should close up, and cover by their formations the attack which he was about to make on the Brussels road. For this latter service he had set apart three divisions of Reille's corps amounting to 15,750 men, with 1865 of Pire's light cavalry, and four batteries of foot and one of horse artillery,—in all 38 pieces of cannon,—and with these he now advanced, in formidable array, against the Prince of Orange.

As was to be expected from the great disparity of numbers, the first attacks of the French were everywhere successful. The Prince of Orange fell back upon the position which he had selected in front of Quatre Bras, and there maintained himself for a while with considerable bravery. But first the village of Piermont, and then the farm of Gemioncourt, were, after a respectable resistance, carried, and the wood of Bossu alone afforded cover to the troops which fought for the junction of the four roads. It was now, when the hearts of the Belgians were failing them, and their gallant leader felt the critical nature of his position, that the apparition of a dark red mass moving over the high grounds that look down upon Quatre Bras operated on all who beheld it like magic.

This was the 5th division, with Sir Thomas Picton at its head, and consisted of two British brigades, the 8th and 9th, the former under Sir James Kempt, the latter under Sir Dennis Pack, with one brigade of Hanoverians—the 4th—of which Colonel Best had the charge. Moreover, there accompanied these stout footmen two batteries of artillery,—one Hanoverian, under Captain Von Rittberg, the other English, under Major Rogers; and the whole defiling by the Namur road, drew up in two lines, the British brigades forming in front, the Hanoverians in reserve.

The brigade of Pack consisted of the 1st battalion 42nd, 2nd 44th, 1st 92nd, and 1st 95th; that of Kempt comprised the 1st 28th, 1st 32nd, 1st 79th, and 3rd 1st Royals. The 4th Hanoverian brigade (Colonel Best's—out of its proper place, as it continued to be to the end of the operations) consisted of four *Landwehr* battalions, each mustering on an average about 650 bayonets.

They had scarcely effected their formations when the Duke of Brunswick's corps arrived,—not complete, for neither the artillery nor the 1st and 2nd Light Battalions had joined, but in sufficient force to render less oppressive the inequality which had heretofore prevailed between the combatants.

Indeed, in point of mere numbers the Duke was now superior to his adversary; for he had in the field about 18,000 infantry, 2000 cavalry, and 28 guns. But, when the composition of the respective corps is taken into account, the advantage thence arising will be found to have been less than nothing; for no reliance whatever could be placed on any except his British and German soldiers, and these, when computed together, amounted to scarce 8000 men at the utmost.

The cavalry, in particular, proved in the hour of need utterly worthless. The men were young and inexperienced, and the horses no match for the animals on which Pire's troopers were mounted; nevertheless, the mere show of columns is not without its effect, especially at the outset of a battle; and the Duke of Wellington lost no time in making the most of his.

It has already been stated that the French, after a trifling resistance, made themselves masters of Piermont, Gemioncourt, and of a considerable portion of the wood of Bossu. They had even pushed forward a cloud of skirmishers into a small thicket which lay in advance of Piermont, and gained by so doing momentary possession of the Namur road.

Indeed, their position was at this moment such as to hold out the best promise of ultimate success; nor, perhaps, shall we go beyond the line of probability if we acknowledge, that had D'Erlon's corps been where Ney expected it to be, the left of the Allies must have been very roughly handled, if not doubled up. But D'Erlon was not where Ney had desired him to be, and the Duke saw too clearly the importance of maintaining or recovering the command of the Namur road to hesitate as to the course which it behooved him to follow.

The 1st battalion 95th regiment was instantly moved in the direction of Piermont. These gallant riflemen did not get so far, for Piermont was well secured; but they drove out the light troops which had entered the wood in advance of it, and fully restored the communication between Quatre Bras and Ligny. Meanwhile Ney was not slack to make use of the advantages which he had won.

His right was still safe, though less movable than he could have wished; his left was equally secure in the wood of Bossu; and his centre found a strong *point d'appui* in Gemioncourt, within pistol shot of the Charleroi road; moreover, the whole front of his position was covered by a double hedgerow, so disposed as to afford admirable shelter to his skirmishers; while a succession of heights in rear of Gemioncourt, offered just such a *plateau* for his artillery as would best enable it to sweep the English position, and to cover the formation of his columns of attack, in whatever direction he might prefer to send them on.

The Duke of Wellington returned from his conference with Blücher just before the arrival of Picton's division. He closely reconnoitred the enemy's position, and detected the formation of a heavy column in rear of the wood of Bossu, which had not been observed by anyone except himself. He instantly directed the Prince of Orange to withdraw the guns which stood exposed on the road, and to gather in the Dutch-Belgian infantry, which were scattered somewhat loosely on either side of them.

These movements were hardly effected when the storm burst which swept the 5th regiment of Dutch militia out of Gemioncourt, and forced the defenders of the wood on its right to give ground in all directions. Meanwhile the Duke galloped off towards the Namur road, where he personally superintended the distribution of Picton's division. One regiment, the 28th, proceeded to the assistance of the 5th Dutch Militia; but, arriving too late to secure the farm, it returned to its place in the brigade. The remainder, with the exception of the 1st Battalion Rifle Corps, formed line in front of the Namur road; and, under a furious cannonade from the high grounds in the French position, waited further orders.

These formations were yet in progress when the Duke of

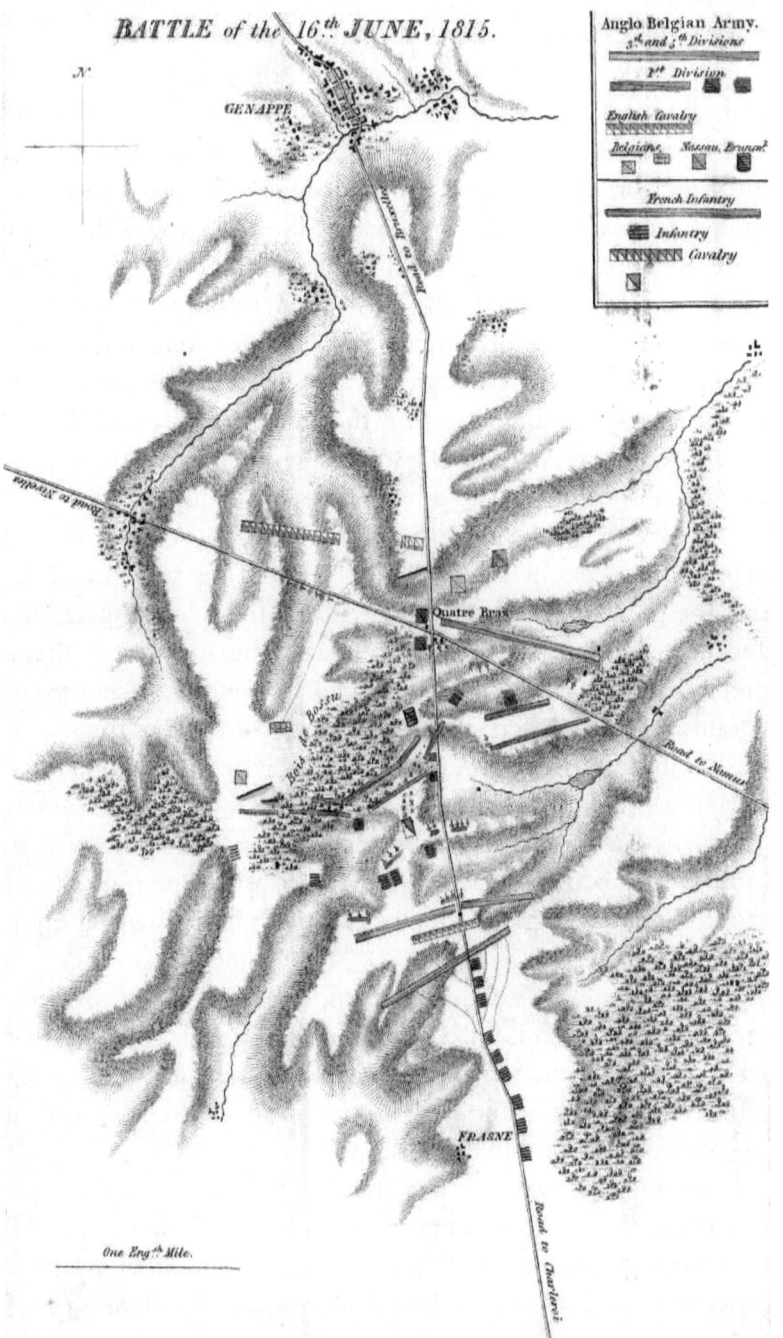

Brunswick's corps arrived, of which one battalion was sent forthwith to support the 95th. They did their duty well, and ably seconded their English comrades in repelling every attack that was made upon the thicket into which they were thrown. But the wood of Bossu on the Allied right was all this while in great danger. Though crowded with Dutch-Belgians, the continued inclination of the fire towards the rear proved that they were not a match for the French *tirailleurs*; and two rifle companies, detached from the Duke of Brunswick's corps, were sent in consequence to reinforce them. Some cavalry were at the same time thrown beyond the wood, to watch what the French might he doing in that direction; and the remainder formed line in support of Picton's division, as a measure preparatory to such an ultimate disposition as circumstances might require,

The French batteries from the heights above Gemioncourt kept up an incessant and a destructive fire. They were so placed that the guns of the Allies could reply to them but imperfectly; and the enemy aware of the advantages thus insured to them, prepared, under cover of this iron hail, to play for a richer prize. Clouds of skirmishers rushing through the hedgerows, and stealing beyond the thickets and woods by which the road was skirted warned the Duke of Wellington that a column was about to advance, whereupon he directed the Duke of Brunswick to move with a portion of his corps, and to interpose himself between Gemioncourt and Quatre Bras, with his left resting upon the road.

At the same time the light companies of Picton's division sprang forward, and lined every hedge, bank, and tree that seemed to offer shelter; and the sharp, quick, and reverberating sound, which tells when light troops are engaged, rang with a ceaseless clamour throughout the valley.

The skirmish was hot, and the Duke, who watched it narrowly, saw the head of an enormous column moving down the road from Gemioncourt. He observed, likewise, that when it arrived at a certain point it broke up into several columns of attack; and that the French *tirailleurs*, encouraged by the approach of their comrades, were gaining ground continually. The Duke had no great confidence in the steadiness even of the Brunswickers. Their natural bravery could not be questioned, but they were deficient in experience; and, having come but recently into connection with their English and Belgian allies, it was hardly to be expected that they should know how far to trust them.

Instead, therefore, of leaving the Duke of Brunswick to offer such resistance as he might, and to retire when overpowered upon his supports, he directed the two brigades of Picton's division to advance, and to meet the assailants half way. Nothing could better accord with the fiery temper of Picton. He put himself at the head of his division; he told them that "there was the enemy, and they must beat him;" and the troops answered with such a cheer as left no room for doubt in their commander's mind respecting the issue.

On they went, leaving the 92nd in reserve to keep the Namur road, and to provide against accidents; and the skirmishers running in, and forming on their proper flanks of each battalion, the fight soon became, what throughout the modern wars of the two nations it has always been, a contest of lines against columns. The lines, as usual, prevailed. Overlapped, and cut down by a volume of fire on three sides, each of the formidable bodies before which the skirmishers had given way, broke and fled; and the British regiments charging with the bayonet drove the enemy beyond the hedgerows, and were with some difficulty restrained from following them up the face of the opposite heights.

Meanwhile the Brunswick corps, which had taken an advanced position on the right of the road, was not left to lean idly on its arms. A French battery commanded the plain, and the casualties occasioned by its well-directed fire were numerous. A regiment of hussars especially, young troops and wholly unaccustomed to war, suffered severely; and every soldier knows that there is nothing so harassing to troops brought for the first time under fire, as a sharp cannonade.

Nothing indeed, except the perfect coolness of their chief, kept these recruits in their places. The Duke of Brunswick rode backwards and forwards in front of them, smoking his pipe, and chatting to men and officers as if they had been on an ordinary parade, and men and officers were alike ashamed to shrink from dangers which their sovereign faced so composedly. But even the Duke's patience gave way at last.

He sent to the commander-in-chief for guns, and four pieces were moved up to his support. These opened their fire, but were so completely overmatched, that in five minutes two were disabled and the other two silenced, after which two columns of infantry, preceded by a battalion in line, advanced along the edge of the wood, while an enormous mass of cavalry crowded the great road and threatened the Brunswickers with destruction.

The Brunswick skirmishers, as well as the Dutch-Belgian infantry, fell back as these columns advanced. The Duke of Brunswick sent off his hussars to the opposite side of the road, and putting himself at the head of a regiment of lancers, charged the French infantry; but these received him with such a steady front that no impression was made, and the lancers retreated in confusion on Quatre Bras. The Duke, perceiving that the enemy was too strong for him, desired his infantry to fall back in good order upon the same point.

They tried to do so, but failed; for the French artillery struck with terrible effect among them, and the *tirailleurs* closing in, supported by clouds of cavalry, the young troops so assailed lost all self-possession and broke. They fled in confusion, some by Quatre Bras, others right through the English regiments which had formed on the left of it; and all the Duke's exertions to stay them failed. It was at this moment that the gallant Duke of Brunswick, while striving to arrest the flight of one of his regiments of infantry, received the fatal shot which terminated his existence.

He fell from his horse, and Major von Wachholtz, the only officer of his staff who was near, caused him instantly to be carried to the rear and laid down in a field while search was made for a surgeon. None, however, could be found, while the deadly paleness of the gallant soldier's countenance told that life was ebbing, though the glazing eye still retained some traces of its natural expression. He asked for water, but there was no water at hand.

He then desired that Colonel Olfermann, his second in command, might be sent for; but before this officer could arrive the continued advance of the enemy compelled his removal still farther to the rear. At last a staff-surgeon came to him, but it was too late. A musket-ball, entering his right wrist, had passed diagonally through his body, and its course was such as to set all surgical skill at defiance. In the forty-fourth year of his age the Duke of Brunswick died, as his father, on the fatal field of Jena, had died before him.

At this juncture the Brunswick hussars were ordered to advance from the left of the road, and to cover the retreat of the infantry. They saw in front of them a mass of French lancers, and as they moved to meet them a straggling fire of musketry somewhat disordered their ranks. It is not improbable that, young and inexperienced as they were, they could not succeed in recovering from that momentary confusion. But however this may be, it is certain that they never so much as closed with the enemy, but turned and fled pell-mell ere a single blow was struck on either side.

The French lancers pursued as a matter of course, and so closely were the two bodies mixed together, that two British regiments, the 42nd and 44th, which stood in line on the left of the road, could not for a moment distinguish between friend and foe. The consequence was a furious charge upon both, in seeking to repel which the 42nd had not time to form square, and therefore suffered severely. The 44th, on the other hand, of which Lieutenant Colonel Hammerton was at the head, never attempted to form square at all; but facing its rear rank round, received the French cavalry with a volley, which was taken up by the front rank as the horsemen swept forward, and completed by the light company, which had reserved its fire, and gave it as the wreck from the leaden storm reeled back beyond it.

The 42nd behaved, as it has always done, with exceeding

bravery and coolness. Notwithstanding that two companies were cut off, and a body of lancers penetrated, into the interval, the square formed itself about them and destroyed them to a man. The 44th, in a feeble line of two deep, proved, that if a regiment of British infantry be but steady and well commanded, it is in any order of formation beyond the reach of hurt from an enemy's cavalry.

Chapter 10

Battle of Quatre Bras—continued

No battle occurs, even in modern times, without affording to individuals the opportunity of exhibiting such feats of heroism as the un-military reader is apt to attribute only to the heroes of romance. The resistance offered by the 2nd battalion 44th regiment to a charge of lancers on the memorable 16th of June, may well be set in opposition to any shortcomings with which, on other occasions and in other lands, the 1st battalion of the same regiment has unfortunately been charged; and the self-devotion of one of its young officers deserves to be held in everlasting remembrance.

They who know how the colours of a regiment, too numerous in our service, are habitually planted, will perfectly understand that in an encounter so conducted as that which has been described, they are eminently in danger of being taken. The enemy, in the present instance, saw their exposure, and dashed, as was to be expected, against them. Many French troopers directed their horses right upon the point where the standards of the 44th were waving; and one more venturous than the rest, bore down upon Ensign Christie, who carried one of them. The point of his lance entered the young man's eye, and penetrated to the lower jaw.

True to his trust, the gallant fellow, amid the agony of his wound, thought only of the honour of his corps. He fell, but took care to fall upon the standard, a small portion of which his enemy tore off with his weapon; but the standard was saved, and the brave Frenchman paid with his life the forfeit of the attempt on which he had adventured. He was bayoneted and shot by the men who stood on the right and left of their officer; and not even the shred of silk, which he lifted from the ground, passed into the possession of the enemy. It went back with the heroes who had saved it, and remains, if he still survive, with Major-General O'Malley, C.B., who, on the fall of Colonel Hammerton, had that day the good fortune to assume the command of the corps.

Meanwhile the column of cavalry, from which this regiment of lancers had been detached, held its course right down the Charleroi road: it hung upon the rear of the Brunswick hussars, among whom, in his endeavour to rally them, the Duke of Wellington got involved, and penetrated to the very edge of a ditch, within which the 92nd Highlanders were lying. The Duke had nothing for it but to put his horse to its speed, and calling to the 92nd to lie down, leaped fairly over them and across the ditch which constituted their post of resistance.

He had his sword drawn in his hand, and turned round as soon as the Highlanders were between him and his pursuers with a smile upon his countenance. The confidence which inspired it was not misplaced; such a volume of fire rose instantly from the roadside that a hundred saddles were emptied, and the residue of the cavalry shrank back—re-forming, however, in a moment, and retiring in good order. But all were not so prudent as to adopt this course. The leading squadrons galloped on till they got entangled among the farmsteads of the village; and though they cut down some stragglers there, they paid dearly for their rashness.

Most of them rushed into a farmyard, which had no outlet except that by which they had entered; to a man they were destroyed by the fire of the Highlanders, and the scattered individuals who endeavoured to cut their way back died, one by one, under the same leaden tempest. An officer named Burgoine dashed at the Duke himself; his horse was shot, and a musket-ball passed through both of his ankles. And such are the casualties of war, that he lay for weeks in the same house where Lieutenant Winchester of the 92nd also lay wounded; and thus the two brave men became personal friends, Mr. Winchester subsequently being the guest of M. Burgoine's family in Paris.

While these things were going on, both sides received by degrees reinforcements, of which both were grievously in want. A considerable portion of Kellermann's heavy horse came into the field, and as neither the Belgian nor the Dutch cavalry could face them, the whole weight of their fury fell upon the British infantry. The 28th, the 42nd, the 44th, and the Royals were all repeatedly charged in succession. Indeed, the Royals and the 28th did not wait to be attacked, but advanced in column, led on by Picton and Kempt, and themselves, contrary to all precedent in war, attacked the cavalry.

This was rendered necessary by the flight of the Belgian infantry, who, driven from the wood of Bossu, could not be rallied, and whose flight exposed the 42nd and 44th to be taken in flank and overwhelmed. Moreover, the hardy footmen had a twofold disadvantage to cope with, inasmuch as the ground where they stood was covered with tall rye, under cover of which the French cavalry made upon them continually, before they could tell, except from the heavy tread of the horses' hoofs, that any enemy was near.

On one of these occasions Picton, who was present with the 28th, appealed to the steady courage of his men through a watch-word, of the value of which only they who know what war is can tell the importance. As the *cuirassiers* were rushing on he shouted, with a stentorian voice, "28th, remember Egypt!" and the men, few of whom knew aught of the exploits of the regiment there, except by tradition, received the omen and replied to it with a cheer.

Not a horseman broke through their ranks; and though the cavalry—not less resolute than their adversaries—actually pitched a lance among the rye, and galloped at it repeatedly, as at a signpost, they were on each occasion received with such steadiness, and with so murderous a fire, that they recoiled from before it. Nor were the other corps engaged one whit less steady or less resolute. The 32nd, the 79th, the 95th—every British soldier, in short, fought that day as if upon the wielding of his single arm, the fate of the campaign depended. It would weary the reader to be told, it defies the utmost powers of the writer to tell, how fiercely the British troops were attacked, how resolutely they received their assailants; though the face of the country, covered with dead and dying, bore testimony to the desperate valour of both parties.

It was now five o'clock, and the French, though baffled in all their endeavours, seemed as little disposed as ever to relax in their exertions. More cavalry had joined them; and in this arm the Allies were so miserably weak, that in spite of the heroism which they displayed, they had, upon the whole, lost rather than gained ground. The enemy now brought forward their infantry in force, and made such progress through the wood of Bossu, that there appeared every probability of their debouching on the flank of the Allied position, which the Dutch-Belgians no longer attempted to cover.

It was evident, likewise, that a reinforcement of artillery had reached them; for the cannonade from the high grounds became more murderous than ever, and several pieces were advanced into the hollow, whence they wrought terrible havoc among the squares which they succeeded in enfilading. Well it was that, at this moment, General Alton's division came up by the Nivelles road, and separated, Halkett's British brigade advancing along the space between the wood of Bossu and the Charleroi causeway, while Kielmansegge's Hanoverians took ground to the left, and supported, and in some measure relieved, the regiments which in that direction had well nigh expended their ammunition.

Ney saw these troops enter into the battle, and sent urgent orders for D'Erlon's corps to close up; and, confident in the belief that these would not be slighted, he boldly pushed onwards every man that he had disposable. The cavalry, as before, rushed down the main road. Through an unfortunate mistake they succeeded in rolling up the 69th regiment, and carrying off the only trophy which they won that day—one of its colours. But an attempt which they made simultaneously upon the 32nd totally failed. and they suffered terribly. Meanwhile, the infantry, clearing the wood, debouched into the open country. They were numerous, resolute, and well supported by a column of *cuirassiers*, upon which Major Kuhlman's battery, of the horse artillery of the German Legion, poured a destructive fire; and they gained ground, driving Brunswickers and Hanoverians before them, till they approached that part of the Allied position where the 92nd were stationed. Major-General Barnes, adjutant-general to the forces, saw the enemy, and rode up to the Highlanders.

He took off his hat, waved it in the air, and crying out, "Now, 92nd, follow me!" struck a spark which flew like electricity from file to file. The Highlanders sprang from the ditch in which they were lying, and, while the bagpipes screamed the Camerons' Gathering, brought their bayonets to the level, and rushed forward. Back and back went the French column.

Once or twice the leading companies endeavoured to make a stand, but the charge of the Highlanders was irresistible, and they broke and fled till the shelter of a hedgerow gave them the opportunity of deploying. From behind that cover they threw in a volley, which did not arrest the assailants for a moment. Colonel John Cameron, who commanded, received indeed a desperate wound, which deprived him of all power to manage his horse, and being thrown heavily on his head, he died.

But his followers, instead of being daunted by that circumstance, seemed but to gather from it an increase of fury. They received, without taking notice of it, another volley from another French column on the flank, which thinned their ranks, but left the survivors as resolute as ever; and these, rushing with a shout through the hedgerow, drove the enemy in confusion back into the wood. They were here halted, and withdrawn under cover of a copse, in order to avoid a fresh charge of French cavalry which threatened them.

It was by this time pretty evident to Ney that success in the battle which he had bravely waged was hardly to be expected.

D'Erlon's corps did not arrive, and he now learned to his horror, that it had been moved to the support of Napoleon, who directed him, in like manner, to bear towards his right, for the purpose of overwhelming the left of the Prussians at St. Amand.

Ney was furious. He persuaded himself that, had the original plan of battle, as given to him early in the morning, been adhered to, he might have secured by this time the entire severance of the English from their allies; and he scouted the idea of being able to disentangle himself from the English, however urgent the call for his assistance might be in other quarters. He therefore reiterated his orders for D'Erlon to close up, and continued his endeavours to gain ground on both flanks, as well from Piermont as through the wood of Bossu. But by this time more strength had arrived for the English.

The 1st and 2nd Light Battalions of Brunswickers came up with two batteries of artillery; and by-and-by General Cooke's British division entered into the battle. The latter, comprising two brigades of Guards, fell in, too, at the very point where they were most needed. They arrived on the skirt of the wood of Bossu just as the French *tirailleurs* were forcing their way through, and a light battalion under Lord Saltoun being let loose, rushed like fox-hounds into the cover, and cleared it.

The battalions followed in the highest possible spirits, despite of the excessive fatigue under which they laboured, for they had been on the march since early dawn, and but for the excitement of a battle must have sunk under it. From that moment the tide of victory was turned. Halkett's brigade on one flank, the Guards on the other, and the regiments of the line filling up the intervals, advanced with the step of conquerors. It was to no purpose that the French cavalry charged these gallant footmen.

Where time to form square was wanting, lines retreated to the edge of the road, and thence, by a well-directed fire, cut down the assailants, who no sooner drew off than the infantry were again in motion, carrying everything before them.

One after another the strongholds which Ney had won in the beginning of the battle were recovered. Piermont fell to the

95th and their comrades of the German Legion; Gemioncourt was retaken by Picton's division; and the Guards effectually made themselves masters of the whole of the wood of Bossu. In a word, Ney was utterly beaten, and retreated, under cover of the growing darkness, to his original position at Frasnes. In front of that place his pickets were planted, while the Duke of Wellington, conscious of his own strength, ordered his followers to bivouac for the night, and waited, full of hope, for the morrow.

Chapter 11

Battle of Ligny

While the English were thus engaged in and around Quatre Bras, a furious combat was in progress a few miles to the left, where Napoleon and Blücher fought with a degree of obstinacy not often surpassed in modern times. Napoleon was the assailant on this occasion, as he had been the previous day. Blücher accepted the battle in a position long previously surveyed, and selected as the fittest for combining the operations of his army with those of the Duke of Wellington. A few words will suffice to describe it.

Nearly parallel with the Namur road, and a little in advance of it, that is, in advance of the road looking in the direction of the French frontier, rises an irregular chain of heights, which, beginning on the west, near the village of Bry, ends somewhat to the east of Balatre. This position, for such it is, has both flanks covered by ravines, through which flow two small rivulets while its front slopes down into the plain, across which, receiving the waters of the other two into its own, passes the stream of Ligny.

A good many villages stand forward from the main position, but they are all considerably removed from it. Bry, St. Amand-le-Haye, St, Amand, and Ligny form a sort of triangle on the left centre, having St. Amand for its apex. Mont Pontriaux, Tongreville, Boignée, and Balatre throw themselves well nigh into the same shape on the right centre. The centre itself—embracing in that term the road from Fleurus and the direct approaches on Sombref—is open. But no hostile column could manoeuvre there as long as the villages should remain in the possession of the defenders; for Ligny on the one side, and Boignée on the other, command the approaches to it; and Tongreville and Mont Pontriaux sweep its further gorge with their fire.

The position or Sombref or Ligny (for by this name the English reader will best recognize it) offered, in a strategetical point of view, many advantages to Prince Blücher. It was not only near the left of the English army, with which it connected itself by the high road from Namur to Nivelles, but so long as he should be able to hold it, he could reckon on his own communications with the line of the Meuse, with Aix-la-Chapelle, and the Prussian states as being secure.

On the other hand, if it should not, on trial, prove tenable; if the Duke of Wellington should not be able to afford in time the full measure of support which was necessary, Sombref on the one hand and Quatre Bras on the other would become mere advanced stations, whence, after offering to the enemy as protracted a hindrance as circumstances would allow, the Allied generals might fall back upon a second line. There were excellent parallel roads of retreat open to both, one leading to Brussels, the other to Louvain; so that by means of these, either in front of the forest of Soignies, or, if need were, still closer to the capital, a junction of their forces might take place.

Moreover the position of Sombref was equally effective against the advance of the enemy, whether he had come by Mons or by Namur. In the former case Blücher could have moved to the support of the English at least as rapidly as, under existing circumstances, the English could move to support him. In the latter, three, perhaps four,, of his corps would have concentrated under cover of the fifth, at the exact point where it was most competent to the English to sustain them; while the latter, in the act of doing so, must have effectually provided against all danger from the side of Charleroi.

Looking, therefore, to the great objects of the campaign, and considering how they were likely to be best attained, there can be but one opinion among competent judges in regard to the fitness of the position of Sombref, though even its comparative advantage as a field of battle would of course depend upon the manner in which the Prussian general should occupy the ground with his troops.

It has been stated that during the operations of the 15th, Zieten's Prussian corps fell back upon Fleurus, and that the French halted in front of that village. The Prussians did not remain in Fleurus. They left, indeed, some troops to keep it, till attacked, and connected them with the villages in rear by means of a body of cavalry; but their infantry were distributed, for the night, among Bry, St. Amand-la-Haye, St. Amand, and Ligny. Early in the morning the main body of the corps took ground to the rear, and formed upon the high grounds above the villages.

Seven battalions of the 2nd brigade drew up in two lines behind the farm and mill of Bussy; the 8th threw itself into this farm, and put it in a state of defence. Two battalions of the six which composed the 4th brigade stood upon the slope between the 2nd brigade and Ligny, while the remaining four occupied the village of Ligny itself. Bry was occupied by two battalions, another being posted a little in the rear in support, and two companies of Silesian riflemen lay, in extended order, among the broken ground between Bry and St. Amand-la-Haye. The remainder of the 1st brigade, of which these formed a part, took post in two lines on the height overlooking St. Amand, with its right on St. Amand-la-Haye, while St. Amand itself was guarded by three battalions of the 3rd brigade.

Finally the six remaining battalions of this brigade formed, in reserve, a little to the northward of Ligny; and the cavalry continued, from its advanced position on the Fleurus road, to watch the movements of the enemy.

These dispositions, which began at an early hour, were completed by eight o'clock; at eleven General Pirch's corps, the 2nd, marched into position; this latter, it will be remembered, having moved from Namur on the first intimation of Napoleon's advance, had bivouacked during the night at Mazy. It was now formed in support of Zieten's corps—one brigade where the

Nivelles road is crossed by an old Roman causeway; another in rear of Bussy and of Bry; a third a little distance more to the left; and a fourth upon the road from Sombref to Fleurus. The cavalry of this corps was massed in rear of the Nivelles road, a good way to the left of Sombref; and its artillery, as well as that belonging to Zieten's, drew up where it was not in reserve on such points as offered the most commanding view of the probable approaches of the enemy.

Last of all, while Pirch's troops were yet settling themselves on the plateaux respectively assigned to them, Thielmann arrived on the ground. He had been on the march since seven in the morning, at which hour his rear quitted Namur; and he now took charge of that portion of the field which lay between Sombref and Balatre. The mass of his troops stood in columns upon the great roads; his skirmishers took charge of the outer face of the line, extending from beyond Balatre, in an irregular curve, all the way to Mont Pontriaux. His artillery was chiefly so disposed as to command the high road where it passes between Mont Pontriaux and Tongrines.

At dawn of day on the 16th Napoleon mounted his horse; and the whole of the French troops which had spent the night in Charleroi, and in bivouac along the banks of the Sambre, marched to join the advanced corps in the vicinity of Fleurus. It takes time, however, to assemble divisions and brigades who may have lain down over night without much regard to order; and hence ten o'clock arrived ere the rear of the French army was so united with the front as to admit of the commencement of a movement in order of battle.

Let us not be misunderstood. Napoleon has been somewhat rashly censured by writers of all nations, as if he had been lax in the distribution of his columns over night, and unnecessarily tardy in bringing them into action in the morning. Lax he certainly was not; that he scarcely made the exertions, which twenty years before he would have made, to sustain the spirits of his men, and close them well up during the night of the 15th, can hardly be disputed. But let it not be forgotten that the exertions of many of his corps, previously to the 15th, had been gigantic; and that whenever you overstrain men's strength, you must make up your mind to a reaction. We doubt whether the battle of Ligny could have been begun many hours sooner than the attack actually took place; and though we blame Napoleon for failing to press his people well nigh beyond their strength, it is not at all clear to us that even if he had done so, the issue of the battle would have been different.

It was about ten o'clock in the morning of the 10th, when the French army debouched in two columns from the wood which covers Fleurus, and formed into two lines facing the town. Pajol's light and Excelman's heavy cavalry constituted the right of the first line, Girard's corps was in the centre, and Vandamme's on the left: the second consisted entirely of the Imperial Guard, with Milhaud's *cuirassiers*—an imposing and very formidable array.

The lines were not, as British lines are, extended by regiments two deep—they were *colonnes serrées,* the favourite formation of the French, and indeed of all the continental armies; and they stood at ease, in their ranks, for a full hour, while Napoleon rode along the line of *videttes* to reconnoitre the Prussian position.

It is difficult to say, among the contradictory accounts which have been given, what Napoleon's real opinions were in regard to the designs of Blücher, and his arrangement of his army in order to accomplish them. The statements which represent him as misunderstanding altogether the object of the Prussian formations, are doubtless incorrect; for it is much more probable that a commander of his experience should give Blücher credit for well disguising his intentions than that, failing to observe them accurately, he should attribute to them a direction altogether out of place.

Be this, however, as it may, he could not but be aware that in order to give himself a chance in the future operations of the campaign, it was necessary to force the Prussians away from the English; and that the only sure mode of doing so would be to overwhelm their right, and so to gain the command of the great road to Nivelles. Accordingly the dispositions of his forces, during the earlier part of the 16th of June, seem all to have had this object in view.

For example, between eleven and twelve he pushed forward his light troops, and with very little trouble made himself master of Fleurus. He then opened a cannonade upon the Prussian cavalry which occupied the high road between that town and the villages on the edge of the plain; and then, after forming his columns, took post upon the high ground above the town, and once more, with equal care and deliberation, scanned the whole of Blücher's arrangements.

It was at this time that he caused Soult to write that dispatch to Ney, of which the latter, not without some apparent reason, has complained. Ney felt that his hands were full; and hence, though it is very possible that Napoleon's plan might, in the abstract, be such as became his own high military reputation, his lieutenant knew that, in the presence of a general like the Duke of Wellington, it was practically out of the question.

Napoleon's orders to Ney were in substance these. He stated, that in half an hour he meant to fall upon Blücher, whose troops were massed between Sombref and Bry; that he had no doubt of making a great impression; but that to complete the victory, and open for him the road to Brussels, it was necessary that Ney should give him a vigorous co-operation. For this purpose it was his desire, that Ney should drive back whatever force might be immediately in his front; and then, instead of following up a partial victory, that he should bring forward his left shoulder, and act upon the right and rear of the Prussians.

At the same time the dispatch gave the agreeable assurance that Napoleon was confident of success; and that in the event of his prevailing before Ney should have had time to make this flank movement, he, in his turn, would bring up the right shoulder, and fall upon Ney's adversaries at Quatre Bras. It is a remarkable fact, that at the very time when the Emperor was reconnoitring Blücher, and meditating these instructions, the Duke of Wellington was with Blücher at the mill of Bussy, arranging

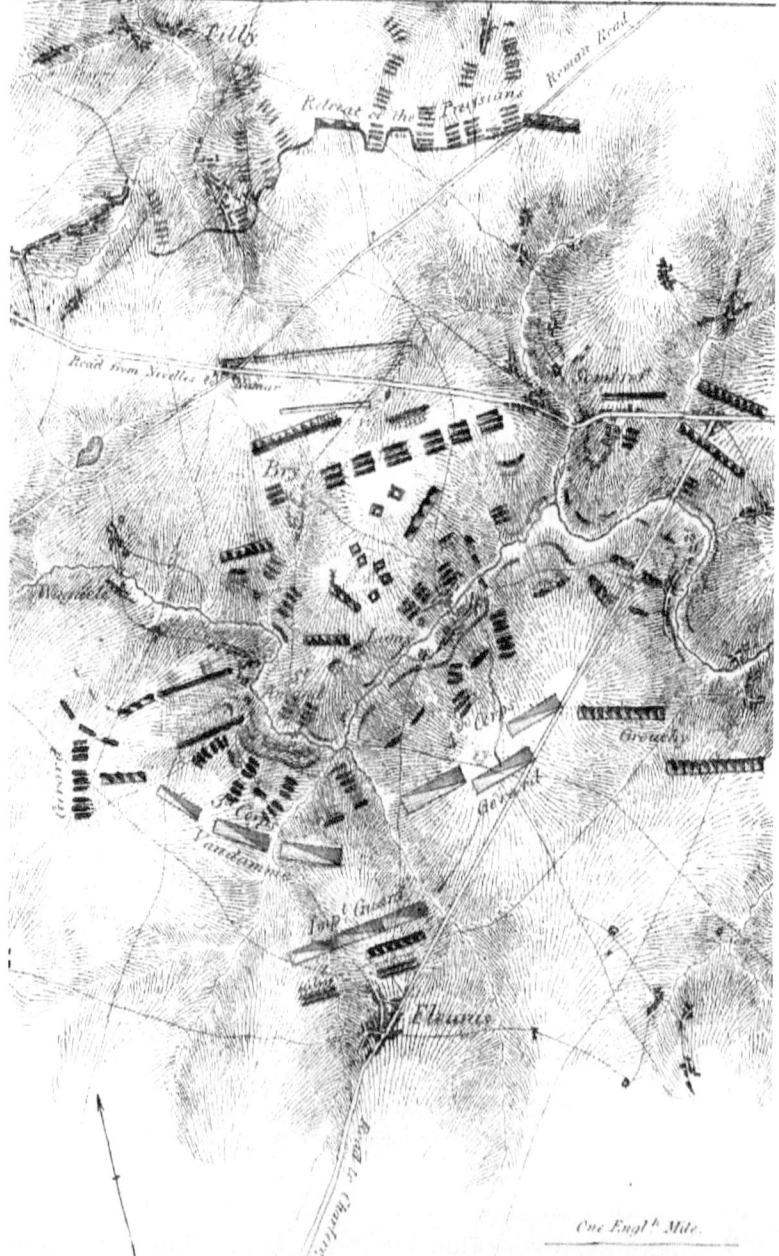

for the co-operation of the two allied armies. So strangely is the great game of war played when masters in the art are opposed to one another; so little are the guiding spirits on either side aware of the obstacles which are in the act of being raised to the accomplishment of their respective designs.

Having cleared the wood of Fleurus, and compelled the Prussian cavalry, under General Roder, to retire beyond the Ligny, the French army formed in three columns of attack, keeping the Guard, 20,000 strong, with Milhaud's *cuirassiers*, in reserve. The left column, consisting of Vandamme's corps, to which was attached Girard's division from the corps of Reille advanced against St. Amand, the salient point in the Prussian position.

In this formation Girard's division constituted the extreme left; next to it moved a division of light cavalry under General Duraont; and then, in continuation of the line, came Vandamme, with his well-arranged infantry. The centre column consisted of Girard's *corps d'armée,* which had the Fleurus road to operate by; and occupied heights on the Fleurus side of Ligny, threatening that village. The right column under Grouchy was made up chiefly of cavalry, and showed front towards the villages of Tongrines, Tongeville, Brignée, and Balatre, protecting Girard against any endeavours of the Prussians to take him in flank, and diverting the attention of the Prussian left from the danger with which the right was about to be threatened. The reserve, composed as has already been described, was halted in two columns; the one upon the right, the other on the left of Fleurus.

With respect to the actual numbers of the forces thus arrayed against one another, it is not very easy to state them accurately. The probability, however, is, that if we take them according to the official lists on both sides, we shall not greatly err: in which case the French may be put down as mustering—of infantry, 50,885; of cavalry, 13,100; of artillery, 7,218; in all 71,203 men, with 242 guns: whereas the Prussians displayed, deducting 1,200 lost in the operations of the previous day, 83,417 men with 224 guns. But the slight numerical superiority of the latter was more than compensated by the comparative inexperience of their troops, of whom many were now for the first time about to come under fire: and it is past dispute that for the mere purposes of a battle, they were not placed exactly as the rules of war would seem to dictate.

The heights of Fleurus, of which the French were in possession, immediately overlooked the ridges of the Prussian position. Troops descending from them were, moreover, sheltered by woods and ground which was much broken; and the villages which the Prussians had occupied, or at least the more advanced of them, lay on the French rather than on their own side of the valley. The heights of St. Amand and Ligny were, on the contrary, open and exposed throughout.

Troops covering them, even on the more elevated points, offered a sure mark to artillery planted above Fleurus, and every battalion which should move down to support the troops in the villages must do so under a murderous fire. It was this fault, indeed, in the position which the Duke pointed out to Blücher while they stood together; but the latter either did not perceive, or chose to disregard it. He said that his men liked to see the enemy with whom they were going to be engaged; and the Duke could not press the argument farther than by observing, that "with English troops he should have occupied the ground differently."

About half past two o'clock the battle began. The advance of Vandamme's columns was covered by a murderous fire of artillery, to which the Prussian batteries from the heights between Ligny and St. Amand replied; but the position of the French guns was far superior, and the practice of their gunners proved to be excellent. Supported by this cannonade, which passed over their heads, Vandamme's people pressed on, and in spite of a stout resistance from the troops in occupation of the village succeeded in obtaining possession of it

They forthwith debouched on the face of the slope; but were met with such a shower of grape from the batteries above, that their order became almost immediately confused. Forthwith four battalions of Prussian infantry charged them; and after a fierce encounter a portion of the village was recovered—the Prussians occupying the lower part, the French holding tenaciously to the higher.

Meanwhile all the guns on either side that could be brought to bear opened their fire. It was a species of battle in which the French had, for many reasons, the advantage; and the corps which held the upper part of St. Amand being largely reinforced, a renewed attack was made upon the Prussians in the hollow. It was repulsed again, and again renewed; but being once more set in motion, with increased numbers, it succeeded. The truth is, that the Prussians lost as many men in the act of feeding the village, as fell in the defence of it.

Brigade after brigade, and regiment after regiment, was decimated while descending the heights to its proper field of battle; and the whole came in consequence into action so broken that they could not make the most of their valour. The consequence was, that alter sustaining an enormous loss, General Steinmetz, who commanded in this part of the field, was forced to retire, and took post, with the remains of his division, on the ridge between Sombref and Bry.

Meanwhile the village of Ligny became the scene of a very fierce and varied struggle. The French, concealed by the tall corn which grew in the vicinity, advanced towards it in front and by the left flank in great numbers, and made their rush so suddenly, that they won all the gardens and hedge-rows which immediately skirted the village. There they established themselves in spite of the utmost exertions of the defenders, who advanced to the point of the bayonet, and fought desperately.

But the enemy were not to be repulsed: and foot by foot the garrison yielded ground, till the farther extremity of the town alone remained to them. At this moment, several houses, including an old chateau, took fire, and the scene became terrific in the extreme: the roar of musketry was incessant; while from cither side the batteries on the high grounds poured down shot and shell, as if the sole desire of the cannoneers had been to destroy life, without pausing to inquire whether they were friends or foes who fell beneath them. And now came a strong reinforcement to the Prussians—running, as their comrades about St. Amand had done, the gauntlet all along the slope.

They were full of energy, however, and seemed to disregard the havoc that had been made in their ranks; and they fell with such fury upon the French that the latter gave way before them, and the village was in ten minutes recovered. Again, for a space, the rattle of musketry was suspended, while the troops on either side sought shelter to take breath; but the roar of cannon was incessant—and though the Prussian salvos did not fall harmless, the slaughter occasioned by those of the enemy was much more tremendous.

In this manner the battle raged for a full hour and a half upon the Prussian left. The right remained comparatively unmolested; for it did not enter into Napoleon's plan to drive them back upon the English, from whom, on the contrary, it was his earnest wish to divide them. But, though Blücher's real object was to keep his ground till supported, it was not in his nature to fight a purely defensive battle. He had lost St. Amand and St- Amand-la-Haye; because the latter, though not so severely pressed, had, in the general retreat of Steinmetz's brigade, been abandoned.

Blücher determined to recover them; and, the better to facilitate this manoeuvre, he directed the 5th Brigade of General Pirch's corps to seize the village of Wagnele, and to operate thence against the enemy. At the same time a considerable body of cavalry was moved towards the slope, and the whole combining their movements with great exactitude, went forward to the fray. But here again the radical defect of Blücher's position made itself manifest: the columns were smashed by the fire of the enemy's cannon ere they reached the points of attack, and their valour, however impetuous, failed in consequence to produce the desired results.

The attack of St. Amand-la-Haye was repulsed with great slaughter, as was a second attempt made in the same direction about half an hour subsequently; and the brave old Prussian could not but look with anxiety towards the road by which his communications with the English army must needs be maintained.

Animated by the success which had thus far attended their endeavours, the French pushed on, and well nigh without firing a shot, made themselves masters of Wagnele. Blücher saw this, and saw at the same time that there needed but a movement in force from that quarter to overwhelm his right; he therefore withdrew more and more his reserves from the centre, and combined another attack for the recovery of the three villages. The proceeding was not lost upon Napoleon: he also detached a division of the Young Guard, with a brigade of lancers from Pajol's cavalry, and a battery of cannon to his left, and directed them not only to support Vandamme, but to communicate, if possible, with Ney by the Nivelles road. This counter-movement succeeded, however, only in part.

Blücher, putting himself at the head of the column which had been formed for the attack of St. Amand-la-Haye, exclaimed, "Children, behave well—don't allow 'the Nation' to mock you again. Forward, in God's name."

And forward they went, with such resolution that all resistance went down before them. They swept aside the troops that covered the approaches to the village; they poured through the street into the churchyard, and fairly lifted the French out of both; indeed, it was not without difficulty that their officers restrained them from following the flying enemy up the slope of their own position.

In like manner the cavalry which supported them on the right broke through and dispersed a portion of the enemy's horsemen whom it encountered; while a battery of twelve-pounders, which supported them on the left, was so intent on the work assigned to it, that before the artillerymen were aware a troop of French dragoons came upon them. Not a gun, however, was lost, nor could the enemy so much as cut the traces or drive away the horses. The gunners, ceasing to fire, attacked these intruders with their rammers and handspikes, and fairly drove them off.

So far Blücher's movement had succeeded. To give it weight

he had much denuded his left and centre of their reserves; and he felt, that were Wagnele in like manner retaken, no serious damage was likely to result from his having done so; but, unfortunately, Wagnele was not retaken. Tippleskirchen's brigade, which went boldly to the work, consisted of very young troops, which passed, indeed, victoriously through the centre of the village, but failed when it became necessary to deploy on the farther side of it.

Among the high corn that grew there clouds of French skirmishers lay, who opened upon the column such a storm of fire as threw it into considerable confusion: and the support coming up somewhat rashly, increased rather than diminished the evil. The result was, that companies so crowded one upon another, that, exposed as they were to a murderous fire, they could not form line. They fell back, therefore, through the village: and a heavy column of the enemy following them close, Wagnele remained in the hands of the French.

CHAPTER 12

Battle of Ligny—continued

The flight of the Prussian column which had charged Wagnele led, as a matter of course, to a second attack by the enemy on St. Amand-la-Haye. Of St. Amand itself they still retained possession; and now in front, and on cither flank, they poured their troops upon St. Amand-la-Haye, in numbers and with a pertinacity which defied contradiction. Once more the Prussians were driven out, only that they might re-form, and with fresh supports rush again upon the prize, and once more the street, and indeed every house in the place, became the scene of a deadly combat. But it was not in this direction exclusively that the battle raged. Ligny had seen a little fighting—it was destined to see much more, and the initiative in the game of death was taken by both sides simultaneously.

The 4th Prussian brigade, commanded by Count Henkel, was in possession of the village; the 3rd brigade, under General Von Jagow, supported it. Two battalions of this latter force were directed to pass through, and to advance in column against the enemy, who had shown a considerable force along the slope beyond. The battalions moved by a sort of defile, and were scarcely clear of the houses when they found themselves in presence of a heavy column of French infantry, on the advance, as it seemed, to attack the village.

Both columns came simultaneously to a halt, yet neither deployed: indeed, the nature of the ground was such as scarcely to admit of a deployment. But though leading companies on either side opened their fire—a blunder from which it was impossible that to one or the other harm should not ensue. One of those accidents, which more or less occur in all battles, caused the evil to overtake the Prussians.

While other battalions were coming up to their support, a cry arose that the enemy had penetrated by a different direction into the village, and that the churchyard was in their possession. You cannot argue troops so circumstanced into the exercise of right reason. Some of those in the rear turned round, and unfortunately fired towards the churchyard.

The sound of firing heard in that direction confirmed the belief that the column was taken in reverse, and its communications with the main body cut off; and, some French guns having been brought to bear, and throwing in at this moment a well directed shower of grape, all order and consistency in the ranks were abandoned. The men turned and fled in confusion, their own groundless fears paralysing them; and half of the village was actually won by the enemy ere the fugitives could be convinced of their error.

The fight in and about Ligny was not unobserved by Blücher. He saw the advance of his column, its check, panic, and ultimate retreat; and, feeling the importance of keeping the village under the turn which the battle had taken, he ordered General Von Krafft, with four battalions which had not yet been engaged, to drive the enemy back. At the same time some changes of position among the artillery took place—batteries which had been exposed all day to the enemy's fire being withdrawn, and others, fresh and well supplied with ammunition and necessary equipments, pushed forward from the reserve.

These latter opened a murderous fire to which the French, who happened to follow the same course at the same moment, replied; and, the advantage of position being entirely on the side of the latter, the Prussians suffered severely. Nevertheless, General Krafft, forming the residue of his brigade into two columns, advanced upon Ligny. Few combats have been waged with more determined gallantry than that which for the space of an hour was maintained in the village.

From house to house, and from inclosure to inclosure, the combatants pressed on, and were forced back alternately; now the Prussians gained ground—now they were headed and rolled to the rear by the French, to whom, as well as to themselves, reinforcements came up every moment; and who, in regard to artillery practice, were decidedly superior; and though many buildings were on fire, and the wounded not unfrequently perished in consequence, the mutual hatred of the contending parties was such, that neither would withdraw. No quarter was either given or sought in the streets of Ligny that day.

Upon the whole, the French had the advantage. They overpowered Von Krafft's battalions, and winning the churchyard, as well as a large stone building advantageously placed for either side, they held them both with the most obstinate valour. In vain was regiment after regiment of the Prussians, which had heretofore been engaged, launched against these two strongholds; they could not make the smallest impression, and were cut down by sections in the effort—till at last Blücher sent down a fresh brigade (Colonel Von Langen's) to sustain them, and the battle became more furious than ever. Colonel Langen attacked the village with infantry, cavalry, and artillery; he succeeded in mastering it, all except that portion which lay on the left of the stream, and even upon that he made for a while a marked impression.

But the progress of the struggle elsewhere had caused Napoleon to look at Ligny with a different eye, and in due time plans were developed which there were no means at hand to derange or counteract.

It was natural that Blücher should be peculiarly jealous of his right. He had already sustained a loss of position there, of which it is not too much to say that he entertained an exaggerated opinion; and, believing that his hold upon the English army would be lost if he did not recover it, he drew off every disposable man from his left and centre, that he might make a desperate effort to recover his ground.

With this view he directed General Tippleskirchen to throw himself again upon St. Amand-la-Haye, while, with all the force which could be collected from other quarters, an effort was made to reoccupy Wagnele, and the detached houses and inclosures near it. Among the rest, the hamlet of Hameau St. Amand, forming a sort of salient angle between Wagnele and St. Amand-la-Haye, was furiously attacked by a battalion of infantry, covered on its right by a regiment of hussars. The French appear not to have expected this movement; and their troops, which held the place loosely, as if in reserve, were driven out with much slaughter; but they instantly rallied, and, supported by fresh numbers, became in their turn the assailants.

A desperate battle now ensued. The Prussian hussars, the 10th regiment, did their duty nobly. They charged a French column, and broke it while advancing; but they were carried too far by their ardour, and falling upon the enemy's supports, suffered in their turn, and were dispersed. In like manner St. Amand-la-Haye was four times taken and retaken on both sides. In fact, the whole extent of this flank became the scene of a struggle so sanguinary, that it seemed as if neither general had any other object in view than to make himself master of the irregular line of inclosures which covered it.

All this while Napoleon, from the high ground above Fleurus, was watching with an eagle's eye, the progress of the battle. He saw that Blücher had put out the whole of his strength. He observed brigade after brigade file from the exposed plateau on which the Prussians had arranged their reserves, and as the day was wearing apace, he conceived that the time had come for changing, in some measure, the plan of his operations.

The Imperial Guard, 20,000 strong, with eight regiments of *cuirassiers*, the elite of his cavalry, had not yet come into action. He determined to launch them in one overwhelming mass against the Prussian centre; and with this view put them in motion upon Ligny. But just at this moment Vandamme sent to inform him that a strong body of troops, composed of infantry, cavalry, and artillery, were approaching Fleurus. The direction of their march, moreover, was most suspicious. They seemed to come from Nivelles or Quatre Bras; and instead of bearing down upon the Prussian right, threatened, or appeared to do so, the rear of the French. Vandamme at the same time informed the Emperor, that, alarmed by this apparition, he had been forced to throw back Girard's division; and that unless the reserve were employed to protect his rear, he would be obliged to relinquish the advantages which he had won, and to evacuate St. Amand. Napoleon was perplexed.

He did not know what to make of this corps.. He was apprehensive that it might have been detached by Wellington, and that consequently affairs had not gone well with Ney. Under this impression he suspended the advance of the Guard, midway, while he sent out staff-officers in whom he could trust, to ascertain both the composition and the design of the strange column. This sudden check of the Guard in its march, together with the withdrawal of a portion of Girard's guns, created a belief among the Prussians that the enemy were retreating. Immediately Blücher directed a fresh attack, with every disposable man, to be made upon St. Amand; and the fire of cannon and musketry in that direction became more close and incessant than ever.

A brigade of light cavalry, commanded by Colonel Von Marwitz, had some time previously been moved by Blücher to his extreme right, where it formed *en potence,* in two lines, between the Nivelles road and the old Roman causeway. Colonel Marwitz had not long occupied this position ere he was menaced both by cavalry and artillery, the fire of the latter doing him some damage, though the former seemed reluctant to close. Once it threw out a detachment, which was charged and beaten back; and by and by an encounter took place, with similar results, between some *chasseurs à cheval* and a squadron of *landwehr horse.*

There was a good deal to perplex and alarm both parties in these eccentric movements. Marwitz, not knowing what to make of them, pushed forward a reconnaissance, in the course of which some prisoners were taken, and from them it was ascertained that D'Erlon's corps had begun to manoeuvre towards

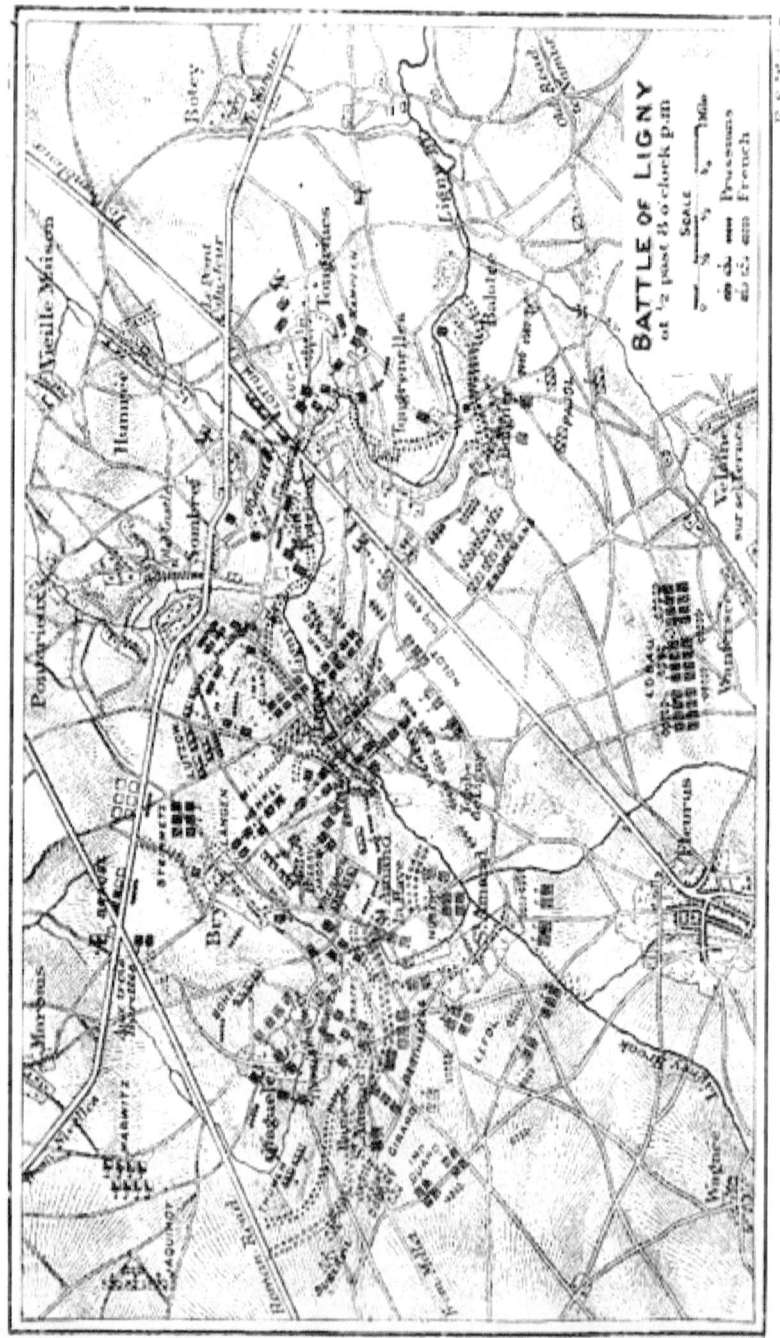

the Prussian right, and that the cavalry and artillery with which the latter had just been engaged formed part of it. These were serious tidings for Blücher. He was already matched upon this point, and though successful on his right, felt that in that direction no serious attempt had been made to force him. He could not fail, therefore, to watch with much anxiety the issue of an operation on which he had no cause to reckon.

It was about seven o'clock in the evening when the officer whom Napoleon had dispatched returned with information that the troops which had alarmed Vandamme and occasioned the delay in the projected attack on Ligny were friends. The fact was, that D'Erlon had been completely paralyzed in his proceedings by the contradictory orders which reached him, now from Ney and now from the Emperor.

The former, having gone on without him to the attack of Quatre Bras, left directions that in the first instance he should draw up in front of Gosselies, intending by and by to bring him down along the main road, and to throw him upon the flank of the Allies. Meanwhile, Napoleon being informed of this halt, and taking it for granted that Ney could do without him, sent an order that he should bring up his left shoulder, and overlap the Prussians in St. Amand. Before the latter instructions could reach him, however, Ney's second message had arrived, and he was already advanced in the direction of Quatre Bras as far as Frasne.

But here the Emperor's messenger overtook him; and he, dispatching the chief of his staff to inform Ney of what had occurred, instantly turned back and took the road to Villers-Perruin. This was an error for which he was not responsible. Villers-Perruin had been expressly named as lying in the route which it behooved him to follow; and the consequence was, that instead of debouching, as he might have done, on the Nivelles road, he made his appearance in the rear of the French line, and discomposed for a time the arrangements of his friends. Moreover another, and that not an unnatural blunder occurred, of which D'Erlon was in some sort the victim. The staff-officer whom Napoleon employed to find out what this unlooked-for corps might be, carried with him no particular instructions such as friends might profit by. Hence D'Erlon had nothing for it except to move, as he was originally desired to do, upon St. Amand; and if he moved cautiously, he cannot, considering the peculiarity of his circumstances, be blamed.

But still worse remained for him. While musing over the circumstance that no specific duty had been assigned to him by the Emperor, Ney's last and most urgent command for his immediate junction at Quatre-Bras came in. He believed that to it he was bound to pay obedience. And so it came to pass, that just at the moment when by a vigorous onset he might have decided the fate of the day, he was once more countermarched on Frasne, almost without firing a shot. As has already been shown, Ney bitterly complained of this, in his letter of the 26th of June to the Minister at War; and there is no denying that for the complaint therein uttered there was much room.

It does not appear that Napoleon experienced much disappointment because of the departure of D'Erlon from the field of Ligny. His plan of battle, was not formed in any dependence on support from that quarter; and as he made no change of disposition in consequence of the tidings which his *aide-de-camp* brought, so it is probable that he took very little notice of them. The case was different in regard to the Prussians.

They felt that it was in D'Erlon's power to work them infinite harm, and therefore when his cavalry, after skirmishing with Marwitz's squadrons, drew off and disappeared, they experienced an amount of relief which those alone can comprehend who may have stood in a similar predicament. They saw that they were safe in St. Amand and the places near, and they hoped to accomplish more than their own safety. Blücher hastened his preparations for an offensive movement against the French left, and calculated on rendering it decisive.

Meanwhile, Napoleon resumed his plan for breaking the centre of the Prussian line. He did nothing, however, in a hurry. On the contrary, he masked the formation of his columns behind the broken road on the right of Fleurus, and the better to deceive the enemy, drew off both guns and cavalry from the immediate vicinity of Tongrine. Grouchy commanded here, to whom General Thielmann was opposed; and the latter, taking it for granted that the enemy were shaken, determined to push them hard. His corps had been much weakened by the withdrawal of portions of it to strengthen the attacks on St. Amand.

Of cavalry he retained but one brigade, Colonel Von Marwitz's being disposed of as has already been explained. His infantry consisted of two brigades, one of which, Colonel Von Kamfen's, occupied the slope between Tongrine and Tongrenelle; while the other, Von Borcke's, held Mont Pontriaux, and communicated by a detached battalion with Stulpnâgel's, in front of Sombref. Thielmann instantly directed General Von Robe to advance Lottum's cavalry along the Fleurus road, and to carry with him a battery of horse-artillery.

There was already a battery of 12-pounders upon the road, close to which the lighter pieces drew up, and the whole opened a furious cannonade upon the French artillery, which was ranged along the opposite slope. By and by a couple of guns galloped forward under cover of two squadrons of dragoons, and a sort of duel commenced between them and an equal number of pieces which the enemy had brought up to meet them. But the fight, besides that it was not very equal, did not last long. Two regiments of Excelmans' heavy horse, which had formed on the French right of the road, suddenly charged the Prussian guns, and the squadrons which protected them.

The latter were ridden down and dispersed, while the guns retreated at a gallop. But the enemy never drew bridle: they pursued the flying horsemen, hewing and cutting at the rearmost, and coming upon the 12-pounder battery before it could be moved, made themselves masters of the cannon. This was a severe blow, and seemed to threaten still more disastrous consequences, which in all probability would have occurred at once, had not General Von Borcke interposed to avert them.

General Von Borcke made a forward movement with the

whole of his infantry brigade. Two battalions were thrown out to line some hedges and stone walls, which running parallel with the high road, flanked the enemy's cavalry; a third took post in column on the road itself. Mont Pontriaux and its outlets were at the same time occupied in force; and two battalions alone remained in reserve. These dispositions, supported by an artillery fire from the high ground about Tongrenelle, checked the enemy, and caused him some loss: he therefore withdrew from this part of the field.

It was about eight o'clock, and the battle continued to rage in and about Ligny with unremitting fury. Langen's brigade having been called away from its position it! front of Sombref, was replaced by that of Colonel Stulpnâgel, who not only had devolved upon him all the duties of a reserve, but was compelled, at the same time, to feed the garrison of Ligny, and to keep open, by means of a chain of skirmishers, the communications with the troops on the right and left. Just then, when General Gneisenau, the accomplished chief of Blocker's staff, rode up to Von Borcke's ground, and was taking a survey from it of the whole field of battle, there arrived from Ligny an *aide-de-camp* dispatched by Von Krafft, and prayed earnestly for assistance. Now Gneisenau had not a single battalion disposable.

He therefore desired the officer to return and say, that for half an hour longer Krafft must hold his ground, let the sacrifice of life be what it might. And it is not a little remarkable that Blücher was at the same moment animating Von Pirch to the defence of St. Amand-la-Haye, though the latter assured him that his men did not retain a single round of ammunition in their pouches.

The Prussians had fought long and gallantly, but the symptoms of exhaustion which they now began to exhibit could not escape the observation of Napoleon. It seemed as if the hour for which he had waited and watched were come; and he was not the man to let it pass unimproved. He moved forward upon Ligny eight battalions of grenadiers of the Guard, with the whole of Milhaud's heavy cavalry, none of which had as yet come under fire. They were all fresh and free from fatigue. Their approach was covered and protected by whole salvoes of artillery, many pieces being brought up from the rear, and now for the first time exploded; and the more to encourage the Emperor in the accomplishment of the crowning manoeuvre, he received tidings of the arrival of Lobau's corps.

This fine body of men, which, having a long way to compass, had been unable to come up in time to play a part in the opening of the battle, arrived just as they were wanted. They numbered about 12,000 of all arms; and being formed into contiguous columns a little to the right of Fleurus, constituted such a reserve as left Napoleon nothing to fear. Their hands, and those of the Guard, were thus completely freed, and he did not permit them to lack employment.

Napoleon, ere he advanced his Guards and cavalry, looked closely, from some rising ground, into the dispositions of the Prussians. He observed that the space in the rear of Ligny was well nigh denuded of troops; and turning to Count Gerard, who stood near, he exclaimed, "They are lost; they have no reserves left."

In a moment directions were given to push on guns, horse, and foot; and a furious roar of cannon soon told that they had been obeyed. The shot from these guns fell like hail among the Prussian troops which were in march to sustain their comrades in Ligny. It tore open sections, and seemed to crush by its weight whole columns; and while men and horses yet reeled beneath it, the Guards appeared emerging from the smoke. In front and by both flanks the village was fiercely assailed.

It was defended with great resolution, in spite of an uncommon disparity in numbers; indeed one regiment even advanced with the bayonet beyond the shelter of the houses, only that it might be charged and overwhelmed by Milhaud's *cuirassiers*. No man amid that struggle staid to notice that thick clouds had for some time been gathering over the field; it was scarcely felt when the rain came down in torrents that the storm had burst. But neither the war of the elements nor the obstinate valour of the Prussian infantry arrested the progress of the assailants, who, with loud cries of "*Vive l'Empereur!*" carried the long-contested post.

While the force which thus broke through his centre was mustering, Blücher had directed, and to a certain extent carried into effect, a fierce attack on the French left. The manoeuvre was, however, but partially in progress, when messenger after messenger came at speed to recall him to Sombref, on which Napoleon was said to be marching at the head of his guard. Blücher flow back to the spot where danger was described to be most imminent; and finding three cavalry regiments belonging to Zeiten's corps intact, he directed them to charge the head of the column.

They did so; but scarcely with sufficient spirit. The enemy's fire was so close and well delivered, that many men and officers fell beneath it, and the remainder wheeling about, went off as rapidly as they had approached. This had occurred twice, when Blücher in person rallied his broken squadrons, and himself led them the third time into action. But the French were not to be moved: they poured in again such a musketry-fire that the cavalry recoiled from before it; and the field marshal carried away by the tide, galloped, like the rest, to the rear.

Just then his horse received a mortal wound, which entered the noble animal's left side near the saddle girth. Blücher felt that his charger was checked, and, applying the spur, caused it to make two or three convulsive plunges forward, but beyond this the strength of the animal would not carry him. It reeled and staggered under its ride, while close behind might be heard the tramp of the French *cuirassiers* as they thundered in pursuit.

"Nostitz," cried Blücher to his *aide-de-camp*, "I am lost: save yourself;" and as he spoke his horse fell, rolled upon its right side, and half buried him under its weight. But Count Nostitz paid no regard to the generous advice thus given. He leaped from the saddle, held the bridle of his own horse with his left hand, and drawing his sword, placed himself over the body of his fallen commander, determined to defend him as long as life remained, and if he could not save to die with him. He had scarcely done so when the *cuirassiers* came pouring up How they failed to notice him it might be hard to say. Probably they were too much intent on overtaking and destroying the mass to pay heed to an individual, whom, if they saw him at all, they doubtless imagined to be wounded: but, however this may be, they rushed past without offering to him or to his chief the slightest molestation.

Nostitz, of course, stood stock still. It was not his business to attract attention; and the better to hide the General from curious eyes, he threw a cloak over him. But his heart beat quick when again the sound of horsemen drew near, and he beheld the French galloping back, right over the ground which they had previously compassed. This time, however, they did not come as conquerors. The Prussians having rallied, charged them vigorously, and the ranks of the *cuirassiers* having been disturbed in a previous pursuit, they retreated with precipitation.

Now then Count Nostitz hastened to make the case of the field marshal known to his followers. Half a dozen stout troopers sprang to the ground: they removed the dead horse by sheer strength; and lifting their general from the ground, laid him upon one of their own chargers and bore him off. Blücher was insensible when first extricated from beneath his dead horse; but his consciousness slowly returned as his gallant *aide-de-camp* guided him towards a column of infantry, which received him in charge, and moved off with him to the rear just as the French had begun to renew their attack, and Prussian resistance was constrained to grow lax before it.

Chapter 13

The Night after the Battle

The battle of Ligny was lost. This triumph to the French arms had been occasioned by the success of a manoeuvre which was not properly guarded against, perhaps because it does not seem to have occurred to the Prussian general that it would be attempted. But the defeat was neither a rout, nor, by reason of the manner in which the blow fell, were its consequences further to be deplored than that morally they told in favour of the French and against the Allies.

That alone of which Blücher was apprehensive, and to guard against which he had weakened every part of his line save one, was that he should be forced into a line of retreat which might separate him from the English; and the direction taken by the Imperial Guard in the last and crowning charge upon Ligny sufficiently insured that no such calamity should befall him. The Prussian army was in some sort pierced; that is to say, there was free access to the assailants up the face of the heights as far as Sombref; and any retreat undertaken amid the first panic of the moment would have necessarily carried the fugitives into two diverging roads.

Luckily for them, however, the battle had been maintained till the last glimmering of twilight died out; and the Prussian officers took advantage of the darkness to reorganize, to a certain extent, their shattered masses, and withdraw them simultaneously along the roads that had been previously agreed upon.

The Prussians were fairly broken in the centre. They held

Sombref, it is true, with great tenacity; neither did the enemy succeed throughout the night in making a lodgement there, but they kept it merely as a place of arms, by means of which the communication between the extreme flanks might be preserved. The enemy, on the other hand, not only threatened this place but turned round upon the villages among which so much fighting had been maintained, and compelled the Prussians to withdraw with precipitation from the whole of them.

Meanwhile General Thielmann, on the extreme left, as he had never been seriously attacked, nor of course suffered as the others had done, resolved to make a diversion in favour of his more hard-pressed comrades. Accordingly he debouched from Mont Pontriaux, and commencing a stout battle in the dark, carried for a while all before him. The French skirmishers were driven in by two battalions. These next encountered a regiment of dragoons, which charged them, and was repulsed. By and by, on two separate occasions besides, similar attacks were made upon them with a similar result; and finally, encountering a portion of Lobau's infantry, they took it in flank and overthrew it.

These were gallant exploits, and much aided the exertions of Generals Von Jagow, Krafft, Von Pirch, and others, who fought to extricate their people from inclosures which had ceased to be tenable. But the Prussian loss was necessarily severe. Over and above the fugitives, of whom every army engaged throws oft' an abundant crop, there had fallen in the fight about 12,000 men, and 21 pieces of cannon remained in the enemy's bands. The field of battle was likewise abandoned, though gradually. The right wing assembled in tolerable order in and about Bry; the centre maintained Sombref, with a hollow road which communicated between that place and Bry.

These gradually filed off towards Tilly, on the road to e leaving Thielmann's corps on the right to cover the movement. As was to be expected, the retrogression of masses such as these did not take place without difficulty or molestation. The enemy's cavalry hung upon their rear, forcing the battalions to march in squares, and giving ample occupation to the horse, who bravely succoured them by the flank. But they made no serious impression; indeed, they were repeatedly driven off, and more than once were pursued to the villages which had been the scene of the day's terrific contest.

The result was, that, about midnight, Vandamme's corps (the 3rd) bivouacked in advance of St. Amand; Gerard's corps (the 4th) lay upon its arms in front of Ligny; and the Guards occupied the heights of Bry. Before Gerard's corps, and nearer to Sombref, Grouchy's cavalry halted; while Lobau's corps, which had been less engaged than the rest, slept around its fires in the valley behind Ligny.

With respect to Napoleon himself, whether it was that his bodily strength failed him, or that he saw the hopelessness with jaded troops of any further exertion, he ceased in a moment to harass the Prussians. He did not so much as feel for them with patrols, having persuaded himself that they were in full retreat, and had taken the road which he wished them to take. He rode back to Fleurus, and there spent the night.

While the Prussian army was thus fiercely engaged with the main body of the French under Napoleon in person, the allies maintained their ground against Ney at Quatre Bras; and ultimately. as has been related in a previous chapter, compelled him to fall back beyond the position which he had occupied at Frasne previously to his advance in the morning. Historians, by the silence which they maintain on the subject, seem indirectly to teach that the Duke of Wellington was too much occupied all this while with his own battle to pay any regard to that which Blücher was waging.

This is a great mistake: the Duke knew that his chivalrous ally had made up his mind to fight. Neither could he be ignorant, from the appearance of the enemy's masses, on which he looked down from the mill of Bussy, of the time when in all probability the struggle would begin. He returned, therefore, to his own people, calculating surely on events which came to pass almost exactly as he had foreseen. Moreover, the fields of action were near enough the one to the other to permit his seeing, from each height as he ascended it, the smoke of the battle of Ligny rise in thick volumes over the intervening woods. From time to time, likewise, when a lull occurred where he himself was stationed, the sound of the French and Prussian cannonade reached him plainly, and he was well pleased to perceive that it continued on the whole stationary; thus indicating that the Prussians did their duty as became them, and well sustained the military character of their nation.

However, as evening wore on, these sounds denoted that the battle was rolling backwards; and sundry dispatches, sent to him by Lord Hardinge (Sir Henry Hardinge in these days, and attached to Prince Blücher's headquarters), informed him of every ebb and flow throughout the mighty struggle. Moreover, he saw, through his glass, the failure of that cavalry-charge which led to Blücher's misfortune, and immediately preceded the general retreat of his army. Indeed the Duke was quite aware of almost all that was passing on the heights of Ligny, and learned after nightfall, from a short note written by Hardinge while he lay mutilated in a cottage, that the Prussians were overmatched.

Still it was impossible to guess the precise extent to which fortune had declared against them; and circumstanced as his own army was he could not, till day should dawn, venture to send out patrols, or by any other direct means strive to open a communication with Blücher. But the Duke was nowise disconcerted by this. His troops were arriving from hour to hour in large numbers. All the cavalry, with the mass of the British and German infantry, was either on the ground or near enough to be brought up as soon as they might be required; and thus concentrated, he knew that in any case it was competent to him to fight or to retreat, as should seem most expedient on the morrow.

Having, therefore, seen his outposts well arranged, and left no point uncared for which seemed to demand attention, he withdrew to a fire near the roadside and sat down. Other generals would have been oppressed with anxiety as to what the morrow might bring forth. Had it been Napoleon, in the days of his early glory, of whom we now write, it would have probably been our duty to describe him as poring over a map and measuring with a pair of compasses the routes and distances from one portion of the district to another. But the Duke seems always to have possessed the rare, and, to an officer, the invaluable quality of relaxing his energies as soon as the call for them was over, and turning his thoughts into any channel which happened to invite them.

On the present occasion a regiment of cavalry, the 12th, happened to come up soon after he had taken his seat. It was commanded by one of the bravest soldiers, though of the gentlest nature, that over wore a British uniform, Lieutenant Colonel the Honourable Frederick Ponsonby, who, passing over to salute his friend and beloved commander, found him busily engaged in the perusal of some English newspapers.

A packet had just reached him, and the Duke began upon them forthwith, reading aloud, and indulging in many a good joke at the expense of the fears of the home government, as they were there described. To speak of such a man as at any moment liable to be surprised, is to exhibit a marvellously slight acquaintance with human nature. He who is surprised must lose self-possession; and if he be attacked in some manner upon which he had never calculated, his means of repelling the attack will be to seek. But the loss of self-possession can hardly be predicated of one who, amid the hurry of active operations, and in the very middle, so to speak, of a battle, is able to amuse himself and all who come near him, as the Duke amused that night his staff, and the gallant soldier who joined himself to their company.

The night of the 16th, which the Prussians employed in executing an orderly retreat, was spent by the British army in quiet. When this expression is used to denote the condition of men who lie, or sleep, on the ground of a lately-fought battle, the reader, not practically acquainted with war and its results, must accept it as a mere term of convention. It means, that there are no alarms from the enemy—no braying of bugles or rolling of drums amid the hours of darkness—no cry of "Stand to your arms!" or other notices expressive of danger near at hand: but of quiet, in the proper acceptation of the word, troops circumstanced as were the Allied regiments on the field of Quatre Bras know little.

Not to speak of the perpetual interruptions to sleep, occasioned by the arrival of new-comers from the rear, the heavy tramp of horses passing, the rattle of steel scabbards, and the lumbering sound of cannon and ammunition-wagons, there are sounds upon the night-air which effectually break in upon the composure, even of the veteran.

When the battle has been carried into the night it is impossible to collect the wounded, and bestow them all in places of shelter; and very piteous are the groans and cries which some of these poor fellows send forth in their agony. Neither is it an agreeable thing to find the regiment or battalion of which you are a member halted, and desired to make itself comfortable, in a field wet with the blood, and cumbered with the bodies of the slain.

Moreover, food and water may alike be wanting; and hungry men will, in spite of much fatigue, prowl about, as far as a regard to personal safety will admit, in search of these things. As the proceedings incident on these contingencies give its peculiar hue to the soldier's manner of existence, it may not be amiss to permit one of the body to explain. A private of the 11th Light Dragoons, who with his corps had compassed that day about forty English miles, and arrived at Quatre Bras just after the firing had ceased, thus describes the manner in which he spent the night:—

> "The horses," he says, "had not tasted water since the march began, and the darkness was such as, combined with their own weariness, hindered our men in general from going in search of it. Again the habits of the old soldier prevailed with me; and knowing that on the efficiency of my horse my own would absolutely depend, I resolved, at all hazards, to fetch him some water. Accordingly I proposed to my comrade that we should steal away together; and he consented the more readily on my putting him in mind, that

the same process which gave refreshment to our chargers might insure a good supper for ourselves.

"Armed each with a pistol, and carrying a sack and leathern bucket in our hands, we stole from the bivouac, and having previously noticed a village about a mile distant, we made for that. We entered, and found the stillness of the grave; but by and by, observing a light in the window of one of the houses, I knocked at the door, and we were admitted. My astonishment may be conceived when the first object that met my gaze was a French grenadier, fully accoutred and sitting in the chimney corner. It was no time for hesitation, so I cocked my pistol; whereupon he rose, bade us welcome with perfect composure, and, pointing to his knee, informed us that he was wounded. Perceiving that he spoke the truth, I desired him to sit down again, adding an assurance that he had nothing to fear; and as he took me at my word, and began once more to smoke his pipe, I addressed myself to the master of the house: but it was to no purpose that I demanded food and drink; he assured me that the French had swept his cupboard bare already, which proved in the end not to be in strict agreement with the truth; for while I kept him in talk my companion descended to the cellar, and soon returned, bringing with him a part of a ham, a loaf of bread, and some butter. With these we judged it expedient to be satisfied; so wishing both our host and the wounded Frenchman good night, we repassed the threshold and took the direction of the camp.

"One object of our excursion was thus accomplished, but another, at least as important, remained unfulfilled. We had not discovered any water, and we were loath to return to our panting horses without it. We looked about, therefore, in various quarters; and at length, to our great joy, discovered a wet ditch. From that we filled our buckets; and the poor brutes seemed to thank us, as they sucked it up, for the care which we had taken of them. Neither did we conceal from our officers and comrades the treasure on which we had fallen. A party was at once sent out under our guidance; and the chargers of the 11th fared that night in consequence better, I am apt to believe, than those of most of the other regiments then in position."

It is the custom in the English army, and probably in the other armies of Europe, that troops in the field shall stand to their arms an hour before daylight. The stir which usually accompanies this arrangement had not yet occurred, when there began at the outposts an irregular firing, concerning which it was not easy to guess of what it might be the prelude. Staff officers rode to the front, and among them Picton, who ascertained that one of the enemy's patrols had shown itself between the pickets; that the shots fired on the English side were answered by a similar salute from the enemy; and that the fusillade thus taken up near Piermont had been carried all along the extent of the line.

It cost some lives, which proved to have been wantonly sacrificed for no movement of attack was meditated; but it was not permitted to continue. The French, like the English, had taken the alarm. They, too, had officers of rank at hand, and both parties exerting themselves to put a stop to the annoyance, it soon ceased.

And now the Duke was in the field. He had mounted his horse at the first streak of dawn, and arrived at the outposts just as Captain Wood, of the 10th Hussars, who had the advanced picket of his corps, was in a condition to convey to him some valuable information. Being planted on the Namur road, Captain Wood had taken upon himself, as soon as there was light, to push forward a patrol in the direction of the Prussian field of battle, and had thus ascertained that the Prussians were no longer in occupation of it.

The Duke immediately ordered a squadron of the same regiment, under Captain Grey, to repeat the experiment. He sent with them Lieutenant Colonel the Hon. Sir Alexander Gordon, one of his *aides-de-camp*, in whom he had great confidence; and having fully instructed him in all that he desired to have done, mounted a height, and stood to observe the issue. He saw Gordon move cautiously along the high road, and a French *vidette*, who occupied the face of the hill of St. Amand, circle as if to give notice to his own people of the proceeding.

He observed that other French troopers showed themselves, and retreated; and by and by Gordon and his escort disappeared over the ridge. Gordon executed his mission with equal sagacity and success. He penetrated as far as Sombref, where General Zieten still lingered, and obtained from him an accurate account, as well of all that had occurred on the previous day, as of Blücher's intentions regarding the future. With this intelligence he rode briskly back, and reached the Duke of Wellington unmolested.

CHAPTER 14

Movement on Mont St. Jean

It had formed part of the original plan of the campaign, concerted some time previously to the advance of the French army, that the Allies should fight a battle on or about the ground where the operations of Ligny and Quatre Bras took place; and that in the event of disaster, or the chances of their fighting to advantage failing, that they should fall back and reunite on the skirts of the forest of Soignies. In pursuance of this design Blücher, with the main body of his army, followed in retreat the great road by Tilly upon Wavre, leaving General Zieten in Sombref, with directions not to stir till the morning of the 17th.

In the expectation likewise that Wellington would find some means of communicating with that officer, he desired him to say that the Prussians were in good heart, and that they would not fail to support their friends wherever the latter might determine to make a stand. Meanwhile General Thielmann, after waiting till the last brigade had got clear of the villages on his right, drew off in good order towards Gembloux. He began his march about three in the morning, and accomplished it without being once required to face round his rear guard or bring a gun into battery; and he found the place, on his arrival, filled with Bülow's corps, which, making great exertions as soon as the real nature of Blücher's position became known to them, had come up from Hannut during the night.

Thus far the ultimate objects which both Blücher and Wellington had in view were as little interfered with as if no battles had been fought They were still in connection—having Brussels in their rear, and all their communications with England, Holland, and Germany safe. Not a magazine or depôt of any kind had fallen into the enemy's hands; and while the English felt emboldened by the remembrance of their successes over night, the Prussians gave the best proof that failure had not disheartened them.

Accordingly, having received from Colonel Gordon a distinct account of all these things, the Duke of Wellington made preparations to withdraw to a position which, as has already been explained, he had carefully examined, and of which he had caused a plan to be made out ten days previously.

There was no occasion for haste, however, and the Duke made none. The troops, on the contrary, were ordered to cook their dinners, after which, about an hour before noon, the infantry began to take ground to the rear. But there were other divisions than those which occupied the plateau of Quatre Bras to be put in motion, and the baggage, which in great quantities covered the roads, must needs be moved off. Concerning these last-mentioned objects of care, explicit directions were issued. All the paths leading to and through Genappe were ordered to be cleared; and every cart, wagon, pack-horse, and carriage not absolutely required for the use of the army, was swept back towards Brussels. Then followed a Memorandum to Lord Hill to the following effect:—

17th June, 1815.

The 2nd division of British infantry to march from Nivelles to Waterloo at ten o'clock.

The brigades of the 4th division, now at Nivelles, to march from that place on Waterloo at ten o'clock. Those brigades of the 4th division at Braine-le-Comte, and on the road from Braine-le-Comte to Nivelles, to collect and halt at Braine-le-Comte this day.

All the baggage on the road from Braine-le-Comte to Nivelles, to return immediately to Braine-le-Comte, and to proceed immediately from thence to Hal and Bruxelles."

The spare musket ammunition to be immediately parked behind Genappe.

The corps under the command of Prince Frederick of Orange will move from Enghien this evening, and take up a position in front of Hal, occupying Braine-le-Château with two battalions.

Colonel Estroff will fall back with his brigade on Hal, and place himself under the orders of Prince Frederick.

Having arranged these points the Duke proceeded to settle the order in which his army should retire, and he directed it to effect the movement in two columns; the brigades which constituted each being instructed, in case of pressure, to halt and form up alternately, so as to show, everywhere, a good front to the enemy. Meanwhile the infantry pickets stood fast, extending all the way from the Bauterley road, a little beyond the right of the wood of Bossu, to the left of the Thyle road, within which the farm of Piermont lay.

And the better to deceive the enemy the cavalry took up a position on the Namur road, where it formed in two lines, the light cavalry in front, the heavy in rear. And now in the full blaze of day, under a burning sun, over the face of which, however, heavy clouds soon began to collect, the Allied army moved off. It is impossible to conceive a march performed with greater deliberation or in better order.

One column of infantry, with its guns, followed the high road; and in spite of the, delay occasioned by the narrowness of the bridge over the Genappe, and the not less inconvenient size and shape of the street to which it conducts, the whole mass, comprising two British and one Dutch-Belgian divisions, besides unattached brigades of Brunswickers and a battalion of the 95th Rifles, gained the opposite side of the defile without appearing to have been noticed.

The other column took a cross-road which ran westward of the *chaussée* through Sart-à-Mavelines and Bossy upon Wasis, where lower down the stream than Genappe it crossed the rivulet. And now the light infantry gradually fell back, leaving the cavalry at the outposts, which threw out pickets to relieve those of their dismounted comrades, and showed a bold face in every direction. The Duke remained with the cavalry till between three and four o'clock in the afternoon.

He kept his eye all the while upon the. enemy's positions, where everything continued unaccountably quiet; till by and by heavy columns were seen to move along the battle-field of Ligny, and then to separate. One portion went forward on the road to Wavre, another, not apparently of great strength, turned its face towards Namur. The third and greatest moved from Sombref, and keeping the main road, evinced a disposition to fall upon the left flank of the Allies.

When he first caught sight of these threatening masses, the sun was shining brightly, and its rays glanced back from their arms in such strong flashes, that the Duke naturally mistook them for infantry. But a little closer inspection satisfied him that the head of the column, at all events, was composed of *cuirassiers*, from whose steel corselets the light was reflected as if from a thousand mirrors, and it soon became apparent that both there and elsewhere danger threatened.

Ney, too, was in motion. His cavalry, like Napoleon's, preceded his infantry, doubtless because the fact of the withdrawal of the English infantry was known to him; and the Duke, having waited till their advanced patrols had nearly touched his *videttes*, gave orders to retreat.

If the infantry had marched off in brilliant order, the formation assumed by the cavalry, under the immediate directions of Lord Uxbridge, was not lest striking. There was some skirmishing, as a matter of course, on and about the two great roads. The pickets did not come on without firing a few shots; but it was Lord Uxbridge's wish to unite his strength with as little delay as possible, and to carry it intact towards a field where it would be enabled to act to better purpose.

Accordingly he threw his horsemen into three columns; one of which, consisting entirely of heavy cavalry, was instructed to follow the main road, and to pass through Genappe by the bridge. On the right, taking for a while the same route with the infantry, the brigades of Vivian and Vandeleur formed; and to them it was given in charge, that they should move on Thuy and there cross the stream.

The left, also composed of light cavalry, was to make its way to a ford above the town; while the whole were covered by the 23rd Light Dragoons on the left, and by the 7th Hussars—taken from Major-General Sir Colquhoun Grant's brigade—on the centre, and partially to the right. With these columns, and with the corps composing the rearguards, moved several troops of horse artillery, which, on the present as on all other occasions, did good service, and earned for themselves the admiration both of friends and foes.

The retreat of the cavalry was as regular as if it had been a series of movements on parade. Occasionally the rearmost troop or section of the retiring force would be charged; when, after offering as much resistance as they could, the overmatched troopers would gallop back upon their supports. But these never failed them; and once, at least, two whole brigades—Vivian's and Vandeleur's—continued, during a good while, a series of demonstrations which foreboded sharper work in the end. Vivian had drawn up the 18th Hussars upon a somewhat advantageous position; and observing that the enemy would take no denial, gave the word, "Make ready to charge."

Meanwhile the horse artillery attached to his brigade unlimbered, and opened upon the enemy's column a well directed fire. But scarcely was this begun, when the clouds, heavily laden with electric matter, which had gathered over the heads of the combatants in masses, burst. It is well known that the fire of artillery produces this effect; and on the present occasion there accompanied the thunder-storm such a torrent of rain, as in five minutes converted every meadow and cornfield into a bog. The consequence was, that cavalry manoeuvring became henceforth impossible, except upon the hard roads.

Elsewhere the horses sank at every stride up to their knees;

and the 18th, feeling how impossible it was to charge, broke once more into column and moved to the rear.

Amid this furious deluge the troops pursued their march—the enemy hanging on their rear, but never closing with them. The column on the right of the road had, indeed, enough to do to effect the passage of the Genappe without a battle; but the centre and the left both pursued their way almost entirely unmolested.

The 7th Hussars brought up the rear of the force, which moved by the great road, continuing on the French side of the bridge after all the other regiments had passed; and eventually squadron after squadron fell back across the stream, till only one remained. But it was admirably manoeuvred, more especially the troop of which the Earl of Portarlington, then Lieutenant Standish O'Grady, was in command; and narrow as the bridge was, and overwhelming the numbers of the pursuers, not a man or horse remained behind.

And now, for the first time, a somewhat sharp encounter took place. Lord Uxbridge, perceiving that a large force of French cavalry had poured into Genappe, and that it was followed by the great bulk of that portion of the French army which moved by the Charleroi road, determined to make a dash at them; being apprehensive lest, by pushing him too sharply, they might, perhaps, hurry the arrangements of the commander-in-chief. And the ground being particularly favourable to him, he formed his troops so as to make the most of it.

About six or seven hundred yards from the town, and on the summit of a range of heights which overlook it, the heavy brigades of Lord Edward Somerset and Sir William Ponsonby were drawn up. In front of them a little way the 23rd Light Dragoons were halted, and the 7th Hussars formed line just outside the town. These formations might have been completed about a quarter of an hour, when loud shouts arose, and presently the head of a dense column of French lancers emerged from behind the street.

One squadron of the 7th acted as a sort of picket or rearguard to the rest. It was charged in a very irregular manner, by a crowd of horsemen, who dashed, as it appeared, without instructions or order, out of the French ranks. Almost to a man they were made prisoners, and proved to be mad with drink.

The column, however, did not move on—at least in its front. This had halted as soon as the English cavalry came in sight; and as there was no check in rear, and the street was narrow and confined, sixteen squadrons soon became jammed together in a dense mass. It was at this moment that Lord Uxbridge, perceiving the state of things, ordered the covering squadron of the 7th to charge. Doubtless, had the body attacked been different from what it was, or any opportunity been afforded of getting at it by the flank, the charge would have proved decisive.

But the enemy consisted entirely of lancers; and their stationary attitude, so far from affecting them injuriously, told in their favour. With a *chevaux-de-frise* extended, and upheld by the crowds that thronged them in their rear, the leading troop received the hussars as the rock receives the wave. No impression could be made upon them; and though the assailants displayed extreme gallantry, losing a good many men and one excellent officer, they were forced to retire.

Meanwhile the French having established a battery of horse-artillery on the left bank of the Genappe, opened a brisk fire upon the English cavalry reserves, and did some damage, and occasioned more confusion, of which their lancers taking advantage, pushed on; but they made little by their movement in attack. The 7th met them halfway, and drove them back; whereupon they again rallied among the houses, and again were the 7th in their turn compelled to give ground.

Immediately the enemy changed their tactics, and deploying their column, as it gained the end of the street, soon presented such a line to the hussars, that the latter saw the impossibility of coping with it. Nor was it necessary that they should. Lord Uxbridge had waited for this information, and knew how to deal with it.

Causing the hussars to move aside, and to form in a field a

little removed from the road, he launched the 1st Life Guards, supported by the 23rd, at the lancers; and in five minutes the latter were ridden down or dispersed, and fleeing in all directions. The Life Guards followed them into the town, hewing, slashing, and driving everything before them, till they fairly pushed the survivors across the stream, and were themselves with difficulty halted at the edge of it.

From that time the enemy's pursuit was much more cautious as well as more distant. He brought his guns to the front, between which and the English horse artillery a smart duel ensued; but his cavalry threatened much more than they strove to perform, and were easily kept in check by the dispositions which were from time to time made to receive them.

At last, however, Lord Uxbridge having satisfied himself that there was no danger to his flanks on ground so deep as under the heavy rain of the afternoon the fields on either side had become, gradually drew in his regiments, and formed one continuous column on the high road. This he covered with the light cavalry, having the Household Brigade in support; and the whole, without further loss or any serious molestation, filed into position on the heights of Mont St. Jean.

CHAPTER 15

State of Feeling where the War was not

While the war thus swayed to and fro at Ligny, Quatre Bras. and the places adjacent, the state of Brussels and of all the towns in the rear was terrible. From the hour when the leading regiments of the reserve filed out of the Park, the Belgian capital in particular became a scene of the most painful excitement. Backwards and forwards—from street to street—and from house to house—people wandered to ask for news and to retail rumours. Numbers on horseback and in carriages followed the track of the column, and returned one by one, and at intervals more or less wide, to swell the tide of popular alarm;—for they had seen no enemy, nor learned from the reports of others more than that a crisis was impending, and that its results were quite uncertain.

Nor was it exclusively upon the non-combatant part of the population that the call to arms came suddenly. Many officers, and among others Sir Thomas Picton, had reached Brussels only on the evening of the 15th, and on the morning of the 16th found themselves in full march against the enemy. Indeed it is well remembered in Canterbury to this day, that just one week after the gallant leader of the 3rd division dined at the Fountain Hotel on his way to the Low Countries, his body, pierced with wounds, was brought back to the same hotel on its way to the mausoleum within which it now rests.

The hour which immediately succeeded the muster of the

reserve was one of great bustle and interest in Brussels. It takes some time to move a division of infantry out of a town and along a road of not more than ordinary width; and the regiments, though they filed off as fast as their ranks could be formed, went but gradually. Nevertheless the rearmost of the whole disappeared at last, and then the scene shifted.

There was no more bustle now. Park, square, street, Place Royale, and indeed the whole town, seemed to become in a moment deserted, for they who had turned out to take perhaps a last farewell of friends and relatives thus suddenly removed from them, hurried back as soon as the parting was over to the privacy of their own apartments. Hence, from early morning till long past noon, Brussels presented the appearance of a city devastated by plague. The shops were not opened, and no manner of business went on—the very market-people, after lingering for a while beside their unvisited stalls, packed up their wagons again and drove them home.

The troops were all gone—all except a few mounted officers, who, conscious of their ability to overtake their corps at any moment, lingered yet a little while in the society of their kindred or families. One by one these in due time departed; and if a few came back, it was merely to say that the men had been ordered to halt and cook, and that they proposed to join them again at a place called Waterloo. And so the day wore on.

But a good many hours of light were yet before them, when fresh rumours, repeated by sterner tongues, reached the lingerers in Brussels. About half-past two or three in the afternoon, the noise of firing came back upon the breeze. Then were the streets filled again with anxious listeners. Men and women ran to the Park, where it was said that the sounds were most audible; and sure enough there greeted them there a tumult of battle so incessant that it resembled more the sound of distant thunder than the noise of a cannonade.

The terror—the agony of many who heard that sound—no words may describe. To their dying hour they never can forget it; for besides that almost all were more or less interested in the safety of individuals around whom the iron hail was sweeping, the sense of danger to themselves was the more overwhelming that it took no definite form.

Suspense on such occasions is far more difficult to endure than the wildest reality; and when, as the evening drew on, rumours of the most sinister kind began to thicken—when stories got into circulation of defeat to the English and of an immediate advance by the French—the fears, especially of the women, were wrought up to such a pitch as to set all the restraints of common sense at defiance. Nobody could stay at home—all were abroad, listening and marvelling how near or how far away the battle might be; and as darkness itself brought for a while no cessation to the cannonade, so in darkness these unhappy creatures continued to exercise a vigilance which led to no satisfactory issue.

At length the roar of cannon ceased; and, worn out with excitement, people returned to their homes, and by and by lay down. Few, however, had slept; when about midnight there arose such a thunder of heavy carriage-wheels from the streets that all were roused immediately. Hundreds of casements flew open at once, and hundreds of heads protruded from them, looked down, and saw artillery, spring-wagons, tumbrils, and other munitions of war hurrying as fast as horses could drag them through the town.

"It is all over now," cried many voices at once; "the army is defeated, and these are the remains of the artillery trying to escape the fate which has overtaken their comrades."

Then might be seen in the passages of hotels, in the gateways of private houses, and about stable-yards, delicate women as well as timid men, rushing half dressed as from instant destruction.

"Let the carriage be got ready immediately—the French are upon us."

"Who will get me four horses—two horses—one horse?"

"I will give any price for a vehicle, so that it be brought immediately."

Such exclamations as these resounded everywhere; and when the wants of the clamourer were not instantly supplied confusion became tenfold more confounded. At length the truth came out. The artillery which passed with such speed through the town was not fleeing, but advancing. It had come up from the rear by forced marches, and by forced marches was hurrying to the front; so that whatever the ultimate issue of the strife might be, the English were certainly not yet cut to pieces.

Comforted by this assurance, such as had the most courage went back to their chambers and slept. Others sat in their clothes, and kept the carriages and baggage-wagons ready; while the more timid, adhering to the resolution previously formed, hurried off and made the best of their way to England.

So passed the night of the 16th—in anxiety to the bravest—in the bitter agony of fear to those whose nerves were less tensely strung. The morning of the 17th did not bring with it ground of increased assurance to the one class, or any source of comfort to the other; for about six o'clock a body of Belgian horse rushed wildly into Brussels, exclaiming that the French were at their heels. Immediately the whole population was astir again. The carriages and wagons which had stood for several hours in the great square now received their contents and galloped off! The people fled on foot, not seeming to care for anything except the preservation of their lives.

Of the wealthier *burgher* classes , many declared their determination of remaining beside their property, and taking their chance. Others not so philosophical, hastened to conceal such valuables as could be got out of the way, and then, laden with plate, or possibly jewels, fled with the mob. But not altogether universal was this horror of the invaders. Among other acts by which he disgusted the army, Louis XVIII. had summarily dismissed from the service all officers who were not Frenchmen born.

Now, a good many Belgians had served under Napoleon, and were found in the ranks at the period of the Restoration; and these going home to their own country, carried with them an intense hatred of the government which had sent them adrift. Many of them having been cognizant of the plot laid in Elba, were in correspondence to the last with Napoleon's emissaries, and had given the assurance that as soon as the Emperor made his way to Brussels they would pass under his standard, and bring plenty of recruits with them. Such men were of course in ecstasies when tidings of the French successes reached them, though they were not fated to enjoy their triumph many hours.

Such was the state of Brussels when, about seven o'clock, or a little later, an officer attached to the Duke of Wellington's staff arrived from the front. He had been sent back to make arrangements for the distribution of the baggage, which, as has already been shown, was on its march to the rear, and was confounded by the appearances of absolute dismay which everywhere met him. He exerted himself, and not altogether without success, to allay the tumult.

At the same time, when by and by wagon-loads of wounded began to arrive, the fears of some, and the more sickly sentimentalism of others, quite overcame them. In spite of his assurances that there had been no defeat—that the English on the contrary, had stood their ground, and that he had left them hut a few hours previously drawn up in increased numbers to renew the battle—all who had the means took to flight, and in the course of the day Brussels was left to the possession of but a portion of its native inhabitants.

At the period of which we are writing, the communication between England and the Continent, though regular, was not such as it is now. With the difficulties of adverse winds and stormy waters to surmount, even the hardy smugglers from either shore would sometimes be whole days without crossing. Steam navigation was as yet untried in Europe. Packet-boats were indeed well managed and tolerably regular in regard to their days of sailing, but then they could not make the passage under a certain number of hours from Ostend, and might be several days in effecting it.

In London, therefore, there were as yet no authentic tidings to refer to, though a thousand rumours had been afloat ever since the meeting of the Champ-de-Mai, and each new hour added to the number. Now it was of the utmost importance that the English Government and public should not, at so critical a moment, be subjected to a panic; and yet there seemed to be every probability of the evil befalling.

The fugitives from Brussels were not likely to underrate the extent of the danger to which they had yielded; and coming as they did from the seat of war, their tales, however groundless, would be credited. It so happened that among those whom a laudable curiosity or the ties of friendship had carried at this time to the Low Countries, the Right Honourable Maurice Fitzgerald, Knight of Kerry, was one; and he was enabled, by reason of his intimacy with most of the leading actors in the drama, to do his country good service. Though circumstances were these.

The Knight of Kerry had gone from Brussels to Quatre Bras on the morning of the 17th, and remained upon the ground till the cavalry began its retreat. He then returned to Brussels, having promised to visit his friend, Sir Charles Colville, next day at his post, whether at Hal or Enghien, or between them, on the right of the new position which the army was about to take up. In pursuance of this arrangement, he rose very early in the morning; and, accompanied by the late Marquess of Ormonde, got into a carriage.

Important business required, however, that before visiting Colville, he should repair to Ghent; and as he found, upon inquiry, that the direct road might be difficult of passage, he proceeded in the first instance to Antwerp. The Knight's account of all that followed having already appeared in print, there seems no reason why it should not be inserted here; and its details are by far too important, as well as too interesting, to sanction any attempt at abridgment.

"We arrived at Antwerp," says he, "about five in the morning, and after refreshing ourselves, and looking at the cathedral for about an hour, we proceeded to Ghent as fast as we could, and arrived there about two o'clock. We dined with the commanding officer of the 29th regiment, who had been an old acquaintance of Lord Ormonde. We engaged a carriage, and arranged to proceed after midnight for the division of the army under General Colville. I was just entering the hotel between six and seven o'clock, in order to go to bed, when Sir Pulteney Malcolm drove up from Brussels.

"I told him our plan, when he earnestly entreated me to wait till he had returned from the King of France, then at Ghent, to whom he was going to convey a message from the Duke of Wellington. I waited accordingly; on his return he pressed me, in the most earnest manner, to proceed to London, and communicate to the Government what had occurred. He argued the necessity of such a course, from the Duke of Wellington having declared to him that morning, that he would not write a line till he had fought a battle; and from the false and mischievous rumours which had circulated and gone to England, and the total ignorance of the English Government as to what had taken place.

"He said that he was desirous of writing to the First Lord of the Admiralty; but that etiquette precluded his entering into any details on military affairs when the general had not written; that if I consented I would greatly relieve the Government, and do essential public service, as, independently of the Prussian case, of which I knew more than any other individual could communicate to the Government, there were subjects of a most confidential nature, which he would intrust to me to be told to Lord Castlereagh, our Foreign Minister; that he would put me into a sloop of war at Ostend, and send me across at once. I, however, rather reluctantly assented.

"He then told me that he had left the Duke at half-past ten that morning, with the army in position on ground which he had already examined, determined to give battle, and confident of success, and that lie was in military communication with Marshal Blücher.

"We accordingly changed our route, and proceeded at

once to Ostend, where the Admiral wrote a few lines, merely saying that Bonaparte had defeated the Prussians with great loss, that the Duke was in position, as described before, and that he had prevailed upon the Knight of Kerry to convey this dispatch, who also could furnish all particulars which were as yet known for the information of Government.

"We had rather a slow passage. After we were under-weigh, a *gendarme*, with some mail-bags, overtook the vessel, and said reports had just arrived that the Duke of Wellington was driving the French at all points. We proceeded at once, after landing at Deal, to town, and arrived at the Admiralty at half-past four, Tuesday, June 20. Lord Melville had gone to the House of Lords, whither I followed him; and on receiving the dispatch he immediately summoned the Cabinet Ministers from both houses to meet in the Chancellor's room, which they did instantly.

"I was requested to communicate the particulars referred to in Admiral Malcolm's letter. I said, in order to avoid saying anything unnecessary, I desired to know how far the Cabinet was already informed of what had occurred. Lord Liverpool said that they knew nothing. I asked if they had not heard of the battle with the Prussians. He said, 'No.' I then asked, Had they not heard that Napoleon had moved his army? He said that reports by smugglers to that effect had come across, but that nothing was certain.

"I then gave a detail of all the circumstances that had come to my knowledge, and endeavoured to impress on them the utmost confidence in the success of the Duke of Wellington in any battle that might take place. I stated the nature of the driving in of the Prussians on the 15th, as explained to me by the commandant at Mons. I was enabled to describe very particularly the glorious battle of Quatre Bras, as given to me by a gallant officer of the Rifle Brigade, who was near the Duke during its continuance, and who was wounded there; he gave me a very clear account of the action, and affirmed that he had never seen his Grace expose himself so much personally, or so thoroughly direct every part of the operations, in any of the Peninsular fights with which he was familiar. I explained, on Sir Colin Campbell's authority, the Duke's thorough knowledge of the ground which he had occupied on the, morning of Sunday the 18th.

"Ministers expressed their great relief and gratification at the intelligence I had furnished, as the town had been inundated with the most alarming and dangerous rumours, and that from the length of time since they had received any positive intelligence from the Duke of Wellington, considerable anxiety undoubtedly existed, but that I had effectually removed it. On the following morning early I called upon Lord Castlereagh, before he went to his office. I asked him whether he thought I had impressed upon the Cabinet the perfect confidence which I myself felt as to the Duke's success.

"He said I had; but that he wished for a good deal of conversation with me. I then explained to him those particulars which Admiral Malcolm had wished me confidentially to convey, particularly as to what concerned the position and personal safety of the French King, and other points which it is unnecessary to recapitulate. We had a most interesting discussion on the whole state of the two countries as relating to the war. It was certainly gratifying to me to have relieved the anxiety of ministers, and through them of the public; but Sir P. Malcolm certainly lost me the march to Paris."

Such was the state of feeling in Brussels, Ghent, Antwerp, and London at this time. That it was neither unnatural nor greatly to be wondered at, will be freely admitted by all who remember the events as they occurred. Nevertheless, other events were in progress which were destined to prove that it was unnecessary; and of these it remains to narrate the history.

CHAPTER 16

Movements of the French on the 17th of June

The manner in which the Prussian army withdrew from the field of Ligny has been sufficiently described in another chapter. There was no confusion—very little hurry—no dismay; but in squares of battalions the infantry moved off, which the cavalry in some measure covered, besides protecting the guns. Of these latter 21 pieces remained in the enemy's hands. But when we remember that the Prussians brought nearly 200 pieces into the field—that the ground on which they stood was terribly against them, and that darkness had set in before they began to withdraw—our surprise is occasioned, not that 21 fell, but that three times 21 did not fall into the possession of the victors. A battle of 80,000 men a-side, which gives so few trophies to cither party, can hardly be claimed by either as a decisive victory.

Bruised, and for a while insensible, and laid across the back of a trooper's horse, Blücher was borne from the field. He and his guide moved under the protection of an infantry square, which was repeatedly charged, yet never lost its order—possibly because the men knew that the life of their chief was in their keeping; and he was in this way convoyed to a cottage about six miles in rear of Sombref, where surgical assistance was procured.

All the remedies which circumstances would admit of were applied. His wounds were rubbed with brandy: the old marshal having ascertained the nature of the liniment, suggested—that no harm but much good would probably arise from an administration of the medicine internally It is said that, though the doctor refused to give brandy, he allowed a bottle of champagne, under the cheering influence of which the marshal wrote his dispatch. It is certain that, as the bearer was about to depart, he called him back and said—"Tell the King *dass ich hatte kalt nachgetrunken,* and that all will end well."

Meanwhile the two corps of Zieten and Pirch collected at Tilly and Gentinnes, where at an early hour in the morning of the 17th they continued their retreat towards Wavre. They took the road by Mont St. Guibert; and Pirch's corps halted there for some time, so as to give Zieten an opportunity of marching at ease; and between midday and six in the afternoon both were upon the Dyle, and in position. Zieten crossed and drew up in and around Bierge; Pirch kept the right flank, and took post between St. Aune and Aisemont.

Whilst the 1st and 2nd corps followed this line, General Von Jagow with his troops marching after them, and halting at the defile of Mont St. Guibert, Thielmann gathered together his scattered corps, and fell back along the Namur road. He did not, however, prosecute this route beyond the village of Point du Jour, where the cross-road to Gembloux strikes off from the great *chaussée,* but turned the head of his column down the former path, leaving one brigade of infantry and the reserve cavalry under General Hobe to mask, and, if need be, protect the movement. By and by Thielmann opened a communication with Bülow, who, from his remote cantonments at Liège, was only just arriving in the vicinity of the place where the battle had been fought.

The Prussian narrator of this memorable campaign accounts for the tardy co-operation of Bülow satisfactorily enough. The dragoon, it appears, who on the 15th carried the order for his immediate closing in, delivered it safely at Hannut, where, because Bülow was known to be already on the march, it was permitted to lie. But they who so dealt with it either knew not, or had forgotten, that neither a general nor his troops are tied down to one rate of travelling. Had the dispatch been hurried forward, it would have reached Bülow before the march, which he regarded as a mere measure of precaution, was begun; and so, instead of taking twelve hours to perform it, he might have compassed it in six.

As it was, when late in the evening Bülow and his people reached Hannut, the contents of Blücher's letter took away all desire to halt. The troops were allowed one hour to rest, at the end of which they set forward again, and arrived footsore and a good deal exhausted, in the villages about Gembloux a little after midnight.

The junction of Thielmann's with Bülow's corps placed so strong a force on the enemy's flank, that the former did not scruple to give his men ample time to refresh. It was, therefore, two o'clock in the afternoon of the 17th before his march recommenced, and he conducted it to the end without let or hindrance. Meanwhile Bülow, under directions received from Prince Blücher, moved by a different road. Thielmann made direct for La Bavette, on the left of the Dyle, and somewhat in rear of Zieten. Bülow's post was Dion-le-Mont, at the intersection of the roads to Louvain, Wavre, and Gembloux; and the perfect security with which they were all permitted to choose their own paths, and take their own time, showed that the French, though nominally conquerors, had been sorely exhausted in the battle.

It is a remarkable fact in the life of Napoleon—unquestionably one of the ablest military commanders whom the world has ever produced—that he should have permitted his hard-won victory of the previous day to pass from him so imperfectly improved, That his troops were sorely fatigued cannot be doubted. The marches which they had performed and the battles which they fought between the 13th and 16th of June, were indeed enough to break down most men: neither is it to be wondered at if the powers of his own physical frame should have been tried well nigh beyond their endurance.

But the game which he had undertaken to play was altogether so desperate, and the issues of each throw so vitally important, that posterity will never cease to wonder that, even under such circumstances, he should have held his hand at all.

Be the causes what they may, it is certain that the French army, though in possession of the field of Ligny, did not move from it for more than twelve hours after its opponents had retreated. The dawn of the 17th found three whole corps bivouacked in front of the villages which they had won over night; a fourth, that of Grouchy, lay upon the right, not perhaps quite so far in advance, but still ready for prompt action, and the whole of the Guard, as well as Milhaud's cavalry, were comparatively fresh. Nevertheless, Zieten and Pirch were permitted to go off without an attempt made to stay them, and Zieten did not begin his march before the sun was well risen.

Still, not a man moved; not a patrol was sent out to dog the steps of the last Prussian division, or observe whether they held straight for Namur or turned aside from it; and the Emperor all the while was sound asleep in Fleurus. At last, after Thielmann's rear had melted away, and so much time was lost as to render an active pursuit impossible, a division of light cavalry took the direction which he was assumed to have followed.

By and by the 6th division of Lobau's infantry corps marched in support of them, posting itself on the heights of Mazy, far away beyond the point at which Thielmann had quitted the Namur road; and here the cavalry achieved the only success which could with justice be claimed as the result of the victory. They saw before them a battery of guns, retiring along the Namur road; they galloped after it, and as the gunners had not a single round in their tumbrils, they made themselves masters of the whole without loss, while a squadron of Prussian lancers which moved, as it seemed, for their protection, was attacked and put to flight, having about thirty men killed.

The immediate issue of this exploit was satisfactory. The guns were taken, but a long reach of way being explored, empty of travellers, awakened a suspicion among the captors that this could not be the line of the Prussian retreat. General Pajol, who accompanied his horsemen, accordingly struck to the left, and halted at St Denis, where the infantry overtook him. Meanwhile, Excelmans' cavalry being on its march to support Pajol, obtained tidings which induced its commander to bear off in the direction of Gembloux. There, indeed, he came upon traces of a Prussian bivouac recently abandoned; and so by degrees the conviction was matured that Blücher, relinquishing his hold upon the Meuse, was gone towards Wavre.

Napoleon at the close of the battle had withdrawn to Fleurus for the night, though not till he had left directions for Marshal Grouchy, on whom the command of his right wing devolved, to visit him at an early hour in the morning and receive orders. Grouchy came as he had been desired; but the Emperor instead of instructing him to act, desired him to wait, that they might go to the field together. It was half-past eight o'clock ere they turned their horses' heads in that direction, and when they arrived at the position Napoleon still seemed irresolute. He rode over the field—examined the approaches to St. Amand—gave directions that the wounded should be taken care of—and spoke to the different regiments as he passed them, and was answered with cheers.

He then dismounted, and entered into conversation with Grouchy and Gerard concerning the politics of Paris, and various other general subjects, but gave no orders for a move. At length he directed a reconnaissance to be pushed towards Quatre Bras, and after receiving the report of the officer who commanded it, began, as it were, to recover his energies. Milhaud's *cuirassiers*, one of Pajol's light brigades under Lieutenant General Luberovie, and the 3rd Light Cavalry Division, were directed to take post at Marbais, facing Quatre Bras.

These he supported with the 6th (Lobau's) Infantry Corps, of which, however, one division under General Teste had gone off to St. Denis with Pajol, and with the whole of the Imperial Guard, as well cavalry as infantry; and then he addressed himself to Grouchy, under whose orders he placed two entire corps and a division of infantry, as well as Excelmans' corps and one of Pajol's cavalry divisions.

He desired him to "follow the Prussians, complete their defeat, and on no account permit them to get out of his sight. I am going," he continued, "to unite the remainder of this portion of the army with Marshal Ney's corps, to march against the English and to fight them, if they try to hold their ground between this and the forest of Soignies. You will communicate with me by the paved road that leads to Quatre Bras."[1]

It was to no purpose that Grouchy pointed out how impossible it would be for him to recover the time that was lost, and that, supposing Blücher's rallying point to be Namur, the latter part of the Emperor's instructions were simply impracticable. Napoleon would listen to no remonstrance, and refused to take Grouchy along with him, whereupon Grouchy held his peace, and a series of false operations began.

Grouchy saw Napoleon put the column in motion that was to overwhelm the English at Quatre Bras, and repaired forthwith to the right. He there got the corps of Vandamme and Gerard under arms, and marched them to the point where the roads to Namur and Gembloux diverge; and here his difficulties had their commencement. For a brief space he stood irresolute, till, hearing that a considerable body of Prussians had passed early in the morning through the latter town, he gave orders that the infantry should proceed thither.

While it advanced—as briskly as men can do upon foot—he rode forward and put himself in communication with Excelmans' horse, which were already beyond Gembloux: he found that they had had a slight affair with the enemy, but that little loss had been sustained on either side; and that as the night was closing fast, it was impossible with the uncertain information which he possessed, to attempt much more. Accordingly he contented himself with pushing forward three regiments, two of which took post at Sart-à-Walhain, while the third was thrown out as far as Perwez; the remainder of his troops, with the exception of General Soult's brigade of Pajol's cavalry and Teste's infantry division, he halted, some in front, others immediately

---

1. Grouchy'a Remarks on Gourgaud's Work.

in rear of the town. As to Pajol and Teste, they, after lingering for a while at St. Denis, returned to their original ground at Mazy, near Ligny—a strange blunder, for which no good reason has ever been assigned.

From his headquarters at Gembloux Grouchy addressed his first report to Napoleon. It was dated ten o'clock at night, and has been preserved. It describes the Prussians as retiring in two columns, one by way of Sart-à-Walhain upon Wavre, the other through Perwez, as the writer supposes, towards Liège. It informs Napoleon that he had sent out parties to discover by which route the mass was moving, and promises that, should the result of these inquiries show that Wavre was the main object with the enemy, he would follow close upon their heels, and prevent them from reaching Brussels, and so joining Wellington.

In like manner the marshal states that if the great body be directed upon Liège, he will take the same line, and fight them wherever he can find them. Moreover, a second dispatch, sent off from the same place at two in the morning of the 18th, demonstrates that, let him be chargeable with what faults he may, indolence was not of the number. He had by that time satisfied himself that there was no Prussian movement towards Liège, and announced that he was going to direct his columns upon Corbreux or Wavre.

Thus far Grouchy had fulfilled the wishes of his master. That he did not overtake the troops of which he was in pursuit may be attributed, partly to the delays in setting out, of which notice has just been taken, partly to the exceeding skill with which the Prussian retreat was conducted. The latter, by keeping possession of the skirts of the battle-field, held the victors in check till their principal columns were safe; they then so distributed their rearguards, that the pursuers were at a loss to decide by what roads it behooved them to follow; and when they did follow, they found everywhere strong corps prepared to meet them, which never gave ground till they had forced the assailants to form up for the attack.

Now such evolutions constitute the very perfection of manoeuvres in retreat. As often as you compel a superior enemy to deploy, you put him to a very serious inconvenience; because columns of march are not formed in a moment, nor are guns limbered up and carried back to high-roads without much loss of time. But it was not in this respect alone that the leaders of the Prussian army showed that they well understood their art. With the exception of 21 pieces the whole of the cannon were conveyed safely to the position at Wavre, where, through the judicious management of Colonel Von Röhl, it became at once effective. It happened that the reserve ammunition-wagons had been parked in good time at Gembloux.

Thither Colonel Röhl during the night of the 16th sent his *aide-de-camp*, with instructions to remove the whole forthwith to Wavre, while he himself set off at once to the latter place, that he might be at hand, as battery after battery came in, to furnish it. But the supply of ammunition, it was judged, might not after all be adequate to the probable wants, of a great operation, and accidents on the way could not be wholly guarded against. He therefore dispatched an express to Maestricht, with orders to the commandant that he should forward without delay, in the common wagons of the country, as much powder, shot, and shells as could be packed in the course of an hour.

Similar instructions were sent to the Governors of Cologne, Wesel, and Münster, while the battering train, which had heretofore been at Liège, was ordered back to Maestricht. All these were judicious precautions; and though the safe arrival of the wagons from Gembloux rendered them unnecessary, the wisdom of him who looked so far before him is not the less to be commended.

Moreover, the morale of the Prussian army was very little affected by its reverses. A good many men, belonging chiefly to the Rhenish provinces, were found to have left their colours, and of the new levies from Westphalia and the Duchy of Berg a considerable number had deserted. Indeed, the total amount of loss sustained by this means is computed to have reached 8,000; but the courage of the residue, the soldiers of old Prussia, of Merk, Cleves, Minden, and Ravensberg, was as high as ever. They reposed unbounded confidence in their general; they believed that, though foiled, he could not be defeated; and, therefore, they looked upon the retrogression from Ligny as a mere change of position.

And well did Blücher deserve this feeling. In spite of his hurts he was on horseback, and among his "children," as he called them, by dawn of day on the 18th; and his order of the day on the 17th had already told them that, though beaten, they were not destroyed.

> "I will lead you against the enemy," so says the conclusion of this characteristic document, "and we will beat him, because we must."

CHAPTER 17

Operations of Retreat, and Pursuit to Wavre

By the evening of the 17th four corps of the Prussian army were assembled round Wavre, in the best order, and well prepared for battle. Two of these occupied a position on the right, and two upon the left of the Dyle; and the lines of retreat by which they had gained them were both covered by strong rearguards posted at Vieux Sart and Mont St. Guibert respectively. Neither was the important business of feeling round about the position neglected. It was of unspeakable importance to open a communication as speedily as possible with Wellington, and the best means of marching troops to his support must needs be ascertained.

Accordingly, while the left was watched by patrols, who traversed the great road till it joined the *chaussée* from Namur to Louvaine, detachments were thrown out by Zieten from the right, which guarded the Dyle to Lamale and considerably above it, and at the same time communicated with the posts at Mont St Guibert. These operations took place during the night; but before the sun went down the country between Wavre and Genappe was examined; and the officer who had the reconnaissance, Major von Falkenhausen, was enabled, from the wooded tracts beyond Seroulx, to observe the advance of Napoleon along the paved road that conducts by Planchenoit and Mont St. Jean upon Brussels.

In consequence of these judicious proceedings, which were ably responded to on the side of the Allies, the two marshals succeeded in communicating with one another, and to a certain extent in settling their plans. The Duke informed Prince Blücher that he would accept a battle on the morrow, provided Blücher could assure him of the support of one corps. Blücher replied that he would come to his assistance with his whole army if the French attacked; and that, if they did not, he would he ready to co-operate on the 19th in a combined attack upon them.

Meanwhile, Marshal Grouchy lay, in somewhat loose order, from Mazy, in front of the field of Ligny, all the way to Gembloux. His patrols extended, to be sure, to Sart-à-Walhain and Perwez; but the strength of his corps was at Gembloux; and two divisions, one of infantry, the other of cavalry, passed the night at Mazy. At five o'clock in the morning of the 18th these latter quitted their ground, and, marching by St. Denis and Grandeley, arrived at Tourinnes, where they had been instructed to wait for further orders.

At eight Excelmans' cavalry began to move; and an hour later Vandamme and Gerard were in march. Strange to say, however, the two corps of infantry were crowded upon the same road, which was not only narrow, but, owing to the recent rains, deep and heavy; and the progress , which they made, tedious and wearisome at the best, was, through the breaking down of a wagon, or some other trivial cause, interrupted, from time to time, altogether.

The route which the infantry followed was circuitous as well as inconvenient. It led to Sart-à-Walhain, which forms the apex of an obtuse angle between Gembloux and Wavre, and could be preferred only because Grouchy did not as yet seem to be convinced respecting the real direction of the Prussian retreat. Indeed it is clear from the whole manner of Grouchy's manoeuvring that he could not as yet divest himself of the persuasion that Blücher looked mainly to the line of the Meuse, and was going to make his stand at Maestricht.

But while his infantry were toiling through the muddy lane

on which he had placed them, Excelmans overtook the Prussian rearguards not very far from Wavre itself. He immediately entered with them into a skirmish, while, at the same time, he sent back to inform his chief of what had occurred; and the latter being satisfied that to look farther to the right would he useless, brought up his shoulder and marched upon the Dyle.

There occurred, however, previously to the arrival of Excelmans' messenger, an event which well deserves notice, and of which, had proper use been made, the battle of Waterloo might have been productive of results less immediately decisive than those which ensued upon it. Grouchy had stopped to breakfast in Sart-à-Walhain, and about eleven o'clock was joined by General Gerard, who, impatient of the tardy pace of his corps, had ridden forward. The two generals were conversing in the house of M. Rollaert, a notary, when Colonel Simon Lorieu, Chief of the Staff to Grouchy's wing, came in from the garden, where he had been walking, and stated that a heavy though distant cannonade could be heard.

Grouchy and Gerard hurried instantly out of doors, and caught at once the well-known sound. They appealed to M. Rollaert as to whereabouts he supposed the firing to be; and he stated that it seemed to him to come from the direction of Planchenoit and Mont St. Jean. The French generals looked at one another, and at the officers by whom they were surrounded, and all seemed' to arrive, as if by intuition, at the same conclusion—Napoleon had attacked the English, and the battle was begun. And now arose the question—how did it behoove them to act? Gerard suggested that it would be well to march towards the cannonade, and to connect their own operations more closely with those of Napoleon.

Grouchy did not conceive that the manoeuvre would be justifiable in the face of the instructions which the Emperor had given him, and amid the uncertainty in regard to Blücher's position with which they were surrounded. Each chief had its partisans, who argued stoutly on both sides—one party pointing out that bad roads and a woody country offered serious obstacles to the endeavour—the other professing their ability as well as their desire to surmount them; but the result was that Grouchy adhered to his own view of the case.

It was his duty, he said, to keep the Prussians in view, and to fight them; and this he could not hope to do with success were he, as Gerard finally proposed, to detach one of his corps, and, having the Dyle between them, to operate with the other. Accordingly, the march of the infantry was not delayed; but requesting Gerard to hurry it as much as possible, he mounted his horse and rode towards the advanced guard.

Grouchy was yet *en route,* when an *aide-de-camp* from the main army overtook him, and put into his hands a dispatch, of which the subjoined is a free translation:—

> Camp in front of the Farm of Caillou,
> 18th of June, ten o'clock in the morning.
> Sir, the Marshal,—The Emperor has received your last dispatch, dated Gembloux, in which you make mention of only two Prussian columns as passing to Sauvencères and Sarravalines, the other reports speak of a third and strong column as having gone by St. Gery and Gentinnes to Wavre.
> The Emperor charges me to inform you, that he is just about to attack the English, who are in position at Waterloo, close to the forest of Soignies. His Majesty desires that you direct your movements upon Wavre, so that you may approach us and put yourself *en rapport* with our proceedings, and that, securing our communications, you push before you whatever Prussian corps may have taken that direction, and engage them at Wavre, where you ought to be with as little delay as possible.
> Whatever portion of the enemy may have gone off to your right you can follow with light troops, so as to observe their movements, and pick up their stragglers. Inform me immediately concerning the dispositions of your, march, as well as of any news which you may have obtained respecting the enemy; and do not fail to unite your com-

munications with ours.
Le Major-General Duc de Dalmatie.

The tenor of this note seems to be obvious enough. It indicated that Napoleon was jealous of his right, and that he knew better than the individual to whom it was addressed how Blücher had disposed of his army. Still Grouchy was not persuaded by it to deviate from his own previously conceived plans. He continued to move along the Sart-à-Walhain road, and thence by Neuf Sart upon Wavre. Indeed he did more. Instead of bearing towards his left, so as to touch the Dyle in the first instance at Lenulette or Lamale, he directed Excelmans to take ground to his right, and come out upon the high road at Dion-le-Mont.

Thus not only were his communications not connected with those of Napoleon, but they were rendered less attainable than ever; while the Prussians by this order of his advance, were involuntarily led—if not in some sort driven—to connect themselves at once with the English. At the same time it is just to bear in mind that for the support which he gave to the troops of his ally, Blücher had fully provided. Interrupted—perhaps retarded— his flank movement might have been, in which case the completion of Napoleon's overthrow would have probably been deferred a few days; because, beaten as they were in the battle of the 18th, the French could not have kept their ground, though they might perhaps have retreated in something like order.

But there was no power in Grouchy, or in his master, or in both, united, to frustrate operations so well calculated in regard both to their object and details as those which Wellington and Blücher had concerted together. Wherefore, though Grouchy undeniably was in fault, to lay upon him the blame of the disasters which ensued is to act unjustly. He certainly did not make the most of his opportunity; but it was never such as to give to his master a chance of victory, except in the overthrow of the English whom he attacked at Waterloo.

While the French marshal was thus executing a slow and not very well arranged pursuit, Blücher had long begun that series of movements which brought him at a critical moment on the rear of Napoleon's army. Bülow's corps, which had passed the night at Dion-le-Mont, received orders to move, at dawn on the morning of the 18th, through Wavre to St. Lambert, on the other side of the Dyle.

At the same time detachments of hussars were to march by different crossroads along the course of the Lasne. Of these, one proceeded as far in advance as Maransart, while the rest scoured the country, and in a measure blocked up every lane between Mont St. Guibert and the Lasne. The consequence was that communication, even by orderlies, became exceedingly difficult from one portion of the French army to the other; and that Grouchy, who ought to have been alive to every movement of Napoleon's corps, received no tidings of the dangers which menaced it till they had proved fatal.

The result of these reconnaissances having satisfied Blücher that Napoleon kept no very sharp lookout upon his right, and his own rearguard not having warned him of the advance of Grouchy, he determined to commence, without delay, that series of operations which, as he calculated, would enable him to support the English army with three Prussian corps. It was necessary, however, to execute movements of such exceeding delicacy with much caution. The defiles of St. Lambert and of the Lasne—both difficult of passage—were between him and the English right; and on his rear hung Grouchy, with a force of the amount of which he was ignorant.

Whatever was to be done, therefore, must be done with as much prudence as promptitude, so that no risk of disaster might be incurred. Accordingly, as soon as Bülow should have filed through Wavre on his way to St. Lambert, Zieten, who had passed the night at Bierge, was instructed to commence his march upon Fromont and Ohain. Then Pirch's corps was to break up and follow Bülow, while Thielmann, after holding Wavre till the general change of position should be secured, was to tread in Zieten's footsteps and move leisurely upon Ohain.

In pursuance of these arrangements, Bülow quitted his bivouac at Dion-le-Mont by break of day on the 18th. He gained the bridge of Wavre, and passed both that and the town comfortably with his advanced guard; but the head of the succeeding brigade was yet a little way from the river, when a fire broke out in the principal street.

The flames spreading with great fury not only stopped the march—for the street which had taken fire was that which led from the bridge—but they occasioned great alarm lest some of the many ammunition wagons which had been posted in the town should explode; in which case the destruction of the place and of the principal stores of the army would be inevitable. Accordingly the column halted; while whole battalions, casting aside their accoutrements, exerted themselves to subdue the fire. This they eventually did, without loss of life or serious damage to the magazines; but for the loss of time nothing could compensate, and its consequences were felt inconveniently.

Meanwhile the advance of Bülow's corps held its way, and reaching St. Lambert about eleven o'clock, began immediately to pass the defile. It did not wait for the three brigades which the fire had stopped, but entered at once upon the deep and miry paths which alone lay before it. Such operations could not be otherwise than very slow in the performance, and when effected, the brigade seemed to be isolated. A halt in the wood of Paris was accordingly ordered, while cavalry patrols were sent on for the purpose of reconnoitring the enemy, and feeling for the left of the English line.

The delay occasioned by the fire in Wavre was very great. It checked the progress of Bülow's corps several hours, and gave time for the arrival of Grouchy's advanced guard, which pushed some horsemen between Vieux Sart, where the rear of Bülow's column lay, and the Prussian detachment which covered the other road at Mont St. Guibert. It became necessary for the latter to retire, which, assisted by two regiments of cavalry sent out from Wavre, it did in good order, though not without a little fighting. Lieutenant Colonel Von Ledebeer, who commanded this force, halted at a place called the farm of Auzel, near which was the wood of Sorats, an open grove, free from brushwood, and therefore affording considerable facilities of defence.

The movements of the remaining corps will be sufficiently explained in a few words. Zieten filed off from his ground on the left of the Dyle as soon as Bülow's leading brigade had passed through Wavre, and made at once for Ohain. Pirch, on the right of the stream, broke up from his position between St. Anne and Aisemont about noon; his design was to cross by the bridge of Wavre, but the accident already alluded to rendered this operation both tedious and difficult; and before it could be accomplished, the approach of the enemy was announced. Pirch strongly reinforced the detachment which had halted at Auzel, and gave the command of the united force to General Von Brause.

The latter posted his men to the best advantage in and about the wood of Sorats, and maintained a sharp contest with Vandamme's advanced guard; but between three and four in the afternoon, having ascertained that all was right behind him, he ordered a retreat, and drew off his people. They all passed the Dyle, some at one point and some at another; and the enemy's pursuit not being very vigorous, they found time to break down the bridge of Bierge, and to set fire to a mill which, abutting on the right bank of the stream, commanded it.

Bülow's, Zieten's, and Pirch's corps were thus disposed of. They had performed the parts which their commander-in-chief wished them to play, in spite of an accident which could neither be foreseen nor prevented; and though some hours behind their time, were in full march to attack Napoleon's right. Thielmann's alone—and that too seriously weakened by losses in the field, and the disposal elsewhere of several brigades—held the position of Wavre.

With it, Blücher, who was early at Lemale, and with his own eyes examined the nature of the country between that place and St. Lambert, now opened a communication. He sent back Colonel Clausewitz with orders that Thielmann should defend the passage of the Dyle, in case the enemy attacked him; but that if the French either did not advance in force, or crossed the river higher up, he was to leave a few battalions in the town, and to follow the main body of the army. He was to take the road to Coutaire on the Lasne.

If the reader will place a well-marked map of the country before him, he will see that no series of movements could have been better planned than those of which he has just read the description. It was impossible for Grouchy, let him approach the Dyle as he might, to stop the completion of Blücher's design. Had he moved, indeed, as he ought to have done, in two columns instead of one, pushing his left through Mont St. Guibert towards Moustier, and his right by Corbraux towards Le Baraque, he must have gained the command of two stone bridges over the Dyle, and made himself master of the nearest approaches to St. Lambert and Waterloo.

But even in this case Blücher's troops were so disposed, that two corps, those of Bülow and Thielmann, would have given him battle, while the remaining two filed off in the direction of the English left. Probably they might not have arrived in time to fire a shot that night, because the roads by Ohain, and elsewhere to the rear of St. Lambert, were even deeper and less pervious than those in front of it; but their ultimate junction with the English had become a matter of certainty from the moment Blücher got a start of eight hours upon the enemy to whom he was obliged to resign the field of Ligny; whereupon the bravo old Prince felt very much at his ease, in spite of the stiffness which still remained from his bruises of the 16th; and his officers and men nobly aiding his endeavours, the flank march went on as vigorously as circumstances would admit.

CHAPTER 18

The Position of Waterloo

We return now to the Anglo-Belgian army which during the afternoon of the 17th was effecting its retrograde movement upon Waterloo. The march was performed under an incessant fall of rain, and amid a furious storm of thunder and lightning, which added, in no slight degree, to the solemnity of the scene, and filled up the intervals, when from time to time the artillery on both sides ceased to fire. Of the cavalry affair at Genappe sufficient notice has been taken. It was the only encounter of masses which occurred throughout the day, and the skirmishing being mainly confined to patrols which moved by beaten roads, never became very animated.

Enough, however, was done to keep men on their mettle, and to carry them into the bivouacs which they were respectively directed to take up, in a state of considerable excitement. And though it was clear that no great battle could be fought before the morrow, the enemy made here and there demonstrations which compelled similar displays of activity on the part of the English.

For example, after the rearmost cavalry regiment, the 23rd Light Dragoons, had filed off into a hollow on the right of the great road, and taken post beside the orchard of La Haye Sainte, they were suddenly required to form line again, for the purpose of checking the French advanced guard, which pushed boldly up the road after them. The French seeing that the English retreat was ended, did not, however, come to blows. They pulled up on the high ground which intervenes between La Haye Sainte and La Belle Alliance; while two batteries of horse artillery unlimbering, opened a fire upon the centre of the English line.

It happened that Picton's division lay there, and that its fiery chief was not of a temper to take the annoyance patiently; he therefore ordered two batteries, which were near at hand, though not belonging to his division, to take post on a height close to the Charleroi road, and to answer the French fire, not by silencing the guns, but by enfilading a column of infantry which had plunged into a hollow road opposite to them.

The batteries in question, that of Major Lloyd and Captain Cleves, the former British, the latter artillery of the King's German Legion, got the range of their mark at the first discharge; and the havoc which they wrought among a body of men jammed together, and incapable either of retreating or deploying, was terrific. The cannonade lasted about half an hour, indeed till the French column had melted quite away, for the enemy's guns, though they did their best to check it, made no impression.

Night was now beginning to set in. The sun had gone down some time, and twilight grew rapidly darker, when arrangements were begun on both sides for the establishment of pickets, and the planting of sentries and *videttes*. During the progress of a regular campaign, after armies have begun, as it were, to become acquainted with one another, these operations are conducted with the most perfect good-humour, no advantage being taken on either side of a mere blunder, but each civilly informing the other if by chance a wrong direction should have been followed, or too near an approach made to the main position.

This evening a different feeling seemed to prevail: there was positive exasperation on the part of the French, which gradually stirred the bile of their opponents; so that all along the hollow which separated the two armies, a series of skirmishes and single combats went on. These on various occasions took a rather more imposing shape, particularly where parties of cavalry encountered.

A troop of the 7th Hussars, for example, under Captain Heyliger, found itself confronted and annoyed by a body of French light cavalry. Being superior in numbers these would not allow one of Captain Heyliger's *videttes* to keep his ground, but drove them all back as soon as they endeavoured to establish themselves in line with those on the right and left of them.

Captain Heyliger bore with the proceeding for a while. He sent out his men repeatedly, anticipating that the enemy would come, by and by, to see the impropriety of their conduct; but when the course of annoyance was persevered in, he determined in his own way to stop it; he formed his troop, rode at the French outpost, overthrew men and horses, and chased the survivors from the field. The Duke of Wellington was himself an eye-witness to the encounter, and praised the gallantry while he sent to restrain the ardour of the troopers engaged in it.

A somewhat similar affair took place in front of Hougomont, where Lieutenant Von Hugo, of the 2nd Light Dragoons of the King's German Legion, commanded a picket. He likewise was annoyed by frequent incursions into his ground, and by a dropping fire of carbines from the people opposite, and at last saw, as he believed, the beginning of a more formidable danger—the approach of a mass of cavalry belonging to the enemy's advanced guard. He instantly took the initiative; and charging the head of the column before it could deploy, threw it into confusion and forced it backwards.

Nor was it with the mounted pickets alone that this sort of game was played. For a while no sentry took his station till after the interchange of shots between the party from which he was detached and the enemy; so that, as night advanced, the whole front of either position was lighted up by the flashes of musketry. Gradually, however, this irregular fusillade became interrupted; and at last there was silence, except that about their bivouac fires weary men occasionally moved and spoke, and that the roll of wheels, and the clatter of horses' hoofs, told of the coming up of wagons, guns, and ammunition-carts from the rear.

The night of the 17th of June was one of heavy and incessant rain. It seemed, indeed, as if the windows of heaven had been opened again; for, without interruption, the water came down till the whole face of the ground was saturated. Peals of thunder, with frequent flashes of lightning, likewise added sublimity to the scene, which, under any circumstances, would have been, in truth, abundantly solemn.

Amid such a storm the troops on both sides lay down. How it fared with the French has nowhere been accurately stated, though the appearance of their bivouac, as it was seen by our people on the following evening, seemed to imply that provisions were abundant among them; but on the English side food and forage were wanting. Neither, indeed, is this to be wondered at, considering that the operations of the 17th had been retrogressive throughout, and that a movement to the rear, whether pressed upon or conducted at leisure, necessarily implies a still further removal out of harm's way of everything which may not be needed in the hour of battle. But though suffering a good deal from hunger, the fatigue which they had undergone in the course of the two previous days soon closed the eyes both of man and beast; and nowise distrustful of the issues of the morrow, all who were not engaged in more active employments lay down on the wet ground and slept.

With marvellous exactitude the Duke had sent overnight every brigade and corps to the particular post in the position which it was intended next day to hold. A few, and only a few, changes of ground, therefore, took place when the dawn of the 18th came in; and, as these made no alteration whatever in the plan of the battle, and were entirely inoperative both on its progress and result, it seems scarcely necessary, in a sketch like this, minutely to detail them. It may be more to the purpose if we describe, as briefly as a due regard to perspicuity will allow, the manner in which the Anglo-Belgian forces disposed themselves for the impending contest.

About twelve English miles from Brussels, and with the forest of Soignies, about eight miles in width, intervening, lies a narrow tract of country, of which history will long speak as of the scene of the sternest and most decisive battle that has been fought in modern times. It is the field of Waterloo, whereon, within less than 2000 yards of one another, the armies of Napoleon and Wellington slept throughout the night of the 17th of June, and where, on the 18th, they met and fought.

The English position might measure, from one extremity to the other, about two miles, or a little more; it extended from a sort of ridge, on the road to Wavre, overlooking the hamlets of Papelotte and La Haye, to a series of heights of the same character, which rise in the rear of the Château of Hougomont, and throw themselves back as far as Merbe Braine, on the other side of the road from Nivelles to Brussels. The position of the Allies was, therefore, the brow of a slope which dips gradually, like the face of a glacis, into a valley; on the opposite side of which rises another line of heights of like formation, though somewhat more elevated than those upon which the Duke of Wellington was posted. The whole front of the Duke's line was open; there were neither woods nor hedgerows, nor other inclosures, to shelter an enemy's approach, except at one particular part, which deserves a more elaborate description; and the soil being very fertile, the whole surface of the ground was covered with tall corn or rich herbage, or else lay fallow.

The position of Waterloo is not quite in a straight line; a natural curvature of the hills causes the centre to be slightly thrown back, though not sufficiently so either to expose the flanks or to give them a decided advantage in the line of fire; and its left, as the Duke that day held it, would have had no support but for the assumed proximity of the Prussians. With this trivial drawback, however—if, indeed, we are justified under the circumstances in so describing it—the field of Waterloo presents exactly the sort of plateau on which an English officer, aware of the constitution of his army, would desire to bring it into collision with an enemy.

There is abundance of open ground for the formations in which British infantry are always the most formidable. In line or square they have nothing to fear from the assaults of any description of force that can be brought against them; while for such support as cavalry and artillery can give with the best effect, every facility is afforded. Nor is this all. From the top of the ridge the ground slopes backwards, so as to hide the reserves, and to keep the front line itself concealed, till the moment for action has arrived.

And here the Duke, of whose tactics even foreign writers have well spoken, covered his ground, as he was always accustomed to do, showing not a man, except the few that might be required to warn their comrades of the approach of danger; and holding the rest in his hand, as a skilful player holds his cards, that he may deal them out precisely as they are wanted, and lose not one unnecessarily.

Two great roads approach the position from the French side. One of these, which runs from Charleroi and Genappe, cuts it, so to speak, in the centre. It is broad, well paved, but at a point of critical importance hemmed in on either side by high banks. And just where these steeps become most dangerous to an enemy, the farm-house and inclosures of La Haye Sainte abut upon it. The inclosures in question consist of a brick house, with a garden and orchard attached, the orchard running longitudinally along the roadside to the extent of perhaps 100 yards, or a little more. It is surrounded everywhere by a thick hedge, except where a stout brick wall takes up the fence, and going back to the front of the house, forms one side of a quadrangle of buildings.

The other three sides consist of a long barn, which joins on to cow-houses and stables; and these again connect themselves with another wall that rests against the house. The great entrance to this quadrangle is from the high road. There are other doorways which go out into the orchard and garden, but there is no outlet looking up towards the top of the ridge; and as, in the hurry of preparation, those whose especial business it was to see to such matters forgot to break one through, it stood there a perfect redoubt, weak only in this, that the means of throwing in supplies were wanting, except at one point, and that unfortunately turned away from immediate communication with the main army.

It was a formidable post in advance, therefore, and might have been held like Hougomont, but for the occurrence of events which shall be detailed in their proper place; and the Duke did not neglect to occupy it, much to the damage of the French columns, which suffered fearfully in their repeated efforts to carry it.

Moreover, on the opposite side of the road, and but a little in rear of La Haye Sainte, there is a sandpit: it is wide enough to contain 150 men, with ample room to ply their muskets efficiently. That also was filled with troops, who held the ground throughout the whole day, and wrought great damage to the enemy.

The other road falls in obliquely upon the right of the position. It passes from Nivelles, and joins the Charleroi *chaussée* at the village of Mont St. Jean. But this road is efficiently guarded—on the east, or (looking down from Mont St. Jean) the left side, by the inclosures of Hougomont: on the west, or right side, by a wood, along the face of which runs a country road leading to the hamlet of Braine la Leud. The wood is very defensible being sufficiently open to allow troops to act, yet close enough to prevent the advance of a column or the progress of cavalry or guns; and as the country breaks, in its rear, into fresh ridges, or rather swelling downs, the opportunity was afforded of keeping masses so in hand that any *tirailleurs* which might force their way through must be overwhelmed ere time was afforded either to form them up or to support them efficiently.

Of Hougomont itself the description is soon given. It is a *château*, with farm-buildings attached, built in the old Flemish style, with a courtyard approachable through an arched gateway, and a high tower flanking it. The stables are at right angles with this front wall; a barnyard, also walled in, lies behind them; a garden, in like manner walled, adjoins to this; and beyond it, to the east of the mansion, is an extensive walled orchard. A thick wood, surrounded by a strong hedge, and covered with a wet ditch, fronts house, barns, and garden; and is joined on the east by a sort of meadow, fenced in like the rest of the premises.

Attached to the mansion is a chapel, with a large wooden crucifix above the door, which stands at the south-west extremity of this little pile, and faces the altar. Finally, the gardens, laid out in terraces, afford admirable cover to troops if they seek to maintain the place; and as there is a back approach as well as a front one, the lines of communication between the place and the heights which from the English side look down upon it, are abundant.

These two inclosures constituted the advanced works on the right and centre of the English position. The left, as has already been explained, was more open; but even there the farm of La Haye, with the hamlet called Papellotte, though somewhat too much pushed forward, were not without their value; and additional security was given to them by the proximity of the village of Louvain, where, as the road by which he had reason to expect that the Prussians would arrive, the Duke had a sufficient garrison. Thus on the three points by which he must of necessity be assailed, the English general had posts, whence a flanking fire commanded the whole slope—in one direction effectively, because with a double line—in the other to an extent which could not be overlooked or lightly thought of.

The inclosures were all on the slope of the ground, and two of them within point-blank range of musketry. On the ridge itself stood the first line, consisting of Vivian's light cavalry, the 10th, 18th, and 1st Hussars of the King's German Legion on the left of all. Next to them were drawn up Vandeleur's brigade, namely, the 11th, 12th, and 16th Light Dragoons. Then came Picton's infantry division, its left consisting of the 5th Hanoverian brigade, under Colonel von Vencke, to which succeeded Best's, being soldiers of the same nation; and then a little in advance, that is to say on the further side of a road yet to be spoken of, Bylandt's Netherlander, being a brigade of Perponcher's division, consisting of five Dutch and one Belgian battalion.

But they did not stand alone; for about two hundred yards in their rear, so as to give support both to them and Best's troops, stood Pack's brigade, namely, the 3rd battalion 1st Royals, the 1st battalion 42nd, the 2nd battalion 44th, and the 92nd Highlanders. All these had suffered severely in the battle of Quatre Bras, and now took their places in very reduced numbers', but their hearts were stout, and their discipline admirable, and they were all well tried before the day ended

We have thus followed the line from the heights above Louvain to the proximity of the Charleroi road, and we next find Kempt in his place with the 28th, the 32nd, the 1st battalion 79th, and the 1st battalion 95th Rifles. From this latter battalion two companies were detached to hold the sandpit already referred to; while a third company of the same regiment extended itself along a low hedge, which runs in rear of the pit, and passes to an extent of perhaps 150 yards eastward from the road, and in front of the main position. The riflemen attended to their own security by throwing an abattis across the *chaussée*: they trusted to their well-tried weapons to render the task of removing it an arduous one.

From the right of this road the 3rd (Alten's) division took up the line. The 2nd brigade King's German Legion, under Colonel Ompteda, was in immediate connection with the Rifles. It consisted of the 1st and 2nd Light battalions, and of the 5th and 8th battalions of the line. These, with the 1st Light, were formed on the position. The 2nd Light battalion threw itself into the farm of La Haye Sainte, and kept it nobly. They took possession of the inclosures at daylight, and applied themselves immediately to the task of breaking out loop-holes in the walls, and otherwise putting the place in a state of defence; and though, from the lack of intrenching tools, their work was somewhat rudely effected, they found in their own devoted courage a bulwark better than brick walls. They were weak in point of numbers, mustering only 400 men; and their stock of ammunition was scanty.

Next to Ompteda's brigade came that of Kielmansegge. It was composed entirely of Hanoverians, and communicated by its right with the 5th British brigade, of which Major-General Sir Colin Halkett was at the head. This comprised the 2nd battalion 30th, the 1st battalion 33rd, the 2nd battalion 69th, the 2nd battalion 73rd regiments, and formed on the curve of the arc, which now began to bend forward in the direction of Hougomont. And last of all, on the extreme right, came the 1st division (Cooke's), composed entirely of the household troops, of which two brigades were in the field.

These, consisting severally, the 1st brigade, of the 2nd and 3rd battalions 1st Foot-Guards, under General Maitland; the 2nd, of 2nd battalion Coldstream, and 3rd of the 3rd Regiment, under General Byng, were drawn up *en échiquier*, that is, the four columns stood apart as four pieces may be placed upon a draft-board; thus guarding, in part, the inverted face of the position, and in part giving support to the garrison of Hougomont: for that important post had been assigned to them, and they filled it with four light companies, two of these being under the command of Colonel MacDonnel, and two being committed to the guidance of Colonel Lord Saltoun. Moreover, these officers were strengthened by having joined to them the 1st battalion of the 2nd regiment of Nassau, a company of Hanoverian riflemen, and 100 men detached from the battalion of Lüneburg, which formed part of Kielmansegge's brigade.

Such, properly speaking, was the first line of the Allied army early in the morning of the 18th. It was supported both near and at a little distance,—the Guards and Halkett, by the cavalry brigades of Grant and Dornberg immediately; the former comprising the 7th and 10th Hussars, with the 13th Light Dragoons; the latter consisting of the 23rd Light Dragoons and of the 1st and 2nd Light Dragoon regiments of the King's German Legion. The Cumberland Hussars came next, being a regiment separated from Colonel Von Estorff's brigade, which had gone with Sir Charles Colville to watch the road to Hal, and of which there will be occasion to speak by and by.

Then appeared the 3rd Hussars of the King's German Legion, with which, being half of his brigade, Colonel Arentschildt served; for the 13th, which properly belonged to him, had been disposed of elsewhere, and he was too good a soldier to complain. And lastly, so as to cover Alten's and Picton's divisions, came the two heavy brigades—the first, called likewise the Household brigade, on the right of the Charleroi road; the second, called the Union Brigade, in consequence of the intermixture of the corps composing it, and not less efficient as regarded either men or horses, on the left. The former, which consisted of the 1st and 2nd Life Guards, of the Blues, and the 1st Dragoon Guards, was under the immediate orders of Lord Edward Somerset; the latter, comprising the 1st Royal Dragoons, the 2nd or Scotch Greys, and the 6th or Inniskillen, were commanded by Major-General Sir William Ponsonby. Of the rest of the British cavalry mention has already been made; it held the extreme left of the position.

But the Duke had more troops than these, and he posted them as the nature of the ground required. For example, Hill's infantry corps—except that portion of it which had been detached—formed, *en potence,* on the further right of the line. It consisted of one brigade of the 4th division, under Colonel Mitchell, of the main body of the 2nd division, under Sir Henry Clinton, of Du Plat's brigade of the King's German Legion, and Halkett's Hanoverians. These were drawn up partly along that portion of the Hougomont avenue which is nearest to the Nivelles road, partly on the rising ground at the back of it—though a good way below its ridge—and partly on the plateau itself—at once protecting the right, and being in a condition to give support wherever it might be wanted.

Mitchell's brigade, consisting of the 14th, 23rd, and 51st Regiments, had charge of the lower ground: Adams's light brigade, composed of the 52nd, 71st, and 2nd battalion Rifles, with Du Plat's Germans, stood above them, between Merbe Braine and the Nivelles road; while Halkett's Hanoverians, in rear of Adams's, covered the village of Merbe Braine itself, and filled the north side of the plateau.

Finally the reserves, consisting of Brunswickers and Dutch-Belgians, as well horse as foot, formed in a second line from

Merbe Braine to the village of Mont St. Jean; and they were strengthened by the 6th British brigade under Lambert, which, consisting of the 4th, 27th, and 40th Regiments, had just arrived by forced marches from Ostend.

Of the position of the artillery it would be idle to speak. Wherever a gun could see, there it stood. On the extreme left, and attached to Vivian's cavalry, might be seen Sir Robert Gardiner's six guns of the horse-artillery. Above the hamlet of Papelotte were four guns, being the half of Captain Byleveld's Dutch-Belgian battery, and the other half crowned the crest of the ridge just behind Perponcher's infantry. Captain von Rettberg's Hanoverian foot battery occupied the loftiest ridge on the left of the position. Major Rogers's six guns were in front of Kempt, Major Llyod's and Captain Cleves's were with Alton's division. Major Kuhlman's German and Captain Sandham's English guns were attached to Cooke.

All these were in the front line, as were Colonel Sir Hugh Rosse's which took post on the height immediately in rear of La Haye Sainte, with two pieces on the Charleroi road. Major Sympler's German and Captain Bolton's English batteries were with Clinton's division. All the rest of the horse-artillery formed in the morning beside the cavalry. Major Ball's howitzers were there; so were Lieutenant Colonel Webber's guns, so were Captain Mercer's, so were Major Ramsay's.

The Dutch-Belgian and Brunswick artillery took post at first with the corps of which they formed a part, and one of the former, under General Chassé, was thrown into Braine-la-Leud, where it remained all day. Finally, two British and one Hanoverian battery, under Major Benson, Captain Sinclair, and Captain Bram, formed a reserve at Mont St. Jean. But these were only the arrangements incident on the first formation of the troops. In the course of the day every battery present was brought into action, and not even the records of that noble corps can point to an occasion in which they better did their work.

CHAPTER 19

French Position

He takes but an imperfect view of a military position who regards it only from the front, and looks no farther than to satisfy himself regarding the probable difficulty of its approaches. Troops are comparatively helpless; they are necessarily very insecure unless the communications between one part of the line and another be easy, and lines of retreat be open in the event of a reverse. Now, in both these respects the field of Waterloo needs only to be examined with a soldier's eye, and its eligibility becomes at once apparent.

With respect to the means of communicating along the whole extent of his line, the Duke had these in abundance. Besides that the plateau in his front was generally open and level, a road ran there, by which, let the difficulties elsewhere be what they might, it was at all times in his power to march men. horses, and cannon. The road in question leads from Wavre to the Charleroi *chaussée*, and, crossing that, goes on in a curved line till it falls upon the Nivelles road in the rear of Hougomont. though not paved, it is sufficiently made to endure a great deal of trampling, and is constantly used, in winter as well as in summer, as a line of traffic. In rear of this, again, there are other roads; one diverging from the Wavre road along the front of Merbe Braine to Braine-la-Leud; the other stretching from Mont St. Jean towards one of the various paths which pass upwards from Papelotte and La Haye to Brussels.

Moreover, in the hollow which interposes between the

Duke's first line and the ridge of Mont St. Jean, there are no obstacles which might not be surmounted, even by artillery; and the whole extent of the valley is protected from any fire that might come from the French side of the field. The Duke's communications were therefore as secure and as facile as the most nervous could desire; and as regarded his means of retreat, they, too, were abundant.

In the first place, the forcing of his more advanced line, though considering the condition of his army, it must have shaken him terribly, did not necessarily involve the loss of the battle. His second line was quite as tenable as his first; indeed it may be a question whether, but for the proximity of that on which he made his stand, it was not more defensible. He had the villages of Merbe Braine and Mont St. Jean, besides a scattered hamlet which lies to the right of the latter, to fall back upon; and these, like the ground from which he is supposed to have retired, crowned a sloping height, and had a clear glacis before them.

Then the two great roads were at his disposal. To be sure these unite at the village of Waterloo, and become one wide causeway; but it must not therefore be assumed, that only by that can carriages make their way through the forest of Soignies. Three excellent roads at least, with others not unfit for cavalry, traverse the whole width of the forest; and the forest itself is everywhere passable for infantry.

Had the worst, therefore, befallen—had the allied army been driven out of both its positions, the Duke had it always in his power to send off his guns, tumbrils, stores, and cavalry by these roads, while by the simple process of filling the wood with skirmishers, he might have effectually blocked it against every effort of the pursuers; for it is no easy matter to force resolute men through a fine open beech wood, where every tree offers shelter to a sharpshooter; and where, as in this instance, the total absence of brushwood leaves the skirmishers free to choose their own time as well as direction of retreat.

Moreover, the Duke had in his rear *points d'appui* from which Napoleon would have found it impossible to drive him ere the

Austrians or Russians should have made their appearance. With the wreck of the army which he commanded at Waterloo, he could have held Antwerp forever; and though the political consequences of the fall of Brussels might have been serious, they could not possibly avert the doom with which Napoleon was threatened.

Thanks, however, under Providence, to the Duke's masterly arrangements, and to the devoted gallantry of the men whom he commanded, the position of Waterloo was not forced, nor was ever in danger. Nor has so much, as an allusion been made to the possible occurrence of a different result, except for the purpose of showing that he who fought for victory, and won it, was not, therefore, indifferent to or unprepared for defeat.

And now, before we proceed further with, our history, it may be well to cast our eyes over the ground as it was occupied by the enemy, in order to ascertain, as far as circumstances will allow, what dispositions were made by Napoleon, and how far they warranted his acknowledged confidence of success.

It is not worthwhile to inquire how the various divisions of the French army disposed of themselves during the night of the 17th. As soon as the state of the weather on the 18th would permit, they began to put themselves in order of battle, and the ground on which they drew up resembled very much, in its principal features, that which the Duke of Wellington had occupied. About 1600 or 1700 yards removed from the crest of the English position is a range of heights, which passes in a sort of semicircle from Frischermont on the east to a bend in the Braine-la-Leud road on the west, by which Hougomont is overlapped.

It is rather more elevated throughout than that on which the Anglo-Belgian army stood, and here and there it overlooks the latter position considerably; but in no part is it so elevated as to give a commanding view of what lay beyond the Duke's position, far less to offer facilities, by the fire of cannon, to impede the movements of his reserves. The two great roads from Charleroi to Nivelles passed through the French position, as they did through that of the allies. The Charleroi road, indeed, completely intersected Napoleon's line just as it did that of the Duke of Wellington, while the *chaussée* from Nivelles, touching upon his extreme left, bore, though inclining eastward, through the centre of the English right, and would have led any columns that had succeeded in following it between Hougomont and Merbe Braine.

On this side of these downs, as well as on the other, the fields were open and in a state of cultivation. There was nothing to check the advance of troops, except the fire which might be directed upon them from the opposite ridge; and two country paths, passing from the very centre of the position, would have offered facilities for the movement of masses against both the right and the left of the English line if the intervening fields had not been open.

The order of battle, as arranged by Napoleon, threw his army into two lines and a reserve. The first line consisted of infantry, flanked right and left by cavalry, and was composed of the 1st and 2nd *Corps d'armée*, commanded respectively by D'Erlon and Reille. The 1st Corps was on the right. It extended from La Belle Alliance eastward in the direction of Frischermont, and was covered on its extreme right by Jacqueminot's cavalry division, which, facing Ohain, kept the *château* of Frischermont in possession, and threw out patrols so as to guard against the approaches of an enemy.

The 2nd stretched away in a curved line from the left of the same road across the Nivelles *chaussée*, and had its flank protected, just beyond the latter, by Pire's cavalry. D'Erlon's corps comprehended four divisions; Reille's numbered but three. They were both drawn up in a double line of brigades— the first being in advance of the second by sixty yards only; and, strange to say for a French army, which seldom attacks except in column, every battalion was deployed.

Five batteries, comprising eight guns in each, ranged themselves along the front of the right of this line, with a sixth, consisting of 12 pounders, in support, while six guns of horse-artillery took post on the right of Jacqueminot's cavalry. The left was strengthened by the presence of thirty-one pieces, besides six which stood upon the Nivelles road; and on either side of it, and in the direction of Braine-la-Leud, both infantry and artillery were detached.

The second French line consisted entirely of cavalry, with the exception of two infantry divisions forming part of Count Lobau's—that is, the 6th corps. These formed in columns of battalions on the left, or west side of the Charleroi road, and stood with an interval between the head of the one and the tail of the other of about 200 yards. The horse were distributed thus:— Immediately on the right, or east side of the Charleroi road, were drawn up in close columns of regiments by squadrons, two divisions of light cavalry, under Generals Domont and Colbert respectively; to the right of these, so as to support D'Erlon's corps, stood Milhaud's heavy horse; to the left of the road, and in rear of Reille's infantry, Kellermann took his station: these were further, as well as the infantry in the second line, well sustained by artillery, not fewer than 38 pieces being in position on the right of this line, and 23 on the left; and finally, in reserve, the Imperial Guard drew up, infantry, cavalry, and artillery, right and left of the road.

The cavalry of this magnificent corps formed in rear of Milhaud's and Kellermann's divisions—Lefebvre-Desnouettes, with his *chasseurs* and lancers, covering the former—Guyot, with his grenadiers and dragoons, affording support to the latter. The infantry took its ground in six lines of four battalions each, at a distance of twenty yards one from the other, and not fewer than 72 pieces of cannon were distributed among them and the cavalry. Last of all, in a line with the village of Rossomme, stood three batteries of eight guns apiece, which were held in hand to be used as emergencies might arise, and near which the stores of reserve ammunition were parked.

From the above description it will be seen, that for all the purposes of offensive operation the dispositions made by Napoleon were as judicious as circumstances would admit of. If he did not overlap the ground on which the English stood, he was free to move his columns of attack against any part of it which might seem to be the weakest; and his own position was such as to render a direct attack by a force not superior to his own dangerous in the extreme. It is true that his rear was not very well cared for.

He had no line of retreat in the event of a reverse, except the great *chaussées* to Charleroi and Nivelles; and the former, as experience must have already taught him, was by no means pervious throughout. Two country roads, moreover, fell in from St. Lambert on his right, one of which passed immediately in rear of Lefebvre's division, while the other, running parallel with the Lasne stream, traversed a wood, which formed the outskirts of Planchenoit. But retreat was a manoeuvre on which he does not seem to have calculated, and he either did not entertain any fears of molestation from his right, or affected to despise the danger.

And let it not be forgotten, while criticizing his arrangements in the field, that he had a desperate game to play, as well as some grounds of sure hope to rely upon. He knew that defeat must be ruin; and he had been led to believe, that in the ranks of the army immediately opposed to him were thousands who, if they had but the opportunity, would pass over to him as soon as his standards were unfurled. Let him not, therefore, be blamed for arranging his army in order of battle with very unusual display, and throwing all, as he unquestionably did, upon the result of the struggle.

Had he gone a little further, and cast his own life into the same venture, it would have been better for his reputation at this day. However, it is not worth while either to find fault, where the opportunity of amending errors is lost, or to speculate upon contingencies which never come again. Better for our present purpose will it be to set forth in a tabular form the relative strength of the armies which faced one another, and which were about to battle for stakes more momentous than in the history of the civilized world had before been played for. The following may be received as a tolerably accurate account of this matter.

The Duke of Wellington had detached, first, a sufficient number of troops to garrison the fortresses, and next, Sir Charles Colville's corps, including the division of Prince Frederick of Nassau, for the protection of Hal and the great road from Mons which passes through it. He therefore brought into the field:—

	Infantry	Cavalry	Artillery	Guns
British	15181	5813	2967	78
King's G L.	3304	1991	526	18
Hanoverians	10258	467	466	12
Brunswickers	4586	866	510	16
Nasseurs	2880	—	—	—
Dutch Belgians	13402	3205	1117	32
Total	49608	12402	5645	156

Grand Total, 67,655 men, 156 guns.

Napoleon, having detached Grouchy with the troops elsewhere enumerated, confronted these with—

Infantry	48,950
Cavalry	15,765
Artillery	7,233
Total	71,917 men, with 246 guns.

In point of mere numbers the strength of the opposing armies cannot therefore be said to have differed very widely. But if the composition of the corps be taken into account, the preponderance on the side of the French was terrible. Napoleon's soldiers were all enthusiastically devoted to their leader. They were composed of one nation, had one system of tactics, knew their chiefs, were filled with military ardour, had been led to believe that they would find friends in the ranks that stood opposed to them, and counted on victory as certain.

Wellington's army was made up of raw levies gathered from five or six separate sources. Even his British troops were not the men whom he had trained to fight and to conquer in the Peninsula; and as to the rest, they were all in a state of discipline which rendered it perilous, not to say impossible, to manoeuvre with them under fire.

Indeed, the fidelity of some and the animal courage of others were little to be depended upon; and in regard to their systems of moving and forming, there was no uniformity among them. Still the confidence of their leader seems to have been throughout as high, and as conspicuously displayed, as that of his illustrious opponent; and the result of the battle, which it has become my business to describe, shows that on whatever grounds rested, it was not misplaced.

CHAPTER 20

Last preparations—First Shots

The morning of the 18th of June came in lowering and heavy. The rain which had fallen during the night seemed to have relieved the clouds of the weightiest portion of their burthen; but the clouds still covered the face of the sky, and a thick drizzle continued to proceed from them till the day was considerably advanced. The surface of the country was saturated with water A deep clay soil, covered for the most part with standing corn, drank in and long retained the moisture, and offered serious obstacles to the movements of guns, and even to the manoeuvring of cavalry.

Doubtless this circumstance had its weight in keeping Napoleon quiet much longer than his opponent expected. The enemy had shown their strength, and taken up their ground with more than their accustomed display, as early as six o'clock in the morning. But hour after hour stole on, and neither by cannonshot, nor hurra from infantry or cavalry, was any warning given that the battle was about to commence. Meanwhile, the Duke disposed his divisions and brigades beside the various posts on the position which they were intended to maintain.

They were all, however, posted in rear of the ridge, where the infantry lay down, and the cavalry dismounted; and so little was seen of them when the day fully broke, that Napoleon is described to have fallen into the error of supposing that the whole had retreated. It is further said that he was venting his spleen in strong terms when General Foy, whose services in the Peninsula had made him acquainted with the Duke of Wellington's tactics, rode up.

"Your Majesty is distressing yourself without just reason," said he; "Wellington never shows his troops till they are needed. A patrol of horse will soon find out whether he is before us or not; and if he be, I warn your Majesty that the English infantry are the very devil in the fight."

A patrol of horse was not, however, sent out, and neither was it necessary. The rains of the previous day and night having soiled, and rendered dubious the efficiency of their muskets, the English regiments were directed, by portions at a time, to clean their arms; and the process of firing off the charge being at once quicker and more satisfactory than drawing, a good deal of loose fusillading ensued. It seemed to satisfy Napoleon that his game had not escaped; and he proceeded, as has already been explained, to unfold his own troops in their order of battle.

While this was going on, the Duke of Wellington threw some anxious glances in the direction from which he expected to secure the co-operation of the Prussians. He did not look in vain. Long before a shot was fired or a movement of attack hazarded, he had the satisfaction of perceiving on an eminence above Ohain a body of mounted men, which he could not doubt formed a portion of Blücher's army, and of whom he expected in due time to learn tidings.

Nor was he disappointed. In about an hour, or perhaps more, a Prussian patrol entered Smohain, where a picket of the 10th Hussars was on duty; and the officer commanding it being forwarded to the Duke's presence, informed him that Bülow's corps was beyond St. Lambert, and might momentarily be expected. The Prussian officer did not know that the march of Bülow's corps had been retarded in the manner described in a previous chapter; for he himself, being sent out from its advanced guard, assumed, as was natural, that the rear was well closed up.

But his information, though inaccurate in its details, was, in regard to its general purport, correct; and if it led the Duke to anticipate an earlier support than was actually afforded, his

Grace entered into the battle not the less confident, because he knew that his ally was marching to assist him.

It was about this time that Napoleon, having completed the last of his preparations, and dispatched to Grouchy the order, of which a free translation has been inserted elsewhere, rode along the front of his lines. A brilliant staff attended him; and the shouts with which he was greeted, as he passed from regiment to regiment, came up the face of the opposing heights like the rushing of a mighty wind.

They struck no terror, however, into the breasts of the brave men who heard them; on the contrary, the only sensations stirred seem to have been, first, admiration of the magnificent military spectacle before them, and next, a settled resolution to maintain against Napoleon himself the glory which the British arms had achieved against the ablest of his lieutenants. The Duke of Wellington was not less careful to take a last survey of his order of battle ere it should be tried. Having seen that all was right elsewhere, he rode down to Hougomont, and following a lane which passes diagonally through the wood in the direction of La Belle Alliance, stopped for some minutes on the eastern slant of the thicket.

He accurately surveyed from that point the portion of the enemy's masses which was opposite to him, and forthwith caused a few changes to be made in the disposition of the troops which held the inclosure. He withdrew the light companies of the 1st brigade of Guards from the wood, and placed them in the great orchard, while the Nassau battalion and Hanoverian light infantry took up their ground. He likewise caused the light companies of the 2nd brigade to move along the rear of the inclosure, and form upon a lane which runs between the right of the building and the kitchen-garden. This done, he galloped back to the crest of the position, and began to chat to the numerous staff which attended on him, with as much liveliness and as perfect self-possession as if they were about to take part in a review.

With the first dawn of day the pickets on both sides had drawn in their advanced sentries. By and by the French filed up the slope of their own heights, while the English in like manner either returned to their regiments, or joined the irregular line of skirmishers which lay in front of the whole position. There was not much cover for these last—none, indeed, except here and there a low straggling hedge, or a field of rye, the tall grain waving above which might hide them from the immediate notice of the enemy. But there they were extended in loose order, from the rear of the orchard of Hougomont to the back of La Haye Sainte, and again across the Charleroi road, all the way to the row of trees which runs in front of Papelotte and La Haye. The men moved not at all.

Flat upon the ground, in double files, they lay, and conversed cheerily one with another, while the officers passing to and fro kept a good lookout ahead, and told them from time to time to be ready. Now it was seen that the lines on the opposite ridge were changing their formations. Now each battalion threw itself into a column of companies, while two or three, or more, formed a *colonne serrée*: thus showing that Napoleon adhered to that order of attack which, though uniformly unsuccessful against the English, was by him and his lieutenants esteemed the best; and finally, on the French left, just where it threatened the inclosures of Hougomont, one of those masses began to move.

What a moment was that for all who were present in the field, from the commander-in-chief down to the meanest sentinel! Now then, at last, Napoleon and the Duke were on the eve of measuring their swords. He who had triumphed over the most distinguished of the marshals of France was going to throw his renown into the balance against one whom all living generals had acknowledged to be their superior; and to receive a great battle, at the head of raw and disjointed troops, from the best appointed and best disciplined army that even Napoleon had ever led.

What the Duke may have felt will probably never be known. He was calm, and gentle, and collected, as in moments of especial hazard and under a heavy responsibility he had always been seen to be; and if, among the less practised warriors who followed him, there were some whose hearts slightly misgave them, who can be surprised at the circumstance? It is a remarkable fact, that the period of the commencement of the battle of Waterloo has been differently stated by almost all the many writers who have undertaken to give a detailed account of these operations.

Some make the firing begin as early as eight in the morning; others fix the moment of collision at half-past eleven or twelve. In the Duke of Wellington's published dispatch the hour of ten is named; but even here the announcement is rather conjectural than arbitrary, the phrase employed indicating that the writer had not noted the circumstance exactly. One thing alone is beyond dispute—that many hours of precious daylight escaped ere he, to whom time was of unspeakable value, moved to the attack.

We cannot account for this. Napoleon himself has left the statement upon record, that considerations of prudence alone restrained him;-that he was quiet because he could not hope to manoeuvre with either celerity or effect till the ground beneath the horses' feet should have been hardened. Others, and some of them are among the most enthusiastic of his admirers, affirm that he was forced to defer the commencement of operations because the stock of ammunition present with the army would not suffice for more than eight hours of battle.

Be this however as it may, the fact is as remarkable as it is well established, that the British army was not molested till the day had considerably advanced, and that time was in consequence afforded for the accomplishment by the Prussians of a series of movements, which a little more of vigour and forethought on the part of their adversaries might have either frustrated altogether or rendered comparatively useless.

While the French remained thus unaccountably supine, the Duke of Wellington, with characteristic activity, was providing against every possibly emergency that might occur. He was shaved and dressed at two o'clock in the morning; sat down by the light of a lamp to his desk, and wrote many letters, of which three have been given to the public in Colonel Gurwood's invaluable collection.

One of these—to the English minister at Brussels— has for its object the maintenance of quiet in that city. The writer speaks with confidence of the events which were hurrying forward, and assures his correspondent that "the Prussians will be ready again for anything in the morning."

"Pray keep the English quiet," he continues: "let them all prepare to move, but neither be in a hurry nor a fright, as all will yet turn out well."

Another, addressed to the Duc de Berri, gives a brief but clear account of the operations of the 16th, and explains the arrangements which had been made for the protection of the Mons road at Hal. At the same time the Duc is advised to remove with his suite to Antwerp, and to carry thither also the King of France, though only as a measure of precaution.

"I hope," says the field marshal, "indeed I have every reason to believe, that all will go well; but it is necessary to look a good way before us and to provide against serious losses, should any accident occur."

And last of all, the Governor of Antwerp is instructed what to do—that he is to consider the city "in a state of siege, and have his means of inundating the surrounding country ready;" while at the same time he gives free admission to the King of France and his attendants, as well as to any British subjects who may desire to pass through Antwerp on their way to England. Nor was it thus alone that the Duke of Wellington devoted the first hours of that eventful day to the adjustment of matters which bore more intimately upon the arrangements of its later hours.

The spare ammunition, which had been parked over night at Waterloo, was so distributed as to be ready for carriage to all parts at a moment's notice. Apartments were fitted up in every house, both there and along the entire rear of the position, for the accommodation of the wounded. Nothing, in short, was neglected or overlooked which could in any respect contribute to the security of the country, or the efficiency of the force which defended it, while all was done with a cheerfulness and good-humoured alacrity which seemed to forebode the happiest results. Indeed it was part of the character of the Duke of Wellington to inspire every man who approached him with absolute confidence in the success of whatever he undertook, and so remarkable an instance of the extent to which the feeling was carried occurred this day, that it would be unjust to pass it by.

Among other domestic servants who had attended him in the Peninsula, and afterwards followed his fortunes to London, Paris, and Vienna, was a French cook, a man of much science and excellent method in his way. This *artiste* always contrived to get his master's dinner ready at the exact time when it was wanted, and on the 18th of June he applied himself, as usual, to his duties in the kitchen of the house in Waterloo, where the headquarters of the army were established.

Amid the thunder of the battle he never intermitted his task; and when wounded men and fugitives came crowding back, and a thousand voices urged him to escape while he could, he steadily refused either to budge an inch or to intermit his labours. "His Grace had ordered dinner, and would certainly return to eat it. He was not going to disappoint so generous a master for any consideration whatever." And his Grace did come back, as he had promised, and found his dinner not less *recherché* than usual; though the state of his own feelings, victor as he was, could hardly permit him to do justice to it.

Meanwhile the storm which had so long lowered on the heights of La Belle Alliance began to break. From the right of Prince Jerome's division, forming part of Reille's corps, a column advanced towards the south-western boundary of the wood of Hougomont, and as it drew near, the leading companies broke off one by one, and spread themselves into skirmishing order. They moved on, raising from time to time one of those discordant yells which French troops emit as they are rushing to the attack; but the space, which divided them from their opponents was too narrow to afford leisure for much threatening or needless display.

As soon as they arrived within range of musketry, first one, then two or three, and immediately afterwards some half-dozen rifle-shots told that the hedges in their front were all lined. By and by they in their turn began to fire, closing all the while upon the thicket, and in two minutes afterwards an incessant rattle of small arms indicated that the battle was begun.

CHAPTER 21

Attack and Defence of Hougoumont

Of all the tasks to which a writer can apply himself, the description of the commencement of a great battle is, perhaps, the most hopeless. When the affair has begun in earnest—when men's minds are filled with the mighty work before them—it is not so difficult to follow the movements which they make, and to explain and in some sort to enter into the feelings with which they become engrossed.

But to tell how they feel and act while as yet all is expectation and a state of mental excitement, is an undertaking from which even the experienced in such matters will shrink. For though it may read well that men boldly and resolutely met their foes, and gave back the iron hail with which they were greeted, none can tell, till they have actually filled the position, how it fares either with the assailants or their enemies. There may be no especial regard for life or limb.

A thousand situations, even in civil life, may try the moral—aye, the physical— courage quite as much. But the opening of a battle stands quite alone among the states of being in which rational men are liable to find themselves and to speak of it accurately, after the occasion is over, seems to me to be impossible; therefore I decline to record how the French *tirailleurs* on this day went forward to their work—or how the skirmishers who lined the hedge and outer wood of Hougomont faced them, further than by stating that on both sides they bore themselves nobly—the one pressing forward through the open fields, now firing as they went, now taking the best aim which their situation afforded—the other kneeling or standing, behind bush and tree, and from that cover delivering their deliberate shots. But not very long was the action confined to them.

Upon the high ground which overlooked Hougomont, and saw beyond the extremity of its inclosures, stood Cleve's foot-battery of the German Legion, which soon opened its fire with murderous effect; while Major Kuhlman's German, and Captain Sandham's British horse-artillery, which were attached to Cooke's division, and pointed in the same direction, instantly followed the example, making every round tell. They did not, however, keep the game long in their own hands. The batteries of Reille's corps, occupying ground as high as theirs, replied to them with extreme energy; and shots which fell upon the distant ear at first one by one soon mingled in one continuous roar.

The French are good skirmishers. They go to their work like men who understand it, and never permit the grass to grow under their feet. They were up to the hedge in a moment, and by and by, in spite of a brave resistance from the Hanoverians and Nassau riflemen, forced their way through it. The inclosure on the left of the wood soon became, in like manner, full of them; and being fed continually from the column in their rear, they soon, by the mere weight of numbers, gained ground.

Then came Bull's howitzers into play. The Duke, who saw everything, and directed every operation, as if by instinct, gave orders for these latter to join in the fray; and such a shower of shells came pouring into the wood, that no animal courage could withstand it. The practice, too, was beautiful. Over the heads of the defenders—within a couple of feet—every shell passed, and falling right among the crowd of assailants, it scattered death and dismay in every direction.

The French *tirailleurs* could not sustain this fire. They fell back from the fields in front of the great orchard, to which they had made their way in countless numbers, the light companies of the

1st brigade of Guards pressing them severely, while those of the 2nd brigade, advancing from the lane and kitchen-garden on the right of the *château*, rushed like fox-hounds into the wood. Never, perhaps, was skirmish, if such it deserve to be called, conducted at an interval so brief.

The gallant Household troops did not, perhaps, understand so well as the Rifle-Brigade and the regiments of the Light Division the art of fighting in inclosed spaces, but what they might lack in skill they more than made up by their daring—for the shots which they exchanged were muzzle to muzzle, and they very soon cleared the wood of the *tirailleurs* before whom Hanoverians and Nassauers had given ground.

Meanwhile the fire of cannon gradually extended itself from one extremity of the hostile lines to another. The British, seeing their enemies on the slope of the opposite ridge, played into their columns with murderous effect. The French, having nothing but a line of skirmishers to aim at, directed their fire principally against the Allied batteries. Terrific was the noise, awful from time to time the effect of exploding shells and round-shot telling; but the slaughter in the French ranks was double that to which the Anglo-Belgians were exposed; for not a soldier either of infantry or of cavalry, yet showed himself unnecessarily beyond the crest of the English position.

By ricochet it is indeed true that many casualties occurred, but the effect of the direct fire was all in the enemy's ranks, who soon began to exhibit symptoms of impatience under it. It was at this moment that from the extreme right of the French line a column of cavalry moved out, threatening that point in the Allied position where Best's Hanoverian infantry brigade and Von Rottenberg's Hanoverian foot artillery were stationed.

The ground in that direction is of a peculiar formation, seeming to such as look at it from afar to be scarped; and the purpose of this movement evidently was to ascertain whether, during the night, Wellington had intrenched himself. But when Best, anticipating an attack, drew up, in squares, on the brow of the height, the enemy seemed to be satisfied. They immediately fell back again, and the cannonade on both sides went on.

In the meanwhile Prince Jerome had reinforced his skirmishers, and sent them with strong columns of support against the English right of the wood of Hougomont. At the same moment Foy led the whole of his division against its front. Both bodies were at once assailed by such a storm of shot from the British artillery, that they staggered and reeled; indeed, nothing except the concentrated and superior fire which the French brought to bear upon the Allied batteries could have saved them from destruction.

Under cover of this, however, the enemy pressed on; and, in spite of a desperate resistance, numbers so far prevailed, that the light companies of the Guards were forced to give ground, though they fought from tree to tree with an obstinate resistance, which cost them many lives. At last the men were fairly ordered to withdraw—those of the 1st brigade into the orchard on the left of the house—those of the 2nd, partly into the lane which skirts the right, partly behind a haystack which stood at one of the angles of the building, and faced the wood. As a matter of course the assailants grew more and more bold.

They pushed through the wood, skirted it on the right and left, and found themselves in front of a hedge which appeared to them to constitute the only fence by which the buildings were shut in. They rushed at it gallantly, and were gallantly received. Behind that hedge, and about thirty yards removed from it, runs the orchard-wall, which again is flanked on the right by the terraces and low brick fences of the garden; and the whole having been carefully loop-holed, such a storm of fire opened upon the French troops as they had not counted upon, and which they found themselves unable to face. Numbers fell, dead or wounded, while the remainder, recoiling, sought out such shelter as trees and ditches could afford; and for some time endeavoured to maintain from thence a combat which was entirely against them.

It was natural that Jerome, seeing the first successes of his skirmishers, and not knowing the nature of the obstacles which here arrested their progress, should endeavour to feed them largely. Hougomont was felt to be a point of vital importance, and Napoleon calculated that could he but make himself master of that, he might suspend all future operations in this quarter, and turn his undivided strength against the Allied left. Wherefore clouds of men rushed down to sustain the advance, which having won the wood, appeared to be on the eve of winning the *château* likewise; so that the whole face of the slope and the valley and ascent beyond it were crowded.

No arrangement could have been more satisfactory to Major Bull and his gallant companions; they literally swept the field with their shot, and though they could not prevent the influx of multitudes into the wood, they left traces of their practice in crowds of dead and dying, who in five minutes strewed the ground. But the numbers who gained the wood gave, as was natural, fresh confidence to their comrades. The latter, after stealing by banks and hollow ways, round this side and that of all the detached buildings, gradually surrounded the pile, and fairly drove out of the orchard and detached gardens all who survived to retreat inside the courtyard.

The haystack behind which some of the Coldstream light-troops had taken shelter, caught fire; they were forced, in consequence, to give up their vantage ground, and though the gate by which they entered the premises was immediately blocked with every heavy article on which they could lay their hands, time enough to barricade it effectually was not afforded. Dense masses of the assailants rushed against it, and shouted as it flew open; and then began such a struggle as does not often occur in modern warfare.

Not a foot would the defenders yield—not for a moment or two would the assailing party withdraw. At last the bayonets of the Guards carried all before them; and five individuals, Lieutenant-Colonel now Lieutenant General Macdonnell, Captain now Lieutenant General Wyndham, Ensign now Lieutenant Colonel Gooch, Ensign Hervey, and Sergeant Graham, by sheer dint of personal strength and extraordinary bravery and perseverance, succeeded in closing the gate, and shutting the enemy out.

Few prisoners were taken on this occasion; none, indeed, except a few wounded and disabled Frenchmen. They who had forced their way within the barricade died almost to a man; and a great majority of their comrades who pressed on eager to follow them were cut off in like manner by the furious musketry fire that fell upon them; the residue broke and dispersed, some passing to the left, others sweeping back across the Nivelles road; but all presently gathering again under cover of some brushwood, and on patches of broken ground.

They were pounded and pelted by every gun which the Allies could bring to bear upon them; but nothing stopped them; for their own artillery gave them most efficient aid, and under cover of their fire a body, bolder than the rest, crept on amid the concealment which some tall rye afforded, till they got within pistol-shot of Colonel Smith's battery. Now artillery, however effective it may be at a distance, has no chance with infantry in a close fight.

Men and horses dropped beneath the fire of these skirmishers so fast, that Smith was obliged to withdraw his guns into a hollow beyond, and the consequences might have been even more serious had not timely aid been afforded. Lieutenant Colonel Woodford of the Coldstream Guards seeing how the case stood, advanced with four companies of his regiment to meet the intruders. The latter fell back towards the farmyard, behind the wall of which they collected round a strong reinforcement which was in their rear, but they did not long remain there. Woodford charged them in line, and they fled in great confusion.

Woodford, who acted under orders, did not attempt to push his success too far; on the contrary, he entered with his people into the farmyard through a side-door which opened to the lane, and forthwith lent his aid, which did not come undesired, to maintain the pile, which continued to be the object of a fierce attack. For by this time all the French supports, which had been following their leaders in the fray, were in the wood and round about the mansion on every side.

They were in increased numbers at the back-gate, battering and pushing against the stout defences, which Macdonnell and his gallant followers had piled up to secure it; and the fire which they kept up rendered it perilous in the extreme for any man to show his head above the wall. Nevertheless, above the wall many heads were shown; for not only was it loop-holed beneath, but, by means of benches, tables, chairs, everything which they could apply, the garrison had formed a banquet all around the *enceinte,* on which they stood, and from which they delivered their fire with murderous effect.

It was at this moment that one of the enemy's shells, which ceased not to fall about them like hail-drops in a storm, set fire to a part of the mansion. The flames burst forth in terrific majesty; yet they whose duty it was to hold the post paid no regard to them, except that they evacuated room after room as one by one they became ignited. At this moment Sergeant Graham, who stood upon the banquet, and bore himself with unrivalled bravery, begged permission of Colonel Macdonnell to retire for a moment.

Colonel Macdonnell, who knew the nature of the man merely said, "By all means, Graham; but I wonder you should ask leave now."

"I would not, Sir," was the answer; "only my brother is wounded, and he is in that outbuilding there, which has just caught fire. Give me leave to carry him out; I will be back in a moment."

The leave was granted, of course, with eagerness, and Graham, laying down his musket, ran off, lifted his brother in his arms, and placed him in a ditch. He was back at his post before his absence could well have been noticed, and both he and the wounded man survived to thank their commanding officer, and to earn, as they equally deserved, the respect and admiration of all classes of their brother-soldiers.

Scarcely was this feat of nobleness performed, when the enemy, having collected in denser masses, made a new rush against the gate. They failed in bursting it open; but presently upon the top of the wall appeared a French grenadier, who had led the way for the purpose of removing the defences from the interior, and whose bold bearing showed that he would 'not be deterred by a trifle. It happened that Sergeant Graham had given his musket to Captain Wyndham, and was in the act of piling some heavy substance against the gate.

"Do you see that fellow, Graham?" cried the captain.

"Yes, Sir," was the laconic answer; whereupon a log of wood which he carried was dropped, and resuming his weapon, he took aim at the grenadier and shot him dead. None dared to follow where this brave man died, and the enemy forthwith abandoned their attempt on the gate, and turned elsewhere.

Away they now rushed along the inner edge of the orchard. There they found a gap communicating from the wood with the interior of the latter inclosure, and they sprang through it in great numbers, confident that now they should have the edifice in reverse. But Lord Saltoun with his gallant band was here. He did not stop to skirmish—he formed his men in line, and with a shout, rushed upon the head of the column.

A brief but desperate struggle ensued, in which the Guards abated nothing of their accustomed daring, and backwards by sheer force the intruders were borne, leaving many behind who there struck their last blow and fired their last shot. Nevertheless the weight of numbers was overpowering. From other quarters of the wood crowds of men broke in. Lord Saltoun fought as became the descendant of his race, disputing every tree, but was compelled to give ground till in a hollow way, rearward of the inclosure, he found some cover. There he stoutly maintained himself; and it is said that he would have been succoured by the light troops of Alten's division, had not the Prince of Orange interposed in a very characteristic manner to prevent it.

"Don't stir," was his exclamation; "depend upon it that the Duke has seen that move, and will take steps to counteract it."

And his Royal Highness was right. Just as he spoke, two companies of the 3rd Guards were seen to descend the brow of the hill, and to advance along the same hedge by which the enemy were approaching, exactly in front of them. Saltoun saw and felt the advance of his friends. His retreat had drawn the enemy into such a position that they were terribly galled by a flank-fire from the garden-wall; and now he sprang up, and shouted to his men to follow.

They were over the inner side of the ditch in a moment, and the relieving companies pushing forward at the same time, the French were driven back at a pace much more rapid than that which had carried them forward in their tide of success. Lord Saltoun's loss was severe; indeed, more men fell during this brief struggle in the orchard than in the defence of the buildings, though protracted for several hours; but his triumph was complete. He cleared the orchard, reoccupied its front hedge, and effectually secured the important post from risk' on that side; and as his comrades were equally successful, chasing the enemy into the hollow ground from which they had debouched, he felt, as soon as they had joined themselves to his party within the fence, that for the present all was safe. And he was right.

CHAPTER 22

Advance of the French Centre and Left—Flight of Bylandt's Belgian Brigade

While the fields, woods, orchard, and inclosures of Hougomont continued thus to be the scene of a close and desperate strife, the artillery on both sides thundered along the whole extent of each line, and caused many casualties. Under cover of this cannonade Ney formed his columns of attack against the left and centre of the British position, and stood prepared to send them on whenever explicit directions should be given. The force thus concentrated comprised the whole of D'Erlon's *corps d'armée*, infantry and cavalry, as well as Roussel's *cuirassiers*, forming one division of Kellermann's horse, and was to be supported by the fire of not fewer than 72 pieces, which ranged themselves along the brow of the height.

It is not very easy to say, within a few hundreds, of how many men this dense mass consisted. It could not fall short of 16,000—probably it reached 20,000 at the least; but, however this may be, the whole brow of the opposite ridge swarming with soldiers, presented to the troops which occupied the rising ground in advance of La Haye Sainte a grand and by no means an agreeable spectacle. Men ceased to talk except in monosyllables. The skirmishers rose from the ground, knelt on one knee, and threw their firelocks into a manageable position.

The regiments which lay in columns of quarter distance under the reverse descent, stood to their arms and prepared to deploy. General and staff officers reined up their horses on the brew, and bent their telescopes in one direction, while the Duke himself took up a position close to the Charleroi road, whence the entire field spread itself out before him.

As to the artillery, portions of it were massed and arranged so as to enfilade the French columns as soon as they should begin to move; while the remainder either answered the enemy's fire, or continued to plunge shot and shell into every body of troops that presented a tolerable mark,

It was noticed on the English side that, though the enemy seemed to have completed their formations, a pause of some continuance ensued. The fire of cannon did not even slacken, neither were horse or foot put in motion, but mounted officers rode briskly towards the elevated land above La Belle Alliance, and there stood in a group. It afterwards came out, that just as he was about to order the advance of the column, some objects caught Napoleon's eye at a great distance on his right, which troubled him. He saw, or fancied that he saw, in the direction of St. Lambert troops upon the march. Soult, who stood beside him, was appealed to, and pronounced the Emperor to be right.

Others looked, and having a less perfect vision, declared that there were no troops; while a third party exclaimed that, even supposing the Emperor's opinion to be correct, troops in that direction were much more likely to belong to Grouchy than to Blücher. Napoleon assented to this view of the subject, but ceased not to manifest symptoms of uneasiness. Measures must be taken to find out the truth: first, whether there were indeed troops on the heights of St. Lambert; and next, if there were, to ascertain to which side they belonged.

Accordingly, General Domont was ordered to proceed at the head of his division of cavalry towards the right, to form the main body of his own and the whole of Lubervie's *en potence* behind the wood of Paris, and then to push forward with a strong reconnoitring party till he should have satisfied himself as to what was in his front. If Grouchy were near, Domont was to join him, and point but the nearest road by which the English left might be turned; should the Prussians prove to have gained the start, he was to inform the Emperor of the circumstance, and impede the further advance of the enemy by every means in his power.

The circumstances here described befell about one o'clock in the day. Shortly after Domont had set off to execute his orders, a Prussian hussar, who had fallen into the hands of a French patrolling party, was brought before the Emperor. He proved to be the bearer of a letter from Bülow to the Duke of Wellington, acquainting the Duke of the arrival of the writer at St. Lambert. The Prussian hussar was of course examined, and stated that the troops which Napoleon had seen belonged to Bülow's advanced guard; that he himself was a member of Bülow's corps, and had quitted Wavre early in the morning; that Bülow had not been engaged in the battle of Ligny; and that the whole Prussian army had spent the night in the vicinity of Wavre, without having seen, far less suffered annoyance from an enemy.

The Prussian hussar was not more accurate in his information than might have been expected from one in his humble position, but the tidings which he communicated to Napoleon were alarming, though they were scarcely so serious as the truth would have warranted: for the troops seen from La Belle Alliance proved to be, not the advanced guard, but the head of Bülow's main body.

The advanced guard was already through the defiles, and lying in the wood of Paris till its support should come up, while the main body had just begun that difficult and tedious' progress, which, in spite of the best exertions of man and beast, was not completed till an hour before dark.

Before the Prussian hussar came in, Soult, as major-general, had written a letter to Grouchy; and the *aide-de-camp* who was to carry it was mounted and on the eve of starting. The messenger was detained while the major-general added a postscript to his dispatch. The whole ran thus:—

> Field of Battle at Waterloo, 18th, 1 o'clock p.m.
>
> *Monsieur le Marechal,*
>
> You wrote this morning at two o'clock informing the Emperor that you were about to march upon Sart Walhain, whence you intended to proceed either to Corbraux or to Wavre. This movement is agreeable to the dispositions with which you have been made acquainted. Nevertheless, the Emperor commands me to desire that you would manoeuvre constantly and steadily towards us. You can find no difficulty in ascertaining where we are and in so taking up our communications that you may be at hand to fall upon any portion of the enemy's troops which may endeavour to disturb our right, or to crush it. At this moment we are engaged along the line of Waterloo. The centre of the English army is at Mont St. Jean; therefore manoeuvre to join our right.
>
> *Le Duc de Dalmatie.*
>
> P.S. An intercepted letter makes known that General Bülow is preparing to attack our flank. We think that we can perceive his corps on the heights' of St. Lambert. Wherefore do not lose a moment in approaching and joining us, and in crushing Bülow, whom you may catch *en flagrant délit*.

Had this letter, which shows how little Napoleon was beginning to be at his ease, reached the hand for which it was intended in good time, there is no telling to what the results of an obedience to Soult's orders might have led. A series of blunders, however—for the first and gravest of which Napoleon was himself to blame—rendered that impossible. Grouchy was far distant from the road which, in order to serve his master's purposes, he ought to have followed.

Not even then, when the battle of Waterloo was begun, had he fairly struck into his proper line of march; and several hours elapsed ere the head of his column touched the rear of the enemy. Moreover, the whole face of the country between him and the main army was so covered with Prussian patrols, that the messenger, who strove to pass from the one to the other, found it necessary to dodge and turn like a hare in its flight. Grouchy did not receive the major-general's dispatch till seven o'clock in the evening—and was, when he read it, many hours' march from the scene of action. Besides, it was then too late. Napoleon had hazarded his last attack—failed in it, and felt the Prussians on his back.

Grouchy, therefore, deserves to be accounted unfortunate, rather than blameworthy, in not succouring his master in his hour of need: indeed, if he erred at all, it was at the outset, when his error lay in adopting Napoleon's views regarding the line of Blücher's retreat, and adhering to them; whereas it was physically impossible for him, after the above letter was received, to attend to it. Moreover, as has already been shown, no effort on his part could have saved the French army from defeat, however the results of the disaster might have been modified. And failure, either at Ligny or Waterloo, must have proved fatal to Napoleon, round whom on every side numbers were accumulating, against which no efforts of human genius—no display of human courage—could bear up.

The *aide-de-camp* struck spurs into his horse and galloped off; whereupon Napoleon surveyed once more the field of battle, and was about to give the signal, which D'Erlon's corps awaited with impatience—when fresh tidings arrived. A messenger from Domont reported that his patrols had fallen in with some of the enemy's detachments in the direction of St. Lambert, and that he was feeling everywhere for Marshal Grouchy, but could not discover him. It is easy to criticise the dispositions of military commanders, after the occasion has passed by which called for them, and the operations of which we write are ended; but surely there cannot be two opinions in regard to the course which, under such circumstances, it behooved Napoleon to follow.

It was clear, that whether he came in force, or only by detachments, Bülow had got the start of Grouchy; and that to stop him altogether, or at the least so to impede his further progress as that Grouchy might be able to overtake and fall upon him amid the defiles, was a measure of vital importance to the security of the grand army. Moreover, the means of doing so were obvious and close at hand. Bülow could not approach the French rear without passing through the wood of Paris.

A few brigades of infantry, judiciously posted, with abattis thrown across the rides and drives that intersect that wood, might have kept ten times their number at bay for twelve hours; while the cavalry, which now stood uselessly fronting the thicket, ought to have watched its extreme debouches, and been ready to fall upon whatever corps might make their appearance, ere they should find time to form. Napoleon, however, gave no instructions to this effect, neither did Domont apply for them; and so upon the right of his line the French Emperor played all day with danger which he felt to be imminent; and met it at last, when too late, by detaching from a force which had proved incompetent to contend, in its integrity, with the army that was opposed to it.

Having received the communication made by Domont's orderly, and passed some trivial remarks to those about him, Napoleon desired that his grand attack should be delivered. Ney, followed by his staff, rode off at a gallop towards the point where the heads of his columns had halted; and in a few minutes the aspect of affairs underwent a change.

The French accounts of the campaign of Waterloo vary so much among themselves, that it is impossible to gather from them, either in detail or in the aggregate, anything like a knowledge of the truth. The designs of the Emperor, especially, and his plan of battle on the 18th, are differently stated by almost every French writer who has touched upon them. Some say, for example, that the struggle around Hougomont, with which the operations of the day began, was a mistake—that the Emperor did not desire to make any impression on the English right, but intended merely to draw attention thither, while he fell heavily upon the left.

Others, admitting that he was over-persuaded into the rush upon Hougomont, still assure us that of his own gigantic purpose he never lost sight. His object, according to their showing, was to break the Allied centre, and to gain possession of the buildings called La Ferme de Mont St. Jean, or possibly of the village itself, which, commanding the point of junction of the two *chaussées*, would have enabled him to interpose between the English and the nearest way to Brussels. There is no just cause for this controversy. The attack upon Hougomont failed, but does not therefore deserve to be described as a false movement.

On the contrary, the end was of sufficient importance to justify the means. To be sure, the system on which Napoleon acted throughout the day, of delivering his attacks one by one cannot well be defended. He committed an error in suspending his movement against the centre, till the attempt to damage the English right had failed; and he suffered for it. But he suffered much more in consequence of the rash manner in which, uniting cavalry with infantry in his main attack, he hurried the former into action. The blunder may, however, be in some sort accounted for, and probably originated thus.

While the close fighting about Hougomont went on, the enemy kept up from the whole front of their position a heavy fire of cannon upon the Allied line. The brigades which the Duke had found it necessary to form on the exterior slope of the ridge suffered severely; and about one o'clock in the day, or a little later, he caused all on the right of the Charleroi road to fall back, and seek shelter under the ridge, on the interior slope.

It happened that this change of position among the Allies took place just as final orders had been issued for the advance of Ney's columns,—and Ney, or Napoleon, or both, assuming that it was a movement in retreat, hastened to take advantage of it. Accordingly, while D'Erlon's infantry advanced in four columns along the road, and on both sides of it, a large body of *cuirassiers*, which ought to have covered the left, took the lead, and dashing forward as if anxious to overtake the fugitives, and hinder them from rallying, came in contact with troops not yet shaken, and were sacrificed. But it will be best to describe events as they befell.

It might be about two o'clock, when the heads of the masses,

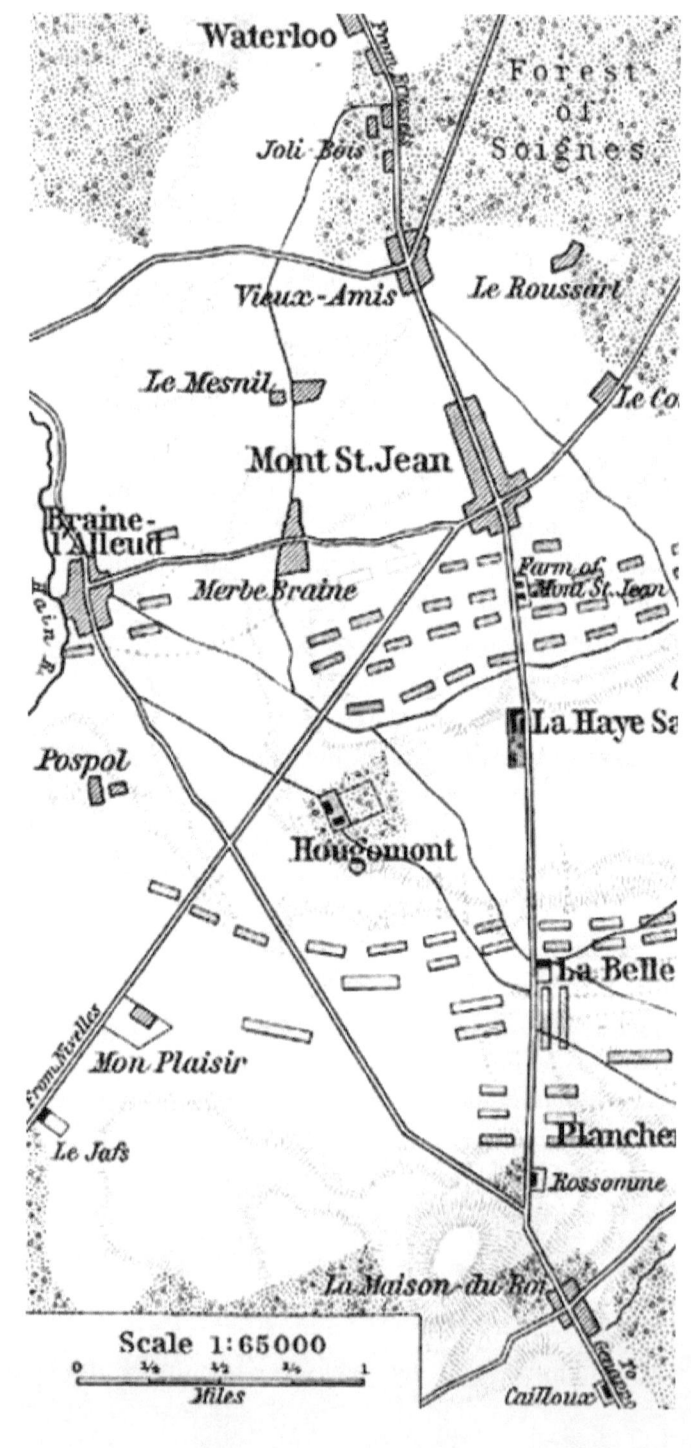

which had hung for awhile like thunderclouds on the brow of the French heights, began to descend. They came on with loud cries of "*Vive l'Empereur!*" in gallant array, and at a quick step, receiving, but as it seemed in no wise regarding, a murderous fire from the Allied artillery. As soon as their rearmost companies dipped over the ridge, the French batteries opened, and such a storm of shot and shell ploughed up the earth along the heights of Mont St. Jean as had never before been witnessed.

The first line of the British infantry halted on the right; the second, having been withdrawn, as just described, did not suffer so much. On the left, where Picton's division, including Bylandt's Dutch-Belgians and Best's Hanoverians, stood, the slaughter was very great; and if these raw foreign troops shook under this iron hail, let not soldiers more accustomed to war blame them too severely. Nevertheless, even Bylandt's division, though it wavered and swayed, still preserved its line intact; while the brigades of Kempt and Pack, formed in columns at quarter distance, looked steadily and sternly before them.

On came the French, shouting, as is their wont, in an ill-assorted and most unmusical chorus; their cries, however, being drowned in the roar of the cannonade, which went forward continually. Now they reached the lowest part of the valley—now they began to ascend the opposite slope; and by and by from the head of each separate column skirmishers ran out in crowds. Between these and the light troops of the Allies a desultory firing began.

The reports of musketry and the short quick puffs of smoke which accompanied them, first attracted attention about the orchard and inclosures of La Haye Sainte. Almost immediately afterwards, similar sights and sounds became distinguishable in front of Papelotte and La Haye; and in a few moments the entire front of the British line, from the Charleroi road to the more remote of the places just named, presented the appearance of an animated skirmish.

The four French infantry divisions which thus advanced to the attack were those of Durette, Marcognet, Alix, and Donzelat. Durette's division was on the extreme right, being flanked only by cavalry; Donzelat was on the left, and moved along the Charleroi road, which, in point of fact, he touched with his left; Alix and Marcognet constituted the right and left centre of the line; Alix being in communication with Donzelat's right. Marcognet with the left of Durette.

It was on Durette's side that the first partial advantage was won. He found himself opposed by a body of Nassau troops, whom his skirmishers forced through the hedges, and beyond the farm-house of Papelotte. Of this they took possession, keeping it till reinforcements arrived for the Nassauers, when they in their turn were expelled; and as the object does not appear to have been very highly esteemed, no especial pains were taken to recover the vantage ground.

On the contrary Durette's troops seemed to accomplish their appointed purpose so long as they amused the battalions which had been posted here, and kept the cavalry that was in support of them on the alert. It was elsewhere that the fighting went on with a ferocity which showed that more than demonstrations were in progress; and many and desperate were the feats of individual daring to which it led.

While Durette's division thus amused itself and that portion of the Allied army which fronted it, the three columns to its right pressed steadily forward, covered for a time by the murderous fire of more than 70 pieces of cannon. They came, not unsupported by artillery—as well as horsemen. Thirty light guns moved in the intervals between them, or up the slope of the height on the other side of the road; and though their fire was mute during the advance, the spectacle which they exhibited was most imposing.

Presently one of Donzelat's brigades took ground to its right, and bore directly upon the farm of La Haye Sainte. It was soon warmly engaged with the companies of light Germans which held that post; and, in spite of a gallant resistance, made its way into the orchard, and sweeping round, enveloped the whole of the inclosures in a blaze of fire. Meanwhile the remaining brigade, pushing along the other side of the road, was met and staggered by the fire of the two companies of the Rifle Brigade which occupied the sandpit. So well these veterans plied their rifles, and so immovable they proved to be, in spite of repeated endeavours to dislodge them, that the brigade, acting, as it seemed, without orders, inclined to its right, and came instantly into contact with the remaining companies which lined the hedge, a little way in the rear of it.

Against these the French *tirailleurs*, by dint of numbers, must have made head under any circumstances; but just as the strife was at its crisis, events befell still more to the French right—which left the Rifles without an alternative. The divisions of Alix and Marcognet pressed on without a check. Their skirmishers drove in the light troops which Bylandt and Best had thrown out to restrain them, and were beginning to open their fire upon the Dutch-Belgian line, when the latter, which had never been steady from the opening of the cannonade, suddenly lost all order, and fairly fled. It was to no purpose that many of the officers exerted themselves to stop the panic.

No regard was paid to remonstrance, reproof, or exhortation; but the whole brigade, turning its back, ran in extreme confusion quite across the crest of the position. Loud were the hisses and bitter the execrations wherewith the brigades of Kempt and Pack greeted them; indeed, it was not without difficulty that the men of more than one British regiment were prevented from firing upon them; but though a battalion of Dutch militia did its best to stop them, and the artillery (likewise Dutch) belonging to the brigade absolutely threw themselves in their way, the fugitives could not be stopped. They fairly ran over guns, men, and horses, and swept all before them.

"See, see!" cried Captain Tyler, General Picton's *aide-de-camp*—who, as well as his heroic chief, was watching from the brow of the hill all that went on—"these fellows won't stand; they are shaking already."

"Never mind," replied Picton; "they shall have a taste of it, at any rate:" and a taste they unquestionably had; but they did not wait for more. They escaped into the valley between the main ridge and the heights that ascend to the village of Mont St. Jean, and never, throughout the remainder of the day, came under fire again.

CHAPTER 23

Attack and Defence of the British Left Centre

Picton's division, which had borne the brunt of the battle at Quatre Bras, was reduced to a mere skeleton. The two brigades of Pack and Kempt—on which alone he could now rely—did not muster between them 3000 men. They consisted of the remains of eight battalions—namely, the 28th, 32nd, 79th, and 95th, under Kempt—the Royals, 42nd, 44th, and 92nd under Pack. Having vented his spleen, against the fugitives, in terms to which his followers were not unaccustomed, Picton deployed the whole into line, and stood to receive the charge of not fewer than 13,000 infantry, besides cavalry. There was a considerable interval, too, between the brigades.

All the space which Bylandt ought to have occupied was vacant, except so far as a cloud of skirmishers managed to blind it; but these, in spite of a stout resistance, were gradually driven in, even the riflemen from the sandpit, the road above it, and the hedge on its right being overpowered. Picton was nothing daunted: he knew that in his rear no infantry stood; and that on his personal exertions, and those of his followers, the maintenance of the centre of the position depended. He rode along the front of Kempt's brigade, therefore, saying encouraging words to the men; and the skirmishers, as they came in, took their proper places in the line as if upon an ordinary parade. And now the head of one of the columns approached.

It looked very formidable; and it was so, both as regarded the number and the composition of the troops; and the shouts with which they rent the air proved that none in all that mass experienced the slightest distrust of their own prowess. Suddenly the fire from the enemy's batteries ceased. Their own people were too much on a level with the English to sanction a further exercise of their skill; and the head of the column halting, its rearmost battalions began to take ground to the right, and to develop a line which, if completed, would have been resistless.

Picton did not wait for such development:—"A volley, and then charge!" shouted he at the top of his Stentorian voice; and such a volley was delivered within thirty yards as rent the force in the midst of its formation: neither was a moment given to recover from the shock.

A double fence or hedgerow separated the belligerents, through which Kempt's brigade rushed, falling, as a matter of course, into momentary confusion, and receiving a deadly fire from the portion of the enemy's mass which was in a condition to act; but order was at once restored as the men gained the open field and, never pausing to calculate how many of their comrades might have dropped, the remainder closed, with a shout, upon all that was before them. It were vain to attempt a description of what followed.

In modern warfare hand-to-hand combats rarely occur—at least with infantry soldiers; and when they do the nature of the weapons with which the combatants are armed renders the struggle necessarily brief; but that day, and in that charge, many a bayonet and sword became bloody enough, for the very colours of one regiment, at least, became the prize for which men contended. So completely were the foemen intermingled, that after the regimental standard of the 32nd had been gathered up by Lieutenant Belcher from a fallen comrade, Ensign Birtwhistle, Lieutenant Belcher was forced to contend with a French officer for the maintenance of it.

The latter fell, indeed, under wounds inflicted by more than his immediate opponent; but they were all delivered by stroke of hand, except the last, which a musket, placed against the side of his head, rendered mortal.

The charge of Kempt's brigade was irresistible. Taken in the act of deploying, the very numbers of the enemy told against them; and they were borne back in a state of confusion such as must be seen to be understood; nevertheless the success was purchased at a dear rate. Picton, struck by a musket-ball in the temple, fell lifeless from his horse, and was instantly carried to the rear by two or three of his followers. He was a thorough soldier in his life, and the manner of his death is not now to be regretted; for he fell, as he himself always wished to do, in the field, and with the consciousness about him of having well done his duty.

But the fall of their leader in no degree discomposed or disheartened his gallant division. Kempt was at hand to supply his place, which he did right gallantly; and the line moved on, driving before it all resistance. Doubtless the 79th had hard work to recover its consistency—which the act of passing through rather a thick part of the hedge, and a warm reception from a cloud of French *tirailleurs*, somewhat discomposed; but a good regiment, like the 79th, may be destroyed—it cannot be defeated. The men soon regained the touch; and then woe to the French soldiers, whether in line or dispersed, that endeavoured to withstand them.

The soldiers of the 5th division were pressing on in this resolute manner, when support suddenly came to them from a quarter on which they did not calculate, and of the manner and occasion of the arrival of which it will be necessary to give some account.

Allusion has elsewhere been made to the premature advance of a portion of Milhaud's *cuirassiers*, who, either because they mistook for flight a prudent move of a portion of the British line, or that their own ardour carried them beyond the limits of their instructions, pushed forward on the left of Donzelat's division, and presently got ahead of it. No doubt the apparition of these steel-clad horsemen in rear of the inclosures which they had been appointed to maintain was not without its effect upon the garrison of La Haye Sainte, whose skirmishers were driven in upon the support sent down to strengthen them, and both suffered severely; for the *cuirassiers* gained the rear of the farm just as a Hanoverian battalion, detached from Kielmansegge's brigade, was approaching the garden fence.

And as these latter happened to be very young troops, they failed to form in time, and were, as well as the skirmishers, with whom they became intermingled, cut well nigh to pieces. Nevertheless, the advantage gained by the destruction of a few companies of untrained infantry was more than counterbalanced by the consequences to which it led.

The Duke having communicated with Lord Uxbridge, the latter put himself at the head of Lord Edward Somerset's household brigade, and led them to a charge of which the results will be imperfectly understood unless the reader have presented to his mind's eye a tolerably correct view of the localities.

The centre of the English position, of which the brigades of heavy cavalry were in support, occupied the broad summit of a range of heights, having in its front the Wavre road, which cuts the road from Charleroi and Genappe at right angles. The Wavre road is to a considerable extent cut into the face of the hill. It is, therefore, as regards the fields on either hand of it, a hollow way, with banks which vary a good deal in regard to altitude, but which, throughout a considerable part of the space of which we speak, are more or less steep.

The farm of La Haye Sainte stands on the farther, that is on the French side of the Wavre road, at a distance of from forty to sixty yards from the top of the hill. It was in the interval which is interposed between the back of the farm and the Wavre road that the *cuirassiers* fell upon the Hanoverian infantry, whom they cut down with great slaughter, and chased to the crest of the hill. Some of the fugitives swerving to the right, escaped across the Charleroi road, and joined themselves to the Rifle Brigade in the sandpit and behind the hedge.

The rest ran wildly towards the main position, and were followed beyond the Wavre road by the right wing of the *cuirassiers*, who, though somewhat confused in scrambling over the hollow way, soon regained their touch.

As a measure of necessary precaution, Kielmansegge's and Ompteda's brigades threw themselves into squares, while two batteries of horse artillery, Ross's and Lloyd's, opened their fire. But the latter had not time to discharge above a round or two when Lord Edward Somerset's brigade came thundering forward, and the *élite* of the horsemen of the rival nations met in close and desperate strife.

The Household Brigade, consisting of the 1st and 2nd regiments of Life Guards, the Royal Horse Guards or Blues, and the 1st Dragoon Guards, was formed in line, having the Blues as a support. The 1st Life Guards were on the right, the 2nd Life Guards on the left, and the Dragoon Guards in the centre. There was a slight obliquity in the plateau whence they moved, which brought the right more quickly in contact with the enemy than the left, though the shock was like the break of a huge wave on the sea-shore—begun, indeed, on one side palpably enough, but almost instantly carried in its impulse to the other.

The left of the *cuirassiers* met it stoutly, and for several minutes the conflict is compared by an eye-witness to the meeting of two flocks of sheep in a confined space, neither of which will give ground. The French right were unable to show the same determined front. They had not yet crossed the hollow road, which curves a good deal in the direction of Hougomont, when the Household Brigade made their appearance. They therefore put their horses to their speed, and found themselves suddenly checked by an impediment which it was not easy, in their circumstances, to surmount.

Nevertheless, they went at the declivity, and were forcing their horses up the opposite bank, when the 2nd Life Guards came upon them. Resistance, in such a situation, was impossible. They wheeled to the right, and galloping across the Charleroi road, went down the hill, through the skirmishers that lined the hedge, some of them even floundering into the sandpit. These latter died to a man; but the rest, breaking through the hedge, and slashing at such of the soldiers of the 95th as lay under it, endeavoured to rally in rear of their own skirmishers, where they were fiercely attacked by the Life Guards, who had followed, helter-skelter, as the enemy fled, and now engaged in a state of as wild confusion as their own.

It is on such occasions that opportunities for individual heroism are afforded, which, however animated the descriptions of them may be, do not, in modern warfare, make amends for the loss of power which attaches to cavalry only while it is massed. Here Shaw, the celebrated pugilist, earned a name for himself by disabling, with his own hand, not fewer than seven enemies; and here he received the multitude of wounds, of the aggregate of which, not of any one in particular out of the number, he died.

The common story is—and Captain Siborne, in his valuable history, has repeated it—that poor Shaw fell from a carbine-ball delivered by a French *cuirassier* from the flank. This is a mistake. Shaw continued with his regiment till the ardour of men and horses carried them whence few were able to return, and reached the position again so enfeebled from loss of blood that he could with difficulty creep to a dunghill beside one of the straggling houses in the rear, where he lay down. Nobody noticed him during the remainder of the struggle; but next morning he was found dead, without one wound about him sufficiently serious in itself to occasion death.

It is an old subject of blame by continental officers, that English cavalry, if successful in a charge, never know when to stop. It is even asserted by Marshal Marmont, in his recent work on the Art of War, that so well known was this disposition to himself and to others, that they have repeatedly, by feigned retreats. drawn English squadrons into positions where a fire of musketry from some copse or the roadside has destroyed them.

Marshal Marmont may be right or wrong in the abstract; but the fact is beyond dispute, that Somerset's noble brigade not only carried all before them, but followed the tide of battle down the bill, regardless of consequences. They neither had any support, nor looked for it; for the Blues, seeing their comrades in the *mêlée*, could not be restrained; and thus the whole soon became intermingled.

Neither did they lack the companionship of the sister brigade, though its first blow fell upon two columns of French infantry, which, mounting the hill a little to the left of Kempt's ground, had become warmly engaged with Pack's brigade: this latter force, it will be remembered, consisted of the Royals, the 42nd, the 92nd, and 44th regiments, which had supported Bylandt's Belgians ere the latter ran away, and were now moved up to fill the space which had become vacant. They stood, the Royals on the right, the 44th on the left of the line, but the left wing of the 44th forming in rear of Best's Hanoverians, the battalion was halted upon the summit in support.

Three skeleton regiments, therefore, were all that could be formed to receive the shock of four strong brigades, which in contiguous columns of battalions advanced against them, and crowned the ridge on which they stood. It was a moment of high emprise to the boldest, and all felt it to be such. Pack rode along his line, not to animate, but to caution his men that they should be steady, while a dozen bagpipes brayed out simultaneously the war-cry of the far north.

On the enemy came. They crossed the hedge; they were within forty yards of the Highlanders, and delivered a fire, of which the Highlanders took no notice. The latter were not yet sufficiently closed up to act according to the customs of their forefathers; and so they marched on till more than half the intervening space was compassed. Then, indeed, such a volley rushed through their closed ranks, that the masses shook as corn waves when a hurricane falls upon it suddenly; and in a moment the bayonets were levelled.

The enemy did not hesitate; they returned the Highlanders' fire, and stood; while the 92nd—a mere handful of men—rushed into the midst of them. Long after that day, individuals who witnessed the charge used to speak of the thrilling sensation which overcame them when they beheld some hundred and fifty or two hundred bonnets and plumes lost, so to speak, amid a crowd of chakos. But lost they were not. Just at this moment Ponsonby's heavy brigade, the Royal Dragoons, the Scotch Greys, and the Inniskillens came up at speed, and, shouting to their dismounted comrades to give place, passed through the intervals of companies and battalions, and fell headlong upon the French.

"Scotland forever!" replied the Greys, as they passed.

"Scotland forever!" replied their dismounted countrymen; and many seized the stirrup-leathers of the troopers, and were borne forward into the heart of the *mêlée*. Never, in the annals of modern warfare, has a cavalry charge been more decisive. The enemy vainly endeavoured to act together. The front was cloven; the centre penetrated; and the rear, while attempting to deploy, as against infantry, utterly dispersed.

In five minutes the whole side of the acclivity was covered with fugitives, who fought singly, or in small groups, to die under the swords of the troopers.

The numbers who fell on that occasion can never be accurately stated. That they were very great the state of the field, both then and subsequently, showed; while 2000 prisoners, with the eagle of the 45th regiment, remained in the hands of the victors. This last was taken by Sergeant Ewart, a brave and expert swordsman, who, seeing it encircled by a band of resolute men, attacked them single handed, and won the prize. It is satisfactory to be able to add that his valour was not left unrewarded. Within a year (how much better if the rules of our service would have permitted the deed to have been done on the spot!) he was promoted to a commission in a veteran battalion.

The Duke's orders to his generals of division and of brigade were explicit—that they should not be induced by any momentary success to advance beyond the rest of the line. Pack, therefore, having with difficulty restrained the ardour of his men and secured his prisoners, sent the latter to the rear, and formed on the ground whence the French had fled.

It was not so with the Union brigade. Ponsonby would have fain followed the example; but the thing was not to be accomplished. In vain the trumpet sounded to halt and rally. Intoxicated with success, and in some instances, perhaps, carried away by their horses, the men paid no heed to the recall. That which the Greys had done on the left, the Royals effected on the right, and the Inniskillens in the centre.

The former corps fell upon that portion of Alix's division which, having advanced upon the space left vacant by Bylandt's flight, had not been opposed to any infantry. It was, therefore, considerably ahead of the column on its right, being through the hedge and across the Wavre road, and seemed in a fair way of penetrating to the village of Mont St. Jean, when the Royals suddenly appeared, mounting the slope at speed, and looking as formidable as "big men on big horses" are apt to do.

The French column seemed to be taken with a sudden panic They had not calculated on finding cavalry here, and were a little confused in consequence of having just passed over broken ground and through the hedges. They therefore made no attempt to form square; but, delivering an irregular fire from the front ranks, endeavoured to escape behind the hedge again. It was a fatal movement.

Long before they could reach the covered places of shelter the Royals were among them; and such a scene of slaughter and confusion ensued as baffles all attempt at description. One regiment, the 28th, did indeed retain some appearance of order. It was immediately in rear of the 105th, and supported it; and round it the fugitives strove to rally. But this was not permitted. The long swords of the British horsemen mowed them down by the score; and the 28th soon became involved in the common confusion.

It was in this charge that Captain Clarke, now Colonel Clarke Kennedy, commanding the centre squadron of the Royals, performed an exploit similar to that which won for Sergeant Ewart his epaulettes. He too saw the eagle of a French regiment, the 105th, surrounded by its guard, and, breaking through, killed with his own hand the officer who bore it. The standard fell, and Captain Clarke endeavoured to catch it, but his horse carried him forward, and he touched only the fringe on the edge of the silk. The pole dropped across the neck of the horse on which his coverer, Corporal Stiles, was mounted, and that good soldier, grasping his trophy, had the honour of bearing it out of the field. Both of these standards now hang, beside many more, in the chapel of the Royal Hospital at Chelsea.

Chapter 24

Cavalry Operations

If the gallant Inniskillens were not equally fortunate with their comrades in seizing standards or bearing other trophies from the field, they were to the full as forward in the fight; and not less successfully so. The right and left wings, consisting each of two squadrons, fell respectively upon the 54th and 55th French regiments of the line, through which they broke with resistless violence, covering the ground with the slain. The numbers of the prisoners whom they made surpassed those taken by the Greys and Royals, for whole companies fled within the British position and surrendered to the infantry, in order to escape from the sharp swords of these horsemen.

And here occurred an incident which, though it has frequently been described before, cannot well be omitted from any narrative which undertakes to tell the story of the battle of Waterloo. A gentleman in coloured clothes had been seen riding, under the hottest of the fire, along the brow of the English heights. That he was not altogether a novice in the game that was going forward his manner of bearing himself seemed to denote, and he suddenly arrived on the flank of the Inniskillens, just as they were about to charge across the Wavre road, shouting, as one might who could have well directed the movement, "At 'em, my lads; at 'em, now's your time!"

It was the late chivalrous and gallant Duke of Richmond, who, though but a visitor at Brussels, could not be aware that a great battle was about to be waged within a morning's ride of him, yet keep at a distance from the field. The Duke had not fewer than three sons in the fight—the present Duke, then Earl of March, Lord George, and Lord William Lennox—and that only one of all these received a severe wound may be accounted a marvellous piece of good luck; for none of the blood of Lennox ever shrank from danger, and all were that day more than usually exposed to it.

The charges of Ponsonby's brigade on infantry, and of Lord Edward Somerset's on cavalry, were delivered almost at the same moment. They were alike successful; that of the Household troops more gradually so, for the *cuirassiers* gave ground unwillingly, but of both the triumph was complete. The right of Somerset's brigade, consisting of the 1st Life Guards and Blues, did not find the same opportunity of being carried away by their own ardour as the regiments on the left. They had the mass of the enemy's horsemen in their front, who, though driven back, retired doggedly and fought till succour arrived.

It was not so with the 2nd Life Guards and the 1st Dragoon Guards. Dashing across the Charleroi road in pursuit of that portion of the fugitives who betook themselves thither, they soon got intermingled with the Inniskillens and the Royals; whereupon both parties, seeming to catch fresh animation from the circumstances under which they met, dashed on, heedful of nothing except the work of destruction. It was to no purpose that Lord Uxbridge sounded to halt and rally; and vain were the glances which he throw behind for the support which was nowhere.

The Greys, which had been directed to form a second line for Ponsonby, were already ahead of their comrades; and Lord Edward Somerset's reserve, the Blues, though better in hand, were hacking and hewing on the flank of the column of *cuirassiers*. What were the light cavalry about? Before the battle began, the brigadiers had been separately instructed to give support, at their own discretion, wherever it might seem to be needed; and never surely was support more required than now, when success had as completely dispersed the heavy brigades as if they had sustained a defeat.

The light cavalry were not so much to blame as their chief seemed to imagine. Vandeleur, who stood nearest with the 11th, 12th, and 16th, was already in motion; but he had a considerable detour to make, in order to avoid a ravine, and though he used his best exertions he arrived late upon the field; for nothing stopped the progress of the Royals and Inniskillens till, with such of the 2nd Life Guards as had tumultuously mingled with them, they plunged into the valley. Then, indeed, a murderous fire from a compact corps of infantry on the right staggered them, and some pieces of cannon, getting their range, told fearfully.

Moreover, a second column of *cuirassiers*, fresh and in perfect order, was seen advancing on the opposite side, and both time and means of forming so as to meet them were wanting. Nothing remained, therefore, but for the victors to wheel about and retire, which they did in great confusion and not without loss, for their horses were blown and the ground beneath their feet was wet and heavy. It would have been well for their comrades on the left had they too pulled up at the same time; but they did not; no musketry fire fell upon them.

The enemy's batteries rained grape, it is true; but the salute seemed to exasperate, not to cow them, and having cut their way to the bottom of their own height, they rushed through the valley and ascended the slope on the opposite side. They were now upon a level with the French guns, and, turning sharp to the left, they swept the whole line, killing the men and sabring the horses as they past. They did not observe, unfortunately for themselves, that a brigade of lancers was in motion, till it arrived obliquely upon their flank in overwhelming numbers. They were overmatched at once, and they knew it.

Meanwhile, on the flank of the Blues and the 1st Life Guards the French had brought a couple of guns to bear. The infantry, likewise, which thronged the orchard of La Haye Sainte, opened a murderous fire, and the two regiments, after sustaining some loss, wheeled round and retreated. They came back in good order, though closely pursued by the *cuirassiers* whom they had just driven back, and were soon safe behind the infantry line, though not till various accidents occurred, among which the fate of Lord Edward Somerset deserves to be noticed.

His Lordship was retiring in rear of his men, when a cannon-shot struck his horse and he rolled over. "Scramble through the hedge," shouted an officer, as he flew past; "you have not a moment to lose;" and scramble through Lord Edward did, without ever rising except on his hands and knees. Well was it for him that he thus disposed of himself, for the next instant the pursuers were up to the fence, and, in spite of a rattling fire from the riflemen who lined it, they soon pressed through.

Simultaneously with the advance of D'Erlon's corps, and its formation into columns of attack, had been the descent of Bachelu's infantry division from its place on the crest of the hill of La Belle Alliance, where it formed the right of Reille's corps. It did not join the onward march, but taking post on the brow of a second range, intermediate between La Belle Alliance and La Haye Sainte, it held itself in readiness to sustain the attacking force, while at the same time it kept up the communication between the right and left wings of the foremost line of the French army.

It was this division which with its musketry fire staggered the 1st Life Guards and Blues, while pressing upon the rear of the *cuirassiers*, and, with the help of the guns which opened on their flank, forced these regiments to retire. But they were all on the west of the Charleroi road, and for the present, at least, escaped the annihilation which seemed to have overtaken the leading regiments of D'Erlon's corps. Even the latter, however, were not without some support.

In spite of the fury with which Ponsonby's troopers had ridden through them, several battalions gathered to a heap on the lower part of the slope, and, though very unsteady, presented, when viewed from above, a not unformidable appearance. They had thrown themselves, as it were, on the line of the retreat of the Greys, Royals, and Inniskillens, and as these regiments, with portions of the Dragoon Guards and 2nd Life Guards, were charged by an overwhelming number of lancers, their destruction seemed to be inevitable. It was at this critical moment that Vandeleur came tip to the rescue, and some sharp fighting ensued.

It has already been shown that, in moving to support their comrades; according to the general, but judicious, instructions of Lord Uxbridge, Vandeleur's brigade was compelled, on account of the nature of the ground, to make a considerable detour to the right. The brigade gained the level at last, and, forming in lines of regiments, pushed forward; the 12th leading, the 16th immediately supporting, and the 11th in reserve. The 12th, with Colonel Ponsonby at their head, galloped down the declivity, and taking note of the infantry column of which the formation was as yet imperfect, rushed, in the first instance, upon that.

They went right through, scattering and cutting down all that encountered them. But they did not halt to complete their victory; their business was to relieve the broken heavy cavalry from the pressure of the French lancers; and hence, though their own ranks were unavoidably confused by the process? of breaking a square, they brought up their left shoulders, and came down with resistless vehemence on the flank of the French cavalry.

They literally rolled up all on whom they fell; while the 16th, with whom Vandeleur advanced in person, charged the front of another line of lancers, and effectually stopped them. Again the impetuosity of English men and English horses carried them too far; they got intermixed with broken parties of the Greys and the other heavy regiments, and went tearing up the face of the French hill like madmen. The 11th, however, kept its order, as did a light brigade of Belgian-Dutch cavalry, which, indeed, attempted nothing more than a mere display upon the crest of the position, and Vivian, sweeping up from the extreme left with his hussars, rendered all tolerably safe.

But the effect of this excessive eagerness in the troops more immediately engaged soon became apparent. The French far out-numbered the Allies in cavalry; a reserve and supports were always at hand, which now coming up in excellent order, once more turned the tide of battle. Back went most of our troopers helter-skelter; the loss was immense, for the horses of the enemy were fresh, while those of the English were blown; and in scattered combat, particularly under circumstances so disadvantageous, swordsmen have little chance against lancers: that any of them succeeded in reaching the crest of the position, and re-forming, as they did, under cover of the infantry, was owing wholly to the excellent practice of the horse-artillery, and the bold front presented by Vivian's hussars.

But the ground was covered with the dead and dying, among whom both Ponsonbys, the general, and the commandant of the 12th were numbered. The former, who was that day very indifferently mounted, stuck fast in a ploughed field, and there perished. A party of lancers overtook him, and, without so much as offering quarter, pierced him through and through; the gallant colonel fared better—that is to say, he survived, though at the expense of an amount of suffering which is only to be described in his own words. After narrating the rush of his regiment through the infantry, he goes on to say:—

> We had no sooner passed through them than we were ourselves attacked, before we could form, by about 300 Polish lancers, who had hastened to their relief: the French artillery pouring in among us a heavy fire of grape, though for one of our men they killed three of their own. In the *mêlée* I was almost instantly disabled in both arms, losing first my sword and then my reins, and, followed by a few of my men, who were presently cut down—no quarter being asked or given—I was carried along by my horse, till, receiving a blow from a sabre, I fell senseless on my face to the ground.
> Recovering, I raised myself a little to look round, being at that time, I believe, in a condition to get up and run away, when a lancer passing by, cried out—'*Tu n'es pas mort, coquin!*' and struck his lance through my back. My head dropped, the blood gushed into my mouth, a difficulty of

breathing came on, and I thought all was over.

Not long afterwards (it was then impossible to measure time, but I must have fallen in less than ten minutes after the onset) a *tirailleur* stopped to plunder me, threatening my life. I directed him to a small side-pocket, in which he found three dollars, all I had; but he continued to threaten, and I said he might search me: this he did immediately, unloosing my stock, and tearing open my waistcoat, and leaving me in a very uneasy posture.

But he was no sooner gone than an officer bringing up some troops, to which, probably, the *tirailleur* belonged, and happening to halt where I lay, stooped down and addressed me, saying, he feared I was badly wounded: I said that I was, and expressed a wish to be removed to the rear. He said it was against their orders to remove even their own men; but that if they gained the day (and he understood that the Duke of Wellington was killed, and that some of our battalions had surrendered), every attention in his power would be shown me.

I complained of thirst, and he held his brandy-bottle to my lips, directing one of the soldiers to lay me straight on my side, and place a knapsack under my head. He then passed on into the action, soon perhaps to want, though not to receive, the same assistance; and I shall never know to whose generosity I was indebted, as I believe, for my life. Of what rank he was I cannot say: he wore a great-coat.

So spoke the brave and gentle Ponsonby, describing in after years the events of that day, and drawing a vivid but true picture of the occurrences which shed both light and darkness over every field of battle; and though in going onward with his narrative events must of necessity be anticipated, the tale is too touching not to be placed on record as it stands.

"By and by," he continues, "another *tirailleur* came up, a fine young man, full of ardour. He knelt down, and fired over me, loading and firing many times, and conversing with me freely all the while." What a situation to be in, and what a strange dialogue—if dialogue that can be called, which appears to have thrown the stream of conversation all into one channel, for the *tirailleur* seems to have been the solo interlocutor, and his communications related entirely to the effects of his own shots, and to the course which the battle was taking!

"At last he ran away, saying—'*Vous serez bien aise d'apprendre que nous allons nous retirer. Bon jour, mon ami.*'"

Thus throughout the whole of the day, from about four o'clock in the afternoon, Ponsonby lay among the dying and the dead. But not even with the flight of the enemy were his perilous adventures ended.

"It was dusk," he continues, "when two squadrons of Prussian cavalry, each of them two deep, came across the valley, and passed over me in full trot, lifting me from the ground and tumbling me about cruelly. The clatter of their approach, and the apprehensions they excited, may be imagined: a gun taking that direction must have destroyed me.

"The battle was now at an end, or removed to a distance. The shouts, the imprecations, the outcries of '*Vive l'Empereur!*' the discharges of musketry and cannon were over, and the groans of the wounded all around me became every moment more and more audible: I thought the night would never end."

But we must draw for the present a curtain over this scene; for the time to describe the field, when nothing but the wreck of the battle covered it, has not yet come.

CHAPTER 25

Second Attack on Hougomont— Advance of the French Cavalry

While this fierce combat was in progress along the centre and left of the British line, the right had not been permitted to breathe freely. Scarcely was D'Erlon's corps launched, when the attack upon Hougomont renewed itself with fresh ardour; reinforcements coming up from both Jerome's and Foy's divisions, to co-operate with the assailants. The latter had never been driven entirely out of the wood, and now, with the help of fresh troops, they regained possession of the whole of it.

This brought them in front of the garden-wall, at a distance of not more than twenty or thirty yards, and they poured upon it such a storm of bullets as rendered the position of the defenders, though exposed only through the loop-holes, a very perilous one. Moreover, they pushed forward on both flanks of the building, pressing Saltoun back through the great orchard, and winning their way along the lane and through the ravine which skirt the chateau on the other side; but on the chateau itself they made no impression. It was held by a garrison, feeble indeed as regarded numbers, but of indomitable courage, which was always ready to meet and to repel the first symptoms of a design to burst open a gate or to scramble over a wall.

The fight had lasted about half an hour, when General Byng, taking note of the progress which the enemy were making, directed Colonel Hepburn, with the 2nd battalion of the 3rd

Guards, to move down the slope and support Lord Saltoun. It was time that this should be done, for Saltoun's party had dwindled to a few men, and these, compelled to give ground, which they did inch by inch, were now making their last stand in a hollow way outside of the orchard altogether.

In a few minutes the aspect of affairs was changed; Hepburn's battalion, fresh and full of ardour, rushed at the orchard fence, and sprang over it; whereupon the French *tirailleurs* fled, and soon got jammed into knots while striving to escape through two or three gaps in the opposite hedge. A well-concentrated fire cut them down while so crowded together, and their loss was prodigious.

The re-occupation of the orchard occurred just about the time that D'Erlon's columns were driven back from the left of the Charleroi road, and was instantly followed by the retreat of the French parties which had penetrated along the lane on the other side of the building. And now occurred a pause in the musketry fire; the French having withdrawn to repair their wreck; while the English stood fast on the position which they had so nobly defended, and sent out their light troops to cover them in a connected order as at the first.

But though the musketry ceased, there was no suspension of the cannonade. On the contrary, the latter seemed to increase in fury along the whole extent of the field, and the gunners on both sides appearing to have caught the exact range, the carnage was fearful. Nor was it the front line alone on either side that suffered; round-shot striking the crest of the opposite hills, bounded off, and fell into the heart of columns which were secure from a direct fire; while of the shells thrown, perhaps the larger portion told in the ranks of the reserves.

Such a plunging fire is exceedingly uncomfortable even to veterans,—to the nerves of young soldiers it is trying in the extreme; yet they stood, upon the whole, marvellously. Of the Belgians, both horse and foot, a good many took to flight; but the English and Germans kept their places gallantly, and the French were equally stern.

The formation of Bachelu's division of Reille's corps on an eminence half way between the ridge of La Belle Alliance and the commencement of the English slope has been already described. The division in question was pushed thus far in advance, partly that it might support D'Erlon's corps in the grand attack on which it had entered, partly that the communications between the right and left wings of the French army might be rendered secure.

A somewhat eccentric movement on the part of this division gave some variety to the operations of the cannonade. It was seen to descend the hill altogether; and by and by the head of a column appeared, pointing in the direction of the farm of La Haye Sainte. Immediately the skirmishers of Alten's division ran down the slope to resist it, and threw such a fire into the leading companies as caused them to swerve to the left. Presently the whole column fell into the same line of march; it moved along the bottom of the hill, sheltered from the fire of the British artillery till it came within a moderate distance of Hougomont, where it began to take the ascent.

Its progress had not been unobserved; a German battery, under Captain Cleves, watched the whole proceeding; and no sooner found a good object at which to aim, than it opened its fire. Three rounds from each of these six guns checked the further progress of the column, and though Bachelu succeeded in restoring order and leading his men again to the attack, a repetition of the same iron shower dispersed them completely. Ranks were broken, and a cloud of fugitives escaped over an intervening ridge, leaving, however, the lower slope of the English height covered with their killed and wounded.

For the better part of one hour subsequently to this repulse, the battle confined itself almost entirely to a cannonade. The French, indeed, threw shells in great numbers, particularly in the direction of Hougomont, which, together with some haystacks that stood near, was soon on fire; and the progress of the conflagration was as sublime to look at as its effects upon the garrison were disastrous. It was compared by those who beheld it from a distance to the burning of St. Sebastian; by such as survived the feats of that day it will long be remembered for the dreadful havoc which it occasioned.

Many wounded men, whom it was found impossible to remove, and whose hurts were so severe as to render them incapable of helping themselves, perished in the conflagration; many more, whose cases were equally desperate, were saved as by a miracle. The fire spread to the west end of the chapel, on the floor of which, principally near the altar, maimed men, French as well as English, were lying. The poor fellows saw the flames burst through; they called for help, but none came, and half-stifled by the smoke, which rolled in upon them in dense volumes, they gave themselves up for lost.

But by some means or another, certainly through no exertions among their comrades, who had not the means of working effectively at hand, and were besides too much occupied to use them had they been near, the progress of the fire became arrested. The flames caught the lower extremities of a crucifix which hung, the size of life, above the doorway; but they never extended farther. Mutilated the image was, and still continues to be, for there it still hangs exactly as at the close of the strife the English Guards left it: but it was not destroyed.

The Flemings said that a miracle had been wrought, and for many a day the more devout among them used to accomplish little pilgrimages to the spot and offer up their devotions; but however this may be, the fact is certain that except upon the feet of the statue no impression was made. Grateful and comparatively happy men were the wounded when, the smoke gradually clearing away, they saw that the danger was passed. They prayed fervently where they lay; and if, amid the excitement of after times, the incident might occasionally be forgotten, it is but common charity to hope and to believe that their forgetfulness could not be perpetual.

The results of the operations, as far as they have been hitherto described, were disastrous enough to the English—to the French they were frightfully so. The infantry of D'Erlon's and Reille's corps was all but disorganized. They had both lost, in killed and wounded, half their strength, and the survivors were necessarily shaken as well in discipline as in spirit. Doubtless it was his knowledge of these facts that induced Napoleon to relieve them by an operation which cannot on any sound principle be justified. He formed his cavalry, of which a large portion had not yet been engaged, into masses, and made ready to send it against the right centre of the English line.

A moment's consideration seemed however to convince him, that till he should be in possession of Hougomont and La Haye Saint, cavalry could not act between them. He therefore directed a fresh assault to be made on the former post by the divisions of Jerome and Foy, while General Donzelat was ordered, at every cost, to gain possession of the latter. But he so arranged his plan of battle, that the advance of the infantry should in some sort be covered by that of the cavalry; and the effect of the combined movement was imposing in the extreme.

The few in that army of raw English levies who were accustomed to the French manner of fighting, knew that a furious cannonade might generally be regarded as a prelude to sharper work. They therefore anticipated, as soon as the fire from the opposite batteries grew thicker and thicker, that more was to follow—and they were not deceived. The Duke had directed his infantry to lie flat on the brow of the hill, while his cavalry stood dismounted, as much sheltered as was possible, behind the ridge; nevertheless round-shot and shell ploughed great gaps in their ranks, and the tumult was awful.

Both infantry and cavalry sustained it with a patience which only British troops can, under like circumstances, display, and bore up against the scarcely less trying effects of the miserable spectacles which everywhere presented themselves; for it is during moments like these that men have time and opportunity to observe the havoc which war has made. On the present occasion, for example, all the slope of their own hill, the valley at its foot, and the rising ground beyond, were studded and strewed with the bodies of the slain.

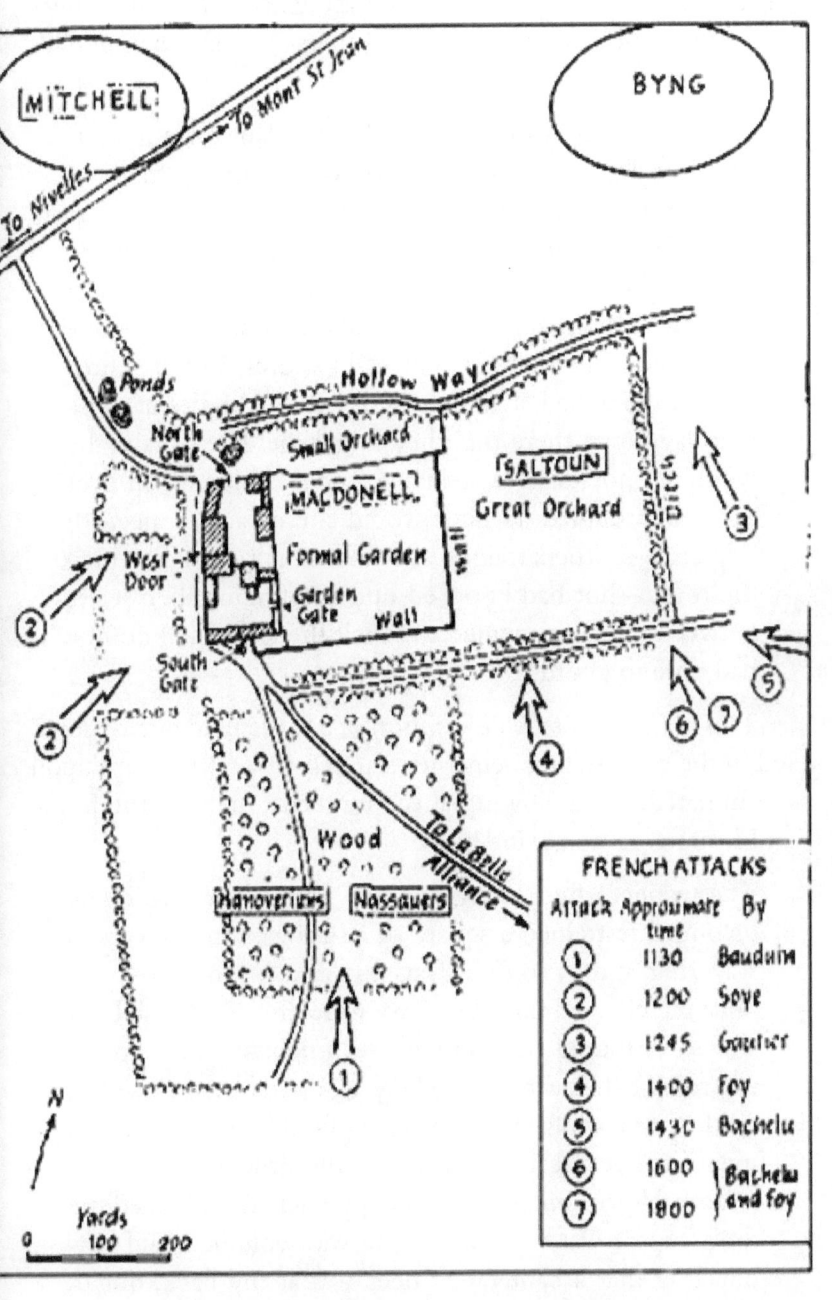

There, too, lay the wounded in their agony, writhing and shrieking where none could afford assistance, while multitudes of horses, some with broken limbs, others dragging their entrails after them, came back to trouble them.

"It was not the least disagreeable attendant on our position," writes a private in a dragoon regiment, "that we stood exactly on such a spot as enabled us to behold the last struggles of the wounded, whose strength only sufficed to carry them a few yards to the rear. There was a long sort of ditch, or drain, some way behind us, toward which these poor fellows betook themselves by scores; and ere three hours were passed, it was choked with the bodies of those who lay down there that they might die. Then again, the wounded horses, of which multitudes wandered all over the field, troubled us. They would come back, some with broken legs, others trailing after them their entrails, which the round-shot had knocked out, and forcing themselves between our files, seemed to solicit the aid which no one had time to afford."

This is a sad but true description of a battle field during some lull in the contest; but, being general, it hardly tells, except upon the initiated. The following anecdote seems more to the point, and I therefore transcribe it:—

The trooper, after stating how the regiment to which he belonged restrained a square of Brunswick infantry from wavering, and by so doing saved it, goes on to say:—
"Having effected this object, we were directed to fall back and to dismount, that our horses might in some measure recruit their strength. Many wounded men passed us while thus resting; but of the case of only one I shall make mention, because it struck me at the time as being very remarkable. An infantry soldier approached, and asked me for a cup of water. I saw that he was wounded, and recollecting that a canteen of beer was at my back, out of which I had been too much engaged to drink myself, I

handed it to him, and desired him to quench his thirst. The poor fellow drank, thanked me heartily, and told me that almost all his regiment—the 28th—was destroyed; then lifting himself from my horse, on which he had been leaning, tottered towards the rear. I watched him, and saw that he had not gone twelve yards before he fell. Almost immediately afterwards his limbs gave a convulsive stretch, and he was a corpse. I went up to him and saw where the fatal ball had taken its course, just above the hip-bone; yet he seemed to die easily, and his voice, not three minutes ere the soul quitted the body, gave scarcely the smallest sign of weakness."

And now, while the extreme right of the Duke's line beyond Hougomont, in the direction of Braine-le-Leud, was threatened by a body of lancers from Pire's corps, crowds of *tirailleurs*, supported by columns in their rear, marched towards the burning *château*, and soon found shelter under the wood. At the same moment, Donzelat's division pushed upon La Haye Sainte, while all the interval between became filled with such a display of horsemen as had never on any previous occasion been looked upon by the most experienced soldier in the Allied lines.

Forty squadrons, of which twenty-one consisted entirely of *cuirassiers*, descended in three lines from the French heights, and at a leisurely pace crossed the valley, and began to mount towards the English position. It was in vain that the Allied artillery tore through their ranks, causing at each discharge great gaps to show themselves. Without once breaking beyond a steady trot, these resolute horsemen continued to advance, their own cannon firing over them with great spirit, as long as they could do so without striking friends as well as foes, till arriving within forty yards of the English guns, they received a last discharge; it was of grape and canister, and told, but it could not stop them.

With a shout, which rent the air, they put their strong horses to their speed, and in a moment the whole of the advanced batteries of the Allies were in their possession. It had been ordered by the Duke of Wellington that his artillerymen should stand to their guns to the latest moment, and then, leaving them where they were, that they should run for shelter behind the squares; for every British and German battalion was by this time in square, and the squares were so distributed along the crest of the glacis as mutually to support one another by covering all the intervals with a cross-fire. I have already told how a young battalion of Brunswickers faltered, and how the coming up of a regiment of British cavalry in its rear restored it to order.

Except in this instance, there was no wavering from one extremity of the line to the other; and as the batteries on both sides had become suddenly mute, and the British infantry, as is their wont, neither spoke nor shouted, a silence more awful than the roar of battle itself prevailed for a moment—but it was only for a moment.

The French cavalry, seeing the calm attitude of an enemy whom they had regarded as entirely overthrown, paused in mid career. The squares looked very formidable, with front ranks kneeling, and the arms of the ranks immediately in the rear levelled to a charging attitude. Nevertheless, the *cuirassiers* would not shrink from the trial. Once again the cry arose, "*Vive l'Empereur!*" and with the noise of thunder they rushed on.

It is impossible to describe with any degree of accuracy the extraordinary scene that followed. The horsemen dashed wildly towards the squares; yet they slackened instead of accelerating their pace as they approached each of them, and at last fell into a walk. Neither did they in any instance dash themselves against the bayonets, but no sooner received a fire, which in the first instance at least was delivered hurriedly, and with imperfect aim, than they broke off from the centre by troops and squadrons, and swept by.

Thus passed the whole line of *cuirassiers*, fairly penetrating beyond the position of the British squares, and seeing before them masses, both of horse and foot, which had not yet been brought into action; while the second and even the third lines, the former consisting of lancers, the latter of *chasseurs*, plunged headlong in the same course, and closely imitated the manoeuvre. The consequence was, that the British infantry became enveloped, and in a great degree hidden, by the enemy, who made, however, no impression upon them, and on whom the file firing, though brisk and well sustained, told with far less effect than they who witnessed and directed it could have previously imagined.

But the British infantry was not left long to sustain the combat single-handed. Lord Uxbridge gathered together as many squadrons as the course of the battle had left available, and launched them against the assailants. They did their duty well, especially the remains of the heavy brigades; and having the advantage of being in good order, they carried for a while all before them. Back over the declivity the French horsemen were borne—*cuirassiers*, lancers, *chasseurs*, all were mingled together, while Uxbridge with his masses hung upon their roar and charged them home; but the pursuers were too few in number to retain the superiority after success had deranged their own ranks.

The enemy rallied under the fire of their guns, which opened as soon as the flight of the horsemen became visible, and assuming the offensive, drove back the English in their turn beyond the squares. And then was played over and over again the game of the previous half hour. Round and round these impenetrable masses the French horsemen rode, individuals closing here and there upon the bayonets, and cutting at the men. But not a square was broken; and a body of cavalry which, had it been wisely handled, might have come in at the close of the day to good purpose, suffered, ere the proper time for using it had arrived, virtual annihilation.

CHAPTER 26

Renewed Attack of Cavalry

The French cavalry was no sooner in motion than the infantry corps allotted for the attack of Hougomont and La Haye-Sainte advanced towards their respective points of operation with great gallantry. On the Hougomont side, as has already been stated, no serious impression was made. Hepburn, with his battalion of Guards, covered the buildings, within which by this time the fire had burned itself out, so that, except in the orchard and by the wood and lane on the other side, not even a partial success was achieved; and even in this quarter the French *tirailleurs* retained their conquests only till the horsemen on the right had begun to give way.

But at La Haye-Sainte the fighting was closer and more desperate, being maintained on the side of the defendants under great disadvantages. The situation and military capabilities of La Haye-Sainte have already been described. The house and outbuildings stand on the slope of the hill about a hundred yards from the Wavre road, and less than half that space in advance of the gravel-pit. The Charleroi road runs between the farmstead and the sandpit, while the orchard stretches downwards to the extent of perhaps three hundred feet, the garden lying on the Mont St. Jean side, and measuring fifty or sixty feet in extent.

There is but one entrance to the court-yard which faces the Charleroi road, and a doorway communicates between the court and the orchard. All on the English right and rear of the pile was solid masonry, through which, by some grievous oversight or another, no aperture had been broken; and the consequence was, that let the battle go as it might, there were no means of reinforcing the garrison except from the Charleroi road. The inconveniences of this arrangement had already been experienced during the pressure of the great infantry attack with which the struggle began. They were still more painfully because more immediately felt now that masses of cavalry swept beyond the farm; indeed, if care had not been taken to strengthen the little garrison during the lull that interposed between the two attacks, the place could not have held out many minutes.

Major Baring, however, having been joined by two companies of green Germans, planted them, together with a detachment from his own battalion, in the garden. With the rest he occupied the house, barn, stables, and other outbuildings, and, abandoning the orchard as too extensive for his force, prepared to make a stout resistance, and hoped to make it an effectual one.

On came the French cavalry, sweeping like a stormy sea up the face of the hill. They soon passed Baring by, driving in the skirmishers which connected him with the main position, and presently Donzelat's infantry moved towards him. They presented a very formidable appearance, marching with a quick yet steady pace along the great road, and covering themselves as usual with clouds of skirmishers. It was not long ere the firing began. The Germans plied their rifles vigorously from loop-hole and window, and over the copings of the wall, behind which they had erected with benches and other articles of furniture a somewhat insecure banquette, and the French replied to them with volleys of musketry.

But the latter soon closed upon the pile, and made determined efforts to force an entrance from the orchard and over the wall wherever it seemed to be accessible. The main attack was of course from the Charleroi road. The assailants found there a large doorway imperfectly, barricaded, and leading into one of the barns. They forced it open, and rushed in with loud cries of "*Vive l'Empereur!*"—but not a man penetrated beyond the threshold. A score of rifles were pointed, and a score of bullets, delivered at the distance of a few feet by steady marksmen, caused a heap of dead to block up in a moment further ingress to the living. The enemy recoiled, and for some minutes contented themselves with pouring into the barn and through the windows and loop-holes a hurricane of shot.

Meanwhile the cavalry having won and lost the whole front of the plateau on which the first line of the Allied army stood, came galloping back in confusion; officers calling to their men to halt and rally, men clamouring as if to drown the voices of their officers; and the English dragoons who hung upon their rear shouting, as is the wont of their countrymen in general, when closing or striving to close with an enemy. Donzelat's infantry could not be expected to look with indifference on such a scene.

Hopes which the rapid and apparently successful progress of their mounted comrades had excited, were all dashed in a moment, and a complete revulsion of feeling ensued. Immediately the whole column began to shake. The retreat commenced, as under such circumstances it usually does, with the rear, who stole off, and melted away company by company. Presently the centre and head of the mass wheeled round, and last of all the parties which had fought so bravely in the orchard and round its walls turned and fled. In five minutes the slope of the English position was once more cleared, and the battle resolved itself for the third time into a languid cannonade.

During the progress of these varied and terrible operations the Duke of Wellington seemed to multiply himself. He was here and there and everywhere—arriving on each point at the precise instant when his presence was most desired, and encouraging the combatants, now by leading on supports, now by the utterance of a few soldier-like words in a calm and cheerful tone of voice.

"Hard pounding this, gentlemen," cried he, as he reined up his horse beside a battalion, through the ranks of which the enemy's shot was tearing; "let's see who will pound longest."

"They fire better than they used to do, I think," was another of his quiet observations, as he stood near a battery and observed with what accuracy the guns from the opposite ridge had got the range.

That he ever threw himself into the heart of a square has not been distinctly proved, neither is it probable; for his duties were those of the commander of a great army, not of a regimental officer. But this much is certain, that from the beginning to the end of the battle he was in the hottest of the fire—exposing himself freely wherever by so doing there appeared to be any chance of accomplishing good—and exhibiting, as throughout life he has always done, the most perfect coolness and self-possession.

How he escaped unhurt is quite inexplicable; how the horse which carried him into the field should have lived to bring him out again, is not less surprising. The officers of his staff, the orderlies which attended him, were killed or wounded to a man. He alone passed through the perils of the day unscathed.

The repulse of Ney's cavalry and the failure of the renewed attempts on La Haye Sainte and Hougomont greatly distressed Napoleon. He himself has spoken of the former as a false movement. He did not intend, at this stage of the battle, to expose the flower of his horsemen to almost certain destruction, and laid the blame of the disasters that followed on Ney's rashness; but the attack having been hazarded, and the troops employed being in full retreat, and, as it appeared to him, in imminent danger, he felt that they must be supported, and for this purpose directed Kellermann to lead his corps of dragoons, *cuirassiers*, and *carabineers* forward.

At the same time, and having a similar object in view, Ney moved Guyot's heavy cavalry of the Guard to the front, and the whole, mustering not fewer than 37 squadrons, formed in rear of the broken force, which had by this time begun to rally. It was beautiful to see how these brave horsemen recovered their ranks, and prepared themselves for a renewal of the struggle; and when they became amalgamated with the fresh squadrons on which they, had rallied, the spectacle presented to the eyes of the looker-on was imposing in the extreme.

These movements in the enemy's line, together with the pushing forward of fresh batteries from the reserve, were not lost upon the Duke of Wellington. He saw that the storm was about to fall where it had fallen already; and, calculating that there could not remain to Napoleon force enough to strike simultaneously in other directions, he determined to strengthen his own centre by contracting the extent of his right wing.

Accordingly Hill, who up to this moment had stood in observation between Braine-la-Leud and Merbe-Braine, was directed to oblique towards his left, which he did, leading Du Plat's infantry brigade of the King's German Legion across the Nivelles road, and closing up Adam with his British regiments immediately in support. At the same time General Chassé was directed to evacuate Braine-la-Leud, and, making a short *détour* by Merbe-Braine, to supply the places of those troops in the second line which the Duke was about to bring into the first. But these changes of position were yet only in progress when a furious cannonade from the opposite heights gave note that the battle was renewed, and in five minutes the whole extent of the field between the Charleroi road and Hougomont was covered with well-dressed lines of horsemen.

To describe how these gallant cavaliers went on—how they swept aside the skirmishers that would have impeded their progress—received but heeded not a well-directed fire of artillery—and charged and wasted their strength in the vain attempt to shake the infantry—would be to tell over again a tale which, having been set forth already, might weary, but could not instruct, in the repetition. Again were the battalions on the brow of the Allied heights thrown into squares which checkered one with another.

Again the British and German artillerymen, after delivering their last fire when scarce twenty yards of space divided them from the enemy, abandoned their guns, in obedience to orders received, and took shelter under the bayonets. Again the French cavalry, instead of charging home, separated from the centres of squadrons, and galloped round the angles of the squares. Not one shook—not one wavered.

"The first time a body of *cuirassiers* approached the square into which I had ridden," writes an engineer officer, "the men—all young soldiers—seemed to be alarmed. They fired high, and with little effect; and in one of the angles there was just as much hesitation as made me feel exceedingly uncomfortable, but it did not last long. No actual dash was made upon us. Now and then an individual more daring than the rest would ride up to the bayonets, wave his sword about, and bully, but the mass held aloof; pulling up within five or six yards as if, though afraid to go on, they were ashamed to retire. Our men soon discovered that they had the best of it; and ever afterwards, when they heard the sound of cavalry approaching, appeared to consider the circumstance as a pleasant change; for the enemy's guns suspended their fire regularly as the horsemen began to crown the ridge, and we suffered so much from their artillery practice, that we were glad when anything put a temporary stop to it. As to the squares themselves, they were as firm as rocks; and the jokes which the men cracked while loading and firing were very comical."

The disposition to treat these cavalry charges as subjects of merriment was not, however, universal in the heterogeneous army of which the Duke of Wellington was at the head. Having failed to make any impression on the front line, which consisted entirely of British and German troops, a large body of the French cavalry passed over the ridge, and sweeping down towards the valley, threatened the Dutch-Belgians in the second line. Great was the commotion in that part of the field, from which whole masses of men began to move off without so much as waiting for musket-shot or stroke of sabre; when Lord Uxbridge again led the wreck of his cavalry to the rescue, and the same scenes which had occurred in the earlier part of the day renewed themselves.

Behind the squares, and in the intervals between, squadrons charged each other, became mingled, and drew off again; till by and by the French, galled by the incessant fusillade to which they were exposed, gave ground. Presently they galloped to the rear, Somerset's brigade pursuing; and Grant's light horsemen, which had come in from the right, following the example, in the direction of Hougomont. But there were infantry columns already on the slope which Somerset could not penetrate. Whereupon Lord Uxbridge, observing that Tripp's brigade of Dutch-Belgian *carabineers* had as yet suffered nothing, having kept its place as long as possible in rear of Mont St. Jean, rode back, and placing himself at its head, ordered a charge.

The *carabineers* heard, but paid no regard to the command: they would not budge a foot; and though Lord Uxbridge upbraided the brigadier, and strove by words and gestures to awaken a right feeling among the men, it was labour lost. Instead of advancing to attack the French, they went to the right about, and, galloping through the 3rd Hussars of the King's German Legion, fairly fled the field. The 3rd German Hussars, weak in point of numbers, and nowise equal in the weight of their horses to the enemy, endeavoured to effect what Tripp's carabineers had avoided. They charged the French heavy cavalry and broke through them; but being outflanked, and sore pressed on all sides, they were forced to retreat.

Seldom has battle-field presented so strange and anomalous a spectacle as that which was offered at the present crisis by the arena whereon the armies of France and England fought. To all appearance the former were masters of the position of the latter. Their cavalry rode round the English infantry at pleasure, and overawed, by strength of numbers, the Allied horse. Scarcely an English gun gave fire. Most of those in the front line were actually in the enemy's possession, the gunners having sought shelter within or along the faces of the squares; while the reserve batteries could not come into action, so completely were friends and foes mingled together. Yet was the *morale* of the English army unbroken.

The infantry stood, wherever placed, as if rooted to the ground. The artillerymen knew that the guns were safe, because they had left neither harness nor limbers in position; and it soon became manifest that the clouds of cavalry which galloped round them were not furnished with means wherewith they might carry off their prize. And if the dragoons held aloof, so to speak, they did so in good order, being conscious that they were not a match for the unbroken strength of their rivals, yet anxiously expecting the moment to arrive when they might meet them on more equal terms.

On the other hand, a soldier's eye could not fail to perceive that there was no reality in the apparent triumph which the French arms had achieved. No infantry columns advanced to secure the ground which the cavalry had won. No batteries ascended the ridge for the purpose of crushing such masses as might be ranged on the opposite side of it. Hougomont on one flank, and La Haye Sainte on the other, rendered all intervals between the Nivelles and the Charleroi roads difficult, and the attempts made to occupy both had failed. It was manifest, therefore, to all who were capable of judging in such cases, that the triumph of the assailants was as remote as at the beginning of the day, and that the Allies, though weakened, were still in excellent plight, and not less determined than ever to hold their ground. Indeed, every minute, as it passed, improved the condition of the latter force as much as it disorganized the former.

The fire of the squares told terribly; while some guns, which crowned the heights above Hougomont, played with fatal precision among the regiments of *cuirassiers* which threatened the Guards, and kept Du Plat's and Adam's brigades on the alert. At last the patience of the French cavalry seemed to fail. After flourishing about for a time, and looking vainly for the support which never came, they fairly wheeled round, and went back, as on a former occasion, at speed, and in great confusion, down the slope into their own valley, and there halted.

It was during this critical moment, when symptoms of wavering on the enemy's part showed themselves, that Lord Uxbridge endeavoured to turn to account some cavalry which had not yet been engaged. The Cumberland Hanoverian Hussars, a well-mounted and handsomely equipped regiment, had hitherto stood at a distance on the Brussels road, rather for show than for use. There seemed to be no very hearty zeal, however, in its commanding officer, Colonel Rulle, who, when the ground to be occupied was pointed out to him, observed that "he did not see what good was to be served by bringing him thither;" but that he would not abide where the commander-in-chief of the cavalry had placed him, nobody went so far as to imagine.

Nevertheless, Colonel Rulle knew better; for scarcely was Lord Uxbridge gone, when, hearing the whistle of some shot about his ears, he wheeled his regiment round and began to withdraw. It was to no purpose that Lord Uxbridge sent an *aide-de-camp* to restrain him; he paid no regard to orders, and seemed deaf alike to remonstrance and reproof, assuring Captain Seymour that he had no confidence in his men, who were, besides, owners of the horses which they rode, and could not afford to lose them. Accordingly, the whole regiment moved off at a brisk trot, though in perfect order, and never drew bridle till they reached Brussels, where they spread a report that the Allied army was destroyed, and that Napoleon at the head of his Guards was advancing.

CHAPTER 27

Continuance of the Battle—Capture of La Haye Sainte

Meanwhile, upon the right of the English line there had been sharp fighting, apart from the defence of Hougomont. Du Plat's Brunswickers being charged by cavalry, stood, after a little wavering, immovable. They were next assailed by a swarm of *tirailleurs en pied,* who, passing through the great orchard, and crowding by its eastern boundary, opened upon the squares a murderous fire. It cut down the gallant Du Plat himself, who fell mortally wounded, the brigade losing at the same time many men and some valuable officers.

And while the ranks yet tottered slightly, because of the gaps which were made in them, a fresh body of *cuirassiers* came on. But the approach of cavalry, though the manoeuvre was thrice repeated, served but to restore to these brave men their accustomed self-confidence. Not a square was broken, not a foot of ground given up; but back behind the shelter of the wood from which they had emerged, the cavalry were time after time driven.

It was at this moment that Adam's brigade, consisting of the 71st, 52nd, and 2nd battalion 95th regiments, with two companies of the 3rd battalion 95th, began to take a prominent part in the struggle: they had reached the reverse side of the slope which looks down upon Hougomont, and were moving upwards to support the Brunswickers, when suddenly the crest of the hill became covered with French infantry, which poured upon the squares. and the artillery stationed near them, a murderous fire. The English gunners fell fast, or retired upon the nearest infantry; and for the first time since the battle began an impression seemed on the point of being made.

The Duke himself at this moment rode through the leaden shower, and put himself at the head of Adam's men. The regiments, by his direction, formed lines four deep; and then, pointing to the enemy on the top of the hill, he said—"Drive these fellows off." No further exhortation was needed. The men raised a shout, and advanced, the 52nd, as the space narrowed, falling so far behind as to form a support to the 71st and 95th; and, gradually quickening their pace as they neared the enemy, they fairly lifted them, so to speak, over the hill.

But it was not intended that they should accomplish more; wherefore Adam, choosing a position with his right shoulder thrown forward, in continuation of Maitland's Guards, brought this part of the line into a sort of curve, and rendered all further attempts by the enemy's cavalry to pierce it utterly fruitless.

In a great battle such as that of which I now write, opportunities for the display of individual valour occur in abundance; though the feats of individuals are so overshadowed by the operations of the mass, that, even if observed at the time, and spoken of for a few days afterwards, they soon pass from men's memories.

It was known and justly estimated, for example, at the time, that Major Ecles, with his company of the 95th Rifles, destroyed more of the enemy's *cuirassiers* that day than he could number men under his immediate command. In like manner a tall, powerful Highlander, Lieutenant John Stuart, of the same noble corps, made himself conspicuous by a hand-to-hand encounter, which, had he been less active and resolute, must have proved his last.

During one of those lulls which occur in all general actions, Stuart and his men lay, in skirmishing order, behind a hedge. About sixty or a hundred yards in front of them, lining in like manner a ditch or hollow, a body of French *tirailleurs* had taken post, and each party continued for a while to watch without molesting the other.

At last a French officer rose out of his own ditch, and either because he really desired to encourage his men, or for the mere purpose of bravado, advanced some space in their front, waving his sword. It would have been easy enough to pick him off, for the Rifles needed no instruction as marksmen in those days; but Stuart would not permit that; on the contrary, his orders were—"Men, keep quiet!" while he himself sprang through the hedge, and ran to meet the French officer.

The latter did not shun the duel. He too was a tall and active-looking man, and in his rapier he had a decided advantage over Stuart, who was armed with the very crooked sabre which it was the fashion in those days for officers of the Rifle corps to carry. The combatants met, and so badly tempered was Stuart's weapon, that at the first pass it broke off, not far from the hilt.

The Frenchman saw his advantage, and prepared to use it. He flourished his sword, as if in defiance, and made a lunge at his adversary's body, which, however, the Highlander received in his left arm, and before a second thrust could be administered, the two men closed. It was the struggle of a moment, and no more—Stuart bore his enemy to the earth, and with the broken piece of his sabre slew him.

These exploits may be regarded as only the by-play in the great drama, of which the action was carried on by a murderous cannonade whereby every regiment in the line suffered, and none more so than the 71st and 2nd battalion 95th. The 52nd came in for its share of loss, and all three, being repeatedly charged by cavalry, repeatedly gave proof of their perfect discipline and indomitable courage. But the time had come when this manner of battle was to undergo a partial change.

It was by this time clear to Napoleon and to the ablest of his lieutenants that a battle of cavalry against infantry and artillery could lead to no decisive results; and that if any impression were to be made upon the English line, a different course of proceeding must be adopted. Something like a lodgement must needs be formed in front of the main position; and this could be done only by taking possession of one or both of the homesteads which acted as advanced posts on the English right and centre. Now, Hougomont had been repeatedly tried, but it seemed to defy the best endeavours of the assailants.

La Haye Sainte had likewise maintained itself well; but La Haye Sainte was not only of smaller compass than Hougomont, but the peculiarities of its position laid it more open to attack and rendered it much less easy of access to support from the rear. Napoleon, therefore, determined to make a great effort in this direction, and sent an *aide-de-camp* to Ney with orders to regulate the movement.

The marshal was nowise indisposed to do his part, but he lacked the means. His cavalry, besides being terribly disorganized, could not act against brick walls and close fences; and the infantry placed at his disposal seemed never to have recovered the effect of their first terrible repulse. Accordingly, he dispatched the chief of his staff to the Emperor with, a request that infantry might be supplied him; and the answer returned bore strong evidence to the unsatisfactory nature of the turn which affairs had taken.

"*Où voulez-vous que j'en procure?*" exclaimed Napoleon, much excited; "*voulez-vous que j'en fasse?*"

And, indeed, the question was become by this time not an immaterial one; for the Prussians were beginning to show themselves, like a threatening cloud, upon the right, and to meet and hold them in cheek Napoleon had already put in motion one whole corps (Lobau's) of the Young Guard.

Colonel Heymes returned to Ney with tidings which, had the latter been a man of ordinary courage and energy, would have cruelly damped his ardour. The Emperor appeared to have lost his self-command; for either there were no reserves available, or he seemed indisposed to bring them into action. Under these circumstances Ney was left without alternative except either to use as well as he could the division of Donzelat, or to give up his last chance of victory. He preferred the former course. Donzelat was ordered to advance against La Haye-Sainte, and to take possession of it. He pushed forward his troops in two heavy columns, covering his advance with crowds of *tirailleurs*, who, driving in the allied skirmishers, soon interposed themselves between the farm and the crest of the position.

Unfortunately for Major Baring, his ammunition, of which he had repeatedly though vainly besought a supply, was by this time quite exhausted. Scarcely three rounds a man remained in the pouches of his followers; and though these gallant fellows nursed them with all imaginable care, it was too manifest that they would not suffice for such an emergency as that which threatened. The furious cannonade with which the enemy prefaced their rush Baring resisted bravely.

As fast as breaches were made in the walls of the garden and the outhouses, his men piled up rubbish and furniture in the spaces; and though their shots came few and far between, not one, as soon as the columns arrived within point blank range, fell harmless. But it was too unequal a contest. The barn and farmhouse took fire. The defenders strove to extinguish the flames, pouring water on them from their camp-kettles; but they could not maintain themselves with their bayonets alone against the swarms by which they were assailed.

To save the lives of the remnant, Baring ordered a retreat, which was effected by twos and threes into the garden. Not even here, however, could a stand be made. The brave Germans were forced to flee, the enemy showing no mercy wherever-they overtook them; for cries for quarter were disregarded at that frightful hour, and frightful atrocities were perpetrated. One or two specimens of the manner in which the French on that occasion used their partial success may not be out of place.

Loath to abandon a post which had been intrusted to him, Baring clung to the farmhouse of La Haye-Sainte long after, in the ordinary sense of the term, it could be said to be tenable. His men had expended their last cartridge; the enemy had won the great barn door, were mounted upon the roof of the building, had torn off the tiles, and were firing down upon the Germans. The cry of these gallant fellows was still the same: "No man will desert you; we will fight and die with you;" and with their bayonets they effectually resisted every endeavour that was made to close. But at last the officers, who had behaved throughout with heroic courage, assured him that farther resistance was hopeless. Then, and only then, he gave the order to retreat.

There was a narrow passage leading through the house to the garden in the rear: as the Germans fell back through this the French broke in from the opposite side, and a hand-to-hand struggle ensued, which cost some valuable lives on both sides. But it was not of long duration. The enemy's pouches were full, those of the Germans empty; and the fire which the former poured down the narrow passage told awfully. On this occasion a young officer seeing a French soldier level his piece at a comrade ran him through. He himself was almost instantly disabled by a musket-shot in the arm, and, in the hurry of his flight and the confusion caused by his wound, he rushed into a chamber and took shelter under the bed.

Two of his men followed, with a dozen Frenchmen at their heels, who never paused to offer quarter. "*Pas de pardon à ces coquins verds*," shouted they; and in a moment the two poor fellows fell riddled with wounds. The young officer who witnessed all this, happily escaped detection; and, lying close for some time, was enabled at the end of the day to return to his friends.

Baring retreated with the remains of his detachment to the main position, and La Haye-Sainte remained in the hands of the enemy. The shouts with which they proclaimed their success bore testimony to their sense of its importance; and forthwith renewed attempts were made to carry Hougomont in like manner.

But one after another they failed. There the English were immovable. There was no let or hindrance to the supply both of arms and ammunition, as these might be wanted; and a well-served artillery gave efficient support to the garrison of the chateau: wherefore the enemy died by hundreds as fast as they renewed their attempts on the place, without making the slightest progress. Nor were the attempts, though resolutely made, against the centre more prosperous. They succeeded, indeed, in driving the rifles from the sandpit which they had so long occupied.

They endeavoured to shake Kempt's brigade by a fire of grape, which these same rifles soon silenced. They collected masses of skirmishers in the orchard and garden, and sent them against the troops which guarded the Wavre road, and who, momentarily expecting a return of the French cavalry, still stood in squares. Such a mode of attack could not but harass, and prove very destructive to life; for the square, though an admirable formation against horsemen, is the worst that can be chosen if the battle be against musketeers.

Wherefore, the Prince of Orange getting irritated, rode up to Colonel Ompteda, and desired him to deploy a battalion into line and charge. Ompteda ventured to remonstrate, but his arguments were overcome. He therefore deployed the 5th battalion and advanced; whereupon the French *tirailleurs* gave way, as he had anticipated, and took shelter in the garden of La Haye Sainte. The line followed, and might have dashed at the fence had not a body of French *cuirassiers* come up at the moment. They fairly rolled the Germans up, and cut the battalion to pieces.

The cavalry attack which proved thus fatal to the 5th line battalion of the King's German Legion was the first of a series which Ney now launched in support of his infantry in La Haye Sainte. They were uninterruptedly renewed for the full space of an hour, and though quite as profitless as those which had preceded them in regard to any impression made upon the squares, they afforded ample opportunity for the display of gallantry on both sides.

Moreover, they were supported, from time to time, with infantry, which crept up the slope, crowned the ridge in loose order, and threw upon the lines and squares that were beyond it a hurricane of bullets. The latter fell in great numbers, and it seemed well-nigh as if the spirits of the Germans were becoming exhausted. It was observed that greater care was taken to remove the wounded from the field than had been exhibited during any previous period in the action, and more than one regiment complained that its ammunition was expended.

Still the strength of the British infantry was unbroken; and the cavalry, though much crippled, exhibited no symptoms of uneasiness. Moreover, though Adams's and even Lambert's brigades had come into action, there was still a reserve, stronger perhaps in numbers than in the composition of the greater portion of it, which had not yet fired a shot. It was manifest, therefore, to both parties that the victory, on which Napoleon early in the morning had counted, was yet to be won; and far as the day had advanced, for it was by this time close upon seven o'clock in the evening, appearances denoted that he had not altogether despaired of achieving it.

CHAPTER 28

Advance of the Prussians—Attack from La Haye-Sainte

All this while the advanced corps of the Prussian army under Bülow was struggling to reach the scene of action against such difficulties as would have tried the endurance of any troops in the world; they won their way slowly and with weary steps from Wavre across the defile of St. Lambert, and plunged by and by into the still more impracticable defile of the Lasne.

Here every step which the men took sank them to their ankles; the horses floundered; guns and carriages stuck fast, and only by manual labour could the latter be extricated: for the soil of this valley being rich and fat, the heavy rains of the 17th had converted it into a swamp; and as the roads which traversed it were without metal or other means of hardening, they, too, became, after a little use, well nigh impracticable.

"We cannot get on," exclaimed the soldiers, worn out with continued exertions.

"We must get on," was Blücher's answer, as he rode from battalion to battalion and from battery to battery, speaking words of encouragement to all. "The English expect us; I have told Wellington that we will be up; and we must get up, be the consequences what they may."

The Prussians are a gallant people, and their courage that day was only to be equalled by their patience. They toiled on; and at last, between four and five in the afternoon, though leading squadron of their cavalry, belonging to the 2nd regiment of Silesian Hussars, passed through the wood of Wavre to a point near Frischermont, whence all the positions and movements of the two great armies then engaged became visible to them.

The detachment in question was commanded by Major Von Lütow, a soldier well trained and of considerable experience in the field. He saw in a moment that the enemy had committed a grievous error in leaving the wood of Paris unoccupied, and rode back to communicate the fact to his superiors. He met by the way General Von Gröllman, who received his report and understood it; and immediately the entire regiment of Silesian hussars, with two battalions of infantry, were pushed forward; the latter threw themselves into the wood, the former drew up in rear of it, and all remained still, though much on the alert, waiting the arrival of fresh reinforcements.

Time passed; and each new hour and moment increased the toil of the Prussians in their march. The defile of St. Lambert became continually more difficult of passage; so that five o'clock had struck before two additional brigades of infantry, with cavalry and guns, reached the high ground that intervenes between the Lasne and Smohain.

These were instantly formed; the artillery in the road, the infantry in the wood to the right and left of it, and the cavalry in the rear; and a brief halt took place. But Blücher, who had intended to await the coming up of more troops, became impatient at the sound of the cannonade in front of Waterloo; and noticing a stir among the enemy's reserves in rear of La Belle Alliance, determined to commence operations at once.

With this view he debouched from the wood, and opened a cannonade upon Domont's cavalry, which preserved its ill-chosen and useless line where some hours previously it had halted. Domont pushed forward, and an affair of cavalry occurred, in which the French had rather the advantage; but the fire of the Prussian guns checked the pursuit, and Domont fell back.

Blücher's attack could not fail to be feeble at this time, because the force at his disposal was very small, but it had the effect of alarming Napoleon, who judged that there must be strong supports behind; and therefore detached General Lobau, with the 6th corps, to resist it: the latter executed this movement with alacrity and precision, while the ground which he vacated was filled up with regiments of the Old and Middle Guard; and now began an affair which, waxing continually more fierce, ended at last in a desperate struggle. To the Prussians engaged reinforcements arrived continually.

At five o'clock, they fought with three brigades of infantry, two regiments of cavalry, and a few guns; at six, they had brought thirty battalions, twenty-seven squadrons, and sixty-four guns into action. It was in vain that Lobau endeavoured to withstand them with sixteen battalions, eighteen squadrons, and forty-two guns. He was forced to give ground; and abandoning Planchenoit against which their principal force seemed to be directed, he drew off in good order towards the Charleroi road.

It was at this critical moment, when his rear and right were threatened, and the enemy in his front stood immovable, that Napoleon received Ney's urgent call for a supply of fresh infantry. He had none to spare; he was even forced to weaken the reserve column which had heretofore been preserved intact, in order to cheek the advance of the Prussians;—and to detach General Duhesme, with two divisions of the Young Guard.

His answer to the marshal was, therefore, such as elsewhere has been described—the reverse of courteous; but it was forced from him. Indeed, his whole bearing at this moment became that of a man who felt his destiny hinge upon the turn of a die. He could not retreat, as other men in his situation might have done; reverse and defeat would be alike fatal to his political existence; and hence there seemed to remain no alternative between complete success and entire destruction.

Accordingly, while Duhesme marched upon Planchenoit, and Lobau resumed the offensive between that post and Smohain, he himself watched with intense anxiety the progress of Ney's attack. It seemed for a moment to go well. La Haye-Sainte was taken; he saw his infantry clustering up the slope. and his cavalry sweep once more over the ridge; and he turned his eyes next in the direction of Planchenoit, where the cannonade grow momentarily more severe. He observed the formation of the Prussian columns which were destined for the attack. He saw Duhesme throw himself into the village; and by and by a warm skirmishing fire told that the action was begun: it was a fierce assault, and it was met as bravely as it was given.

The Prussians forced their way into the churchyard, and lined its walls; they were swept from the roofs and windows of the houses which overlooked it, and, after sustaining a heavy loss, were driven out again. Napoleon observed this, and noticed, at the same time, that the wood of Paris glittered with bayonets, and that along the Wavre road, in the direction of Smohain, and along the rear of the allied posts at Papelotte, fresh columns were advancing. He could not hide from himself the truth—that the next hour must decide his fate; and he resolved to hazard all upon one cast, and to overthrow the English—or perish.

With this view he directed General Drouet to collect as many battalions of the Guard as still remained in reserve, and to lead them forward from the position which they had hitherto maintained, and form them in front of La Belle Alliance. D'Erlon and Reille were, at the same time, instructed to gather together the remains of their respective corps, and to dispose them for a movement in advance simultaneous with that which the Guard was about to hazard.

They were to fall upon the centre of the English line, making good use of the farm of La Haye-Sainte, and to pass column after column from behind the shelter which it afforded till the physical powers of the defendants should be worn out. The Guard, meanwhile, was to pass Hougomont, and to fall upon the left centre of the main English position; while the cavalry—all such, at least, as remained—should move *en masse* in support, to be ready to improve the victory when won.

As a necessary prelude to this closer fighting, every gun and howitzer which could be brought to bear opened its fire, and tremendous as had often before been the shower of shot and shell which they were called upon to sustain, it seemed to the British leader and his noble troops that the present exceeded them all.

Not unobserved by the Duke of Wellington were these preparations made. He had long expected some such crisis to arrive, and on looking round upon the gaps which were already made in his line, and knowing how severely the endurance of the survivors had been tried, it is little to be wondered at if he contemplated the coming struggle with some anxiety.

Often, and with an eager glance, had his eyes been turned of late to the quarter whence he expected the Prussians. He had seen their cavalry patrols early in the day, and not unnaturally reckoned on the speedy coming up of the main body; and when hour after hour rolled on without bringing the co-operation which had been promised, it is not surprising that he should have been anxious— if not uneasy.

At the same time the Duke had perfect confidence in himself and in his army. It had held its ground heretofore nobly—he did not doubt that it would hold its ground still; and he knew that in the event of the worst, there was Colville's division, with the Prince Frederick of Holland's Dutch troops, at Hal; which, though they might not be able to take part in the battle of the 18th, would come in good time to share his fortunes of the 19th, whatever these, might be.

Still, the looks which he cast towards Smohain and along the Wavre road were many and eager; and he finally dispatched Colonel Fremantle, his *aide-de-camp*, to hasten the advance of such corps as he might encounter on that route, and to direct them towards the points in his own line where he felt himself to be weakest.

The cannonade with which Blücher announced his arrival at the outskirts of the wood of Paris, was heard at the English headquarters as well as at the French. How it affected Napoleon has already been explained. On the Duke it operated only thus far—that it caused him to turn his glass in the direction of Planchenoit, which is, however, so completely hidden from view when crossing the heights of Mont. St. Jean, that only the spire of the village church can be discerned.

The Duke gazed, and soon saw the uprising of smoke over the trees. Had the roar of artillery closer at hand been loss incessant, he might have been able, likewise, to detect the fitful progress of the battle; but under existing circumstances the utmost which he could discern was this: that with a greater or a lesser force the Prussian leader was coming into action.

Let it not be supposed that even this remote vision of help was without its effect, he saw that Blücher was true to his word. His troops beheld nothing except the formidable outline of the masses which were collected to assault them, and the incessant flash of the innumerable guns which sent death continually among their ranks. Not a man's heart, however, failed him. Regiments stood to be mowed down like grass before the reaper. Their commanders sent frequent messages to their chief, begging that reinforcements might be furnished, and representing that they were cut to pieces.

But when the answer was, "There are no reinforcements to send you—you must hold out, and all will be well," to a man they obeyed, and faced death as became them; and finally, when the Duke himself rode along the line, encouraging his diminished battalions, and addressing some short, expressive, and appropriate words to each, the enthusiasm of all who heard was raised to the highest pitch. Destroyed they might be, but to break through them was impossible; and the Duke understanding this fully, never lost for one moment his calmness and self-possession.

Meanwhile, on the side of the French, preparations for the final and the heaviest blow which had yet been struck were in progress. Napoleon determined that the Guard should advance in two columns, four battalions composing each, and two being kept as a reserve. One was to bear upon the centre of the English right; the other was to move somewhat in support, though nearer to Hougomont, and therefore more to the French left.

The interval between these masses, as well as that which divided the remains of Reille's from D'Erlon's corps, was to be filled up with cavalry, whose business it should be to sustain the infantry when overmatched, and to make the most of whatever advantages they should succeed in achieving. At the same time, or rather in anticipation of these movements, Donzelat's division, which had gathered in and around La Haye-Sainte, was to dash forward.

If he could but pierce one section of the English line, Napoleon flattered himself that the separated portions would soon give way; and he hoped, by constant attacks upon the centre, either to destroy the troops which composed it, or to draw off from the right such an accumulation of support as would secure in that direction an easy victory. His plan was good, and his manner of acting upon it soldier-like and skilful. Let us see how the Duke disposed the wreck of his army to counteract it.

With the exception of Grant's brigade on the right, and those of Vandeleur and Vivian, which guarded the extreme left of the position, almost all the British and German cavalry was by this time destroyed. The household and hussar brigades could not muster between them two strong squadrons; and Arentschildt's cavalry regiments, as well as those of Dornberg, were not in a better plight. Moreover, the infantry, especially that portion of it which held the ridge above La Haye-Sainte, was diminished to a speck.

Ompteda's brigade had been cut to pieces. Those of Pack and Kempt were reduced to mere skeletons; and Lambert's, though it had come comparatively late into action, was severely thinned in its numbers. By great good fortune the heads of some Prussian regiments showed themselves at this critical juncture on the Wavre road, and Fremantle, meeting them, requested General Zieten, their commander, to act as the Duke had suggested. But Zieten did not feel disposed to isolate his brigade; whereupon Vivian, being aware that there was a grievous want of cavalry in the centre, committed the protection of the left of the line to the new comers, and moved with his brigade in the direction of the Charleroi road.

He was soon afterwards followed by Vandeleur; and the whole

took post in rear of Kruse's Nassauers, who had exhibited much gallantry throughout the day, but were by this time so exhausted that serious apprehensions began to be entertained in regard to their continued steadiness.

Simultaneously with this march of cavalry from the left, a change of disposition was effected on the right, whereby Du Plat's Brunswickers took ground in the direction of La Haye-Sainte, and stationed themselves in continuation between the divisions of Halkett and Alton. Maitland's and Adam's brigades being thus left without support, there presently marched into their rear a Dutch-Belgian division, of which General Chassé was at the head, while Vandeleur's cavalry, passing Vivian's by, drew up as a reserve to the whole. At the same time every gun, which was not disabled either in itself or by the destruction of the artillerymen, took post to the front; and finally the orchard of Hougomont, with the woods and hollow ways that flanked it, were filled with men.

These arrangements were yet in progress, when forth from the inclosures of La Haye-Sainte Donzelat's division came pouring. It were profitless to tell with what daring intrepidity these gallant fellows pushed to the very ridge of the height. They advanced in dense skirmishing order, and kept down so completely the fire of the light infantry which opposed them, that several pieces of artillery succeeded in getting within a hundred yards of the allied line, and plied it with grape.

This terrible fire occasioned great havoc, especially among Kielmansegge's Hanoverians. Two battalion squares suffered from it the annihilation of two whole faces respectively; while the remains of Ompteda's brigade of the King's German Legion may be said to have ceased to exist. No wonder if, under such circumstances, Kruse's Brunswickers wavered, and were restrained from breaking into a disorderly flight only by the resistance which Vivian's horsemen opposed to it.

But assistance came with Du Plat's Brunswickers, though not till the gallant Prince of Orange had rallied the Nassau regiments, and led them to the charge. In this *mêlée* he was himself severely wounded in the shoulder, and the troops, whom his example and that alone had animated to the fight, again gave way. Then came the Brunswickers into the line. They fought bravely, but were in their turn overpowered. The Duke himself rallied them, and Vivian with his hussars kept them in their places, and the battle was renewed. It did not long continue in this direction; for Napoleon had hazarded his last throw elsewhere, and failed.

CHAPTER 29

Attack of the Imperial Guard

The operations thus inadequately described were in full progress, when Napoleon, having formed his Guard in two columns and a reserve, took post in front of the farm of La Belle Alliance, and caused those magnificent battalions to file past. No human being ever knew better than he how to act a part. He spoke to the elite of his troops, many of whom were gray-haired men and covered with the scars of old wounds; and reminding them of former triumphs, told in few but well-chosen words how much was that day expected of them.

Ney was at their head, with Friant, Michel, and others, whom they both knew and respected; and these setting an example of heroic fortitude and self-devotion, the best possible spirit animated the masses. They marched by within a few paces of the Emperor: they answered his appeal with loud cries,—and in due time the face of the slope was covered with masses, which gradually diverged, column after column, each into the line of attack which it was designed that it should follow.

While the Imperial Guard yet covered the ridge of La Belle Alliance, and for a brief space after its roar had passed down on the descent, there was a cessation in the firing of the French artillery, which struck the lookers on upon the opposite height with a feeling of awe. It was like the lull in a storm, which speaks of fiercer blasts to come, when the clouds seem pausing only to collect their strength; and which the mariner observes with increased anxiety, being nowise deceived by it into a forgetfulness of the true nature of his position. In like manner the British troops and their leader perfectly understood that the respite of the moment would be followed by a terrible *denouement.*

They hastened, therefore, to make for the event the best preparations which circumstances would admit of,—and left the issue to a higher power. Wherever the arrangement could be effected without inconvenience, the Duke withdrew his people behind his own ridges, and there caused them to lie down. Where this appeared to be impracticable, there was nothing for it but to keep the ground already occupied, and dare all consequences.

Meanwhile the light infantry threw themselves among the woods of Hougomont, and behind the shelter of every hedge, and ditch, and hollow, that presented itself. The cavalry also shifted its ground, so as to become massed in the centre and on the right of the line—all apprehension in the direction of Papelotte and La Haye being by this time at an end; while the artillery was distributed well nigh in a semicircle, of which one apex rested on the Charleroi road and the other on Hougomont. The following was, therefore, the order in which, at this critical moment, the allied army stood:—

> The first line was held on the extreme left by Prince Edward of Saxe Weimar's division. Upon him the Prussians touched through Smohain; while a portion of their cavalry was coming rapidly into a second line, behind him, by the Wavre road. Best's brigade came next; then Lambert's; then Ompteda and Kruse; Halkett rounded the curve; then came Maitland, then Adam; with H. Halkett and Du Plat touching the orchard of Hougomont. Hougomont itself was filled with Byng's people, while the ravines and difficult country beyond it, falling away in the direction of Braine-la-Leud, were guarded by Brunswickers. In immediate support of these troops stood Kempt's and Pack's brigades in rear of Lambert; Kielmansegge covering Kruse; and the Dutch-Belgian corps of D'Aubrune behind Maitland and Adam; while they in their turn were observed

and supported by the cavalry; the British and German horse being close to the infantry, the Dutch-Belgian considerably thrown back to the rear.

And all were silent as the grave. Fear there was none. The men composing that front line of battle knew no fear; but there was a solemn and serious feeling that a crisis was at hand, and each braced up his nerves to meet it. And they did no more than the occasion required.

The Imperial Guard descended the height of La Belle-Alliance, the two columns into which it had been formed gradually diverging. One bore obliquely to its left, skirted the inclosures of Hougomont, and advanced against the point in the Allied line which Adam held with his brigade. The other directed its march more upon the centre of the position, seeking, as it were, to break the line where Maitland with his Guards took it up.

But the two movements were not quite simultaneous. The column on the French right got a start of full ten minutes—an amount of time if which in the progress of a battle the importance is incalculable. Nor did either of them undertake the combat without assistance; m the contrary, every disposable man, both of infantry and cavalry, joined in this attack. Eastward of the Charleroi road D'Erlon's corps pushed forward in *échelon* of columns, of which that on the left bore down upon Lambert's brigade, while his extreme right was engaged with the Prussians.

Westward of the same avenue, Reille in like manner spread himself; some of his battalions penetrating into the wood of Hougomont, others passing round it further to the right, and a third portion ascending the slope, so as to strike at the centre of the English line. Moreover the whole of the cavalry rode forward in support, with the exception of the divisions for which Bülow had already cut out work, and a hundred pieces of cannon entering into battery on the summit of the nearest ridge halted and unlimbered.

It were vain to attempt a description either of the front thus presented to the English, or of the strong moral effect necessarily produced upon them. They looked round, and saw their own numbers diminished to a fraction: brigades had dwindled into battalions, battalions into companies.

Of the heavy cavalry scarcely enough remained to make, at open order, the show of a line; and as to the Dutch-Belgians, sufficient proof had already been given that, let the cause be what it might, they were not to be depended upon. At the same time let justice always be done to the generals and to the majority of the rest of the officers. No man's gallantry surpassed that day the gallantry of the Prince of Orange. Leader truer to the cause which he served than Chassé—and others whom it is unnecessary to name—it were vain to look for.

And the Dutch soldiers wherever they served alone were, on the 18th of June, 1815, as stanch and brave as they have uniformly proved themselves to be, both as the allies and the enemies of the British army. But their efficiency was marred through the unfortunate intermingling in their ranks of men who had neither taste nor feelings in common with them; and the attempt to force whom into the heart of the Dutch nation was shown, within fifteen years subsequently, to have been idle from the first.

Still, even in the Dutch regiments, marred as they were by the intermixture with Belgians, the English that day put no reliance; and hence the effect of a glance round the field was to satisfy every man who made it that if they were to escape defeat, and consequent destruction, they must owe both safety and triumph to their own exertions.

It has already been stated that so long as the Imperial Guard covered the crest and upper slope of the heights of La Belle Alliance, the French batteries remained quiet: no sooner, however, was the rear column fully beneath the muzzles of the guns than the latter opened with a rapidity, weight, and precision such as they had not exhibited during any previous portion of the day. Round-shot and howitzer-shells tore through the ranks of the regiments which were visible, and struck down mounted men by hundreds.

Even the ricochet of that iron hail brought death into masses which imagined that they were tolerably secure from danger, and sent more than one in full and disorderly flight along the road to Brussels. Vainly did the English artillery, over-matched both in numbers and weight of metal, strive to keep down this storm. Gun after gun was struck and upset, horses were killed, men destroyed; yet the gallant blue-jackets kept their ground as they have always done, and reserved their strength for an occasion which drew rapidly towards them.

Down the slope went the leading column of the Guard, the detached masses of D'Erlon's corps operating an effective diversion in their favour. Now they were in the hollow—now they began to ascend the lower wave of ground which intervenes between the positions of the two armies—now they crown this height, and while their own guns cease firing for a space, those on the external slope of the English position open with terrible effect. Now the shot plunged and smashed among the companies as they went over that ridge! Now one after another their files seemed to be wrenched asunder by the weight of the salvos that greeted them. But they never paused for a moment.

The survivors closed up into the spaces which the dead and wounded had left, and in due time the entire mass was again under cover of a valley; then the French batteries renewed their fire, and so fierce and incessant was it that the uninitiated bystander might have been apt to imagine that a desire to take vengeance on the slayers of their countrymen had animated these vigorous cannoneers. But it could not last long. By and by the leading sections began to breast the English hill. In a few minutes they were so far advanced that their friends did not dare to fire over them, and then feeling, as it were, their hands freed, the English gunners once more plied their trade.

It was positively frightful to witness the havoc that was occasioned in that mass, which did not, however, slacken its pace, or lose, to all appearance, its enthusiasm. There died General Michel, a brave man, whom the soldiers loved and respected; there fell Friant, sorely wounded, and there too the horse of

Marshal Ney, who rode at the head of the column, being struck with a cannon-shot, rolled under his rider. Nothing dismayed, Ney extricated himself from his dead charger, and drawing his sword continued to advance on foot, while a cloud of skirmishers rushing forward, drove in the light troops of the English, in spite of a stout resistance, and crowned the summit.

Rapidly, though at a fearful cost of life, the column passed the line of fire along which the English guns told, and then they became silent. In like manner there was a complete cessation on the side of the enemy—the sharp, quick, and ceaseless tiraillade of the skirmishers keeping up the game of death. To be sure Hougomont, and the woods and inclosures about it sent forth volumes of musketry, while at more remote parts of the line, and especially in the direction of Planchenoit, the cannonade continued in its fury.

But just where the Imperial Guard were moving there was silence, except when the shouts of the advancing veterans broke it. Just at this moment the Duke rode up, and planted himself beside a battery of guns which stood on the brow of the ridge, a little to the right of the ground on which Maitland's brigade were lying. He spoke to Lieutenant Sharpe, and learned from him that Captain Bolton having just been killed, the guns were commanded by the second-captain, Napier.

"Tell him," said his Grace, "to keep a lookout on his right, for the French will soon be with him:" and they were so; for scarcely had the message been conveyed to Captain Napier, when the bear-skin caps of the enemy began to show themselves over the summit.

A cloud of *tirailleurs* instantly opened upon the guns a storm of shot. It was answered by a salvo of grape and canister, which cleared the whole front of the battery in an instant, and forthwith the same iron hail came pouring back into the head of the column which was already within fifty yards of their muzzles. It stands upon record, that these veterans were absolutely astounded when they saw before them nothing more than six field-pieces with the gunners attached, and a few mounted officers in their rear. They did not know that the Duke himself was one of them, neither were they prepared for the apparition which seemed the next moment to rise from the earth to confront them.

For then, whether by the talismanic words which have become a portion of history, or by some other signal, is a matter of no moment, the Duke, and none other, gave the signal to Maitland, which the latter understood, and promptly obeyed. In a line four deep, the brigade of Guards started from the ground. They gazed only so long upon their enemies as to direct their aim, and forthwith threw in a volley, of which, when the smoke had cleared away, the effect was seen: the column was literally torn to pieces. Some hundreds of dead covered the plateau. The rest staggering and reeling endeavoured to deploy, but in vain: for while Napier's guns ploughed through their flanks, Maitland's noble musketeers cut them down by sections.

"Now's the time!" shouted Lord Saltoun, simultaneously with Maitland's order to charge, and in an instant the masses were mingled. Down went the enemy headlong. It was to no purpose that the officers stepped out, waving their swords, and encouraging the men to rally. It was equally in vain that the men themselves struggled to get into order, and answered the fire of their opponents with desultory discharges. Time for formation there was none; but broken, dispersed, and for all offensive purposes utterly useless, these—the very flower and pride of the French army—ran down the slope, with the British Guards close at their heels.

Meanwhile there was close and warm fighting everywhere else. On the left of Maitland, Halkett, on whom the command of Alton's division had devolved, was fiercely engaged with Donzelat's troops, whom he bore back from the forward position which they had taken up, and whence they might have fallen upon Maitland to great advantage.

On his right, also, there was a fierce struggle: for the second column of the Imperial Guard was in this direction winning its way, more slowly indeed than the force which Maitland had overthrown, but not with a less steady and determined movement. In this direction, too, clouds of skirmishers were thrown out, which entered into a close and warm altercation with the British riflemen and some companies of the 52nd which supported them. And here, as well as elsewhere, the English artillery performed prodigies of valour. So sure, so sustained, so deadly was their fire, that the enemy, after passing the skirts of the inclosure, swerved considerably to the right, and taking advantage of a little hollow, pushed under such cover as it could afford somewhat towards the flank of Maitland's troops.

This false movement did not escape Adam, or the officers who served under him. Colonel Colborne (now Lord Seaton), who that day commanded the 52nd, changed the front of his regiment so as to bring its line directly upon the flank of the French column, and paused only till his brigadier should have time to lead up the 71st, so as to head it. Meanwhile, however, Maitland observing the direction which this fresh attack had taken, ordered his men to halt. They did so, and without the slightest confusion; turned, as if by word of command, ran back to the ridge from which they had descended; and at the word "halt!—front!—form!" were once more in perfect order.

It was not so with the troops in the rear. There stood D'Aubrune's brigade of Dutch-Belgians, out of the line of fire, hidden from the very view of the enemy. They had been brought thither, as elsewhere described, in order to support the weakened first line, but that they had no spirit for the fight was now shown.

They heard the cries of "*Vive l'Empereur!*"—they saw the English Guards come rushing back to the ridge whence a moment previously they had gone down with the step of conquerors—and without pausing to learn for what purpose the retrograde movement had been made, they instantly fell into confusion. That they did not in a body follow their comrades to Brussels, was owing to the determined interference of Vandeleur's cavalry, which, closing the intervals of squadrons, would not permit them to pass. But what could be done with such troops?

What possible reliance was to be placed upon them? Happily there was no need to look for succour in this quarter. The 52nd were on the flank of the 2nd column of the Imperial Guard. The 71st and 95th headed it. The three regiments poured such a fire simultaneously into the mass, that it melted like snow under the sunshine. At the same time there was as little disposition in this quarter to abandon the field for trifles as elsewhere.

Moreover, a body of *cuirassiers*, galloping up at the moment, charged the 52nd, which, without changing its four deep line formation, received and repelled the attack, while a squadron of the 23rd light dragoons galloping past completed the confusion among these mailed horsemen which the musketry fire had created. Then too, after Napier's guns had done their work sufficiently, Maitland once more descended from his mountain throne, and the two brigades enveloping the devoted column, swept it from the field.

What a scene ensued! Chassé's battalions, not knowing who were beaten or who victorious, broke their ranks in the rear, and fairly fled—at least some of them—while the English in their front were driving the enemy before them. And so it was everywhere else: D'Erlon's people could sustain the combat no longer; Reille was shivered, and his order entirely lost; indeed, there was wanting only a general advance of the British line to complete the victory. It came in good time.

CHAPTER 30

Close of the Battle—Bivouac of the British Army

It will be necessary for a moment to look back to the proceedings of the Prussians, whom we left bringing their troops into action as rapidly as they could, and though repulsed in an attempt to take possession of Planchenoit, re-forming their masses and preparing again to push them on the village. It was not exclusively in this direction, however, that Blücher strove to bring support to his allies.

Along the Wavre road his cavalry was advancing, and gradually falling in on the left rear of Best's brigade, while lower down, through Smohain and La Haye, other troops, some of them infantry, showed themselves. These materially strengthened the extreme left of the English line, and being comparatively fresh, soon entered into the battle. In particular the Prussian artillery proved of essential service, for the Hanoverian batteries in this direction had expended their ammunition, and, as the infantry and cavalry came up, they descended into the ravine, and prepared to move upon the right of the enemy's line.

Thus, just at the moment when the English had repelled the final attack of the Imperial Guard, when D'Erlon's and Reille's corps were both completely disorganized, when the French cavalry, mowed down by the fire of infantry and cannon, were powerless to resist the rush which Lord Uxbridge was about to make upon them, the gallant Prussians came into play, and a defeat, already achieved, was converted into annihilation; for all means of rallying even a rearguard ceased.

At the same time let it be borne in mind, to the honour of the French, that on the extreme right they still presented a firm and well-arranged front. Lobau's corps was unbroken, and though overmatched, it faced Bülow stoutly. In Planchenoit, likewise, the Young Guard maintained themselves in spite of Pirch's repeated and desperate efforts to dislodge them: indeed, the progress made in this direction was very slow, for the gallant assailants purchased every foot of ground at an expense of life which was-fearful.

Still, the knowledge that he was assailed on the flank and well nigh in the rear could not fail of extinguishing in the mind of Napoleon whatever ray of hope might have yet lingered there. He cast a hurried glance over the field of battle. He saw his Guards coming back in wild confusion, and strewing the earth with their dead. He looked round for his cavalry, and beheld but broken squadrons fleeing for life, yet failing to secure it.

His guns were either dismounted or abandoned by their artillerymen, and there was no reserve on which to fall back. Then it was that the terrible words escaped him, which will be remembered and repeated as often as the tale of his overthrow is told: "*Toute est perdue—sauve qui peut!*" was his last order, and turning his horse's head, he galloped from the field.

It was now eight o'clock in the evening, or perhaps a little later. The physical strength of the combatants on both sides had become well nigh exhausted, and on the part of the English there was a feverish desire to close with the enemy, and bring matters to an issue. Up to the present moment, however, the Duke had firmly restrained them.

For all purposes of defensive warfare they were excellent troops; the same blood was in their veins which had stirred their more veteran comrades of the Peninsula, but, as has elsewhere been explained, four-fifths of the English regiments wore raw levies—second battalions to manoeuvre with which in the presence of a skilful enemy might have been dangerous.

Steadily therefore, and with a wise caution, the Duke held them in hand, giving positive orders to each of his generals that they should not follow up any temporary success, so as to endanger the consistency of their lines, but return after every charge to the crest of the hill, and be content with holding that. Now, however, the moment was come for acting on a different principle. Not by Adam and Maitland alone, but by the brigades of Ompteda, Pack, Kempt, and Lambert, the enemy had been overthrown with prodigious slaughter, and all equally panted to be let loose. Moreover, from minute to minute the sound of firing in the direction of Planchenoit became more audible.

It was clear, therefore, that even young troops might be slipped in pursuit without much hazard to their own safety, and the Duke let his people go. The lines of infantry were simultaneously formed, the cavalry mounted and rode on, and then a cheer began on the right, which flew like electricity throughout the entire extent of the position. Well was it understood, especially by those who, on a different soil and under a warmer sun, had often listened to similar music. The whole line advanced, and scenes commenced of fiery attack and resolute defence—of charging horsemen and infantry stern, such as there is no power, either in pen or pencil, adequately to describe.

It might savour of invidiousness were I, in dealing with this part of my subject, to specify particular brigades or regiments, as if they more than others had distinguished themselves. The case was not so. Everyman that day did his duty—making allowance, of course, for the proportion of weak hearts which move in the ranks of every army, and seize the first favourable opportunity that presents itself of providing for their own safety.

And probably it will not be received as a stain upon the character of British troops if I venture to hazard a conjecture, that in the army of Waterloo these were as numerous as in any which the Duke of Wellington ever commanded. Accident, however, and their local situation in the battle necessarily bring some corps more conspicuously into view than others, and at this stage of the fight Adam's infantry, with Vivian's hussars, had the good fortune to take in some sort the lead. The former followed up their success against the Imperial Guard with an impetuosity which nothing could resist.

They left the whole of their dismounted comrades behind them, and seemed to themselves to be completely isolated, when Vivian's huzzars, whom Lord Uxbridge had ordered on, swept past them. For there was seen on the rise of the enemy's ascent a body of cavalry collected, which gathered strength from one moment to another, and threatened ere long to become again formidable. It was of vital importance that it should be charged and overthrown ere time was given to render it the nucleus of a strong rearguard; and against it, by the Duke's personal command, the hussar brigade was directed. Loudly these rivals in enterprise and gallantry cheered one another as the British horsemen galloped past, and both caught a fresh impulse from the movement.

Adam's brigade moved steadily on; Maitland's marched in support of it; and down from their "mountain throne" the rest of the infantry moved in succession. The cavalry came first into play. It was observed, as they pushed on, that at the bottom of the descent two squares stood in unbroken order. These were the battalions of the Guard which had been drawn up to support the advance of the French columns; and, though grievously incommoded by the swarms of fugitives which rushed down upon them, they still kept their ranks.

A portion of the cavalry wheeled up and faced them. It is a serious matter to charge a square on which no impression has been made, and probably Vivian, with all his chivalry, would have hesitated to try the encounter, had he not seen that Adam was moving towards the further face of one of these masses with the apparent design of falling upon it. He did not therefore hesitate to let loose a squadron of the 10th, which, headed by Major Howard, charged home, and strove, though in vain, to penetrate.

The veterans of the French Guard were not to be broken. They received the hussars on their bayonets, cut down many with their fire, and succeeded in retreating in good order, though not without loss. Moreover, just at this moment one battery, which had escaped the general confusion, opened upon the flank of Adam's brigade, while another came galloping across the front of the 18th Hussars, as if seeking some position whence they in like manner might enfilade the line of advance which the British troops had taken. But these latter were instantly charged, the gunners cut down, and the pieces taken; while the former soon fell into the hands of the 52nd regiment, which changed its front for a moment, and won the trophy.

Darkness now began to set in, and the confusion in the French ranks became so great as to involve, in some degree, the pursuers in similar disorder. The more advanced cavalry got so completely intermingled among crowds of fleeing men and horses, that they could neither extricate themselves nor deal their blows effectually.

Moreover, as night set in, and the Prussians began to arrive at the scene of action, more than one awkward rencontre took place, which was with difficulty stayed. Nevertheless, the pursuit was not checked. Down their own slope, across the valley, up the face of the enemy's hill, and beyond the station of La Belle Alliance, the British line marched triumphant. They literally walked over the dead and dying, the numbers of which they were continually augmenting.

Guns, tumbrils, ammunition wagons, drivers—the whole materiel, in short, of the dissolved army, remained in their possession. Once or twice some battalions endeavoured to withstand them, and a particular corps of *grenadiers à cheval* contrived, amid the wreck of all around, to retain their order. But the battalions were charged, rolled up, and dissolved in succession, while the horsemen effected no higher triumph than to quit the field like soldiers. Still the battle raged at Planchenoit and on the left of it, where Lobau and the Young Guard obstinately maintained themselves, till the tide of fugitives from the rear came rolling down upon them, and they too felt that all was lost.

Then came the Prussians pouring in. Then, too, the Duke,

feeling that the victory was won caused the order for a general halt to be passed; and regiment by regiment the weary but victorious English lay down upon the position which they had won.

It is well known that throughout this magnificent advance the Duke was up with the foremost of his people. Nothing stopped him—nothing stood in his way. He cheered on Adam's brigade, and halted beyond its front. He spoke to the skirmishers, and mingled with them; till at last one of his staff ventured to remonstrate against the manner in which he was exposing himself, "You have no business here, sir," was the frank and soldier-like appeal; "we are getting into inclosed ground, and your life is too valuable to be thrown away."

"Never mind," replied the Duke; "let them fire away. The battle's won and my life is of no consequence now."

And thus he rode on, regardless of the musketry which whistled about him. The fact is, that though he had put a machine in motion which no resistance could stop, he was still determined to superintend its working to the last moment; and the further the night closed in, the more determined he was to observe for himself whatever dispositions the enemy might have made.

Accordingly, keeping ahead of his own line, and mingling, as has just been stated, with the skirmishers, he pushed on till he passed to a considerable distance beyond La Belle Alliance, and there satisfied himself that the rout was complete. At last he reined up his horse, and turned him towards Waterloo. He rode, at this time, well nigh alone.

Almost every individual of his personal staff had fallen, either killed or wounded. Colonel De Lancey, quartermaster-general, was mortally wounded; Major General Barnes, adjutant general, was wounded; Lieutenant Colonel Lord Fitzroy Somerset, Military Secretary, had lost his right arm; and of his Grace's *aides-de-camp*, two, namely, Lieutenant Colonel the Honourable Alexander Gordon and Lieutenant Colonel Canning, were both struck down.

The latter died on the spot, the former survived his mortal

hurt only long enough to learn from the chief whom he served and dearly loved, that the battle was going well. Indeed, the losses that day to England, and to the best of English blood, were terrible. Lord Uxbridge, as is well known, was struck by one of the last shots fired, and suffered amputation of the leg.

Picton, the hero of a hundred fights, was gone whither alone his glory could follow him. But it is as useless to enumerate the brave who purchased with their lives this day a renown which can never perish, as it would be idle to attempt a description of the feelings of the survivors. As to the Duke himself, he has recorded the state of his own emotions in language of which the touching simplicity cannot be surpassed.

> "I cannot express to you," he says in a letter to Lord Aberdeen, written from Brussels on the morning of the 19th, "the regret and sorrow with which I look round me, and contemplate the loss which I have sustained, particularly in your brother. The glory resulting from such actions, so dearly bought, is no consolation to me; and I cannot suggest it as any to you and to his friends."

In the same spirit runs the letter in which he informs the Duke of Beaufort of the fate of his gallant brother.

> "You are aware," he says, "how useful he has always been to me, and how much I shall feel the want of his assistance, and what a regard and affection I feel for him, and you will readily believe how much concerned I am for his misfortune. Indeed the losses I have sustained have quite broken me down, and I have no feeling for the advantages I have acquired."

No wonder if he who thus wrote after the excitement of the battle was in some sort passed away, should have traversed the bloody field in his homeward way silent and sorrowful. It has been currently reported that he could not restrain his tears while he threaded his way back through the slain; and the tale is too honourable to the heart of a great man not to deserve acceptance.

The Duke had followed the flying enemy considerably beyond La Belle Alliance, and was on his way back to Waterloo, when, at a place called the Maison Rouge, or Maison du Roi, he met Blücher. Many congratulations passed between the two generals; and the latter having readily undertaken what the former proposed to him, namely, that he with his troops should follow up the pursuit, the former continued his ride homeward.

Thus was fought, and thus ended, one of the greatest battles of modern times—if its results be taken into account, perhaps the most important battle of which history makes mention. It began amid a drizzling rain, was continued under a canopy of heavy clouds, was lighted up for a few moments by the rays of a setting sun, and did not terminate till after the moon had risen. It was now over; and the sound of firing died away in the distance as fugitives and pursuers rolled onwards.

Not that either silence, or the unbroken beauty of a summer's night, succeeded. Over Hougomont there still curled a lurid smoke, which the ashes of the ruined pile, as yet red and fiery, strongly coloured. Other houses, which had caught fire later in the day, blazed brightly, and threw over the fields immediately contiguous to them a terrible shadow. But perhaps the most hideous sight of all was that which the moon's rays rendered obscurely visible.

"I shall never," says an eye-witness, "as long as I live, forget the adventures of that extraordinary night."

The writer, it is worthy of notice, being a private trooper, had gone forth with a comrade in search of plunder; and he thus describes his proceedings:—

> In the first place, the ground, whithersoever we went, was strewed with the wreck of the battle. Arms of every kind, cuirasses, muskets, cannon, tumbrils, and drums, which seemed innumerable, cumbered the very face of the earth. Intermingled with these were the carcasses of the slain, not lying about in groups of four or six, but so wedged together that we found it impossible in many instances to

avoid trampling them, where they lay, under our horses' hoofs; then, again, the knapsacks, either cast loose or still adhering to their owners, were countless.

I confess that we opened many of these, hoping to find in them money or other articles of value, but not one which I at least examined contained more than the coarse shirts and shoes that had belonged to their dead owners, with hero and there a little package of tobacco and a bag of salt; and, which was worst of all, when we dismounted to institute this search, our spurs forever caught in the garments of the slain, and more than once we tripped up and fell over them.

It was indeed a ghastly spectacle, which though feeble light of a young moon rendered, if possible, more hideous than it would have been if looked upon under the full glory of a meridian sun; for there is something frightful in the association of darkness with the dwelling of the dead; and here the dead lay so thick and so crowded together, that by and by it seemed to me as if we alone had survived to make mention of their destiny.

Nor were the sounds which greeted the ears of the watchful that night more exhilarating. The wounded lay in numbers still more innumerable than the dead; and amid the stillness of the night their cries and low moans became fearfully audible. Of the sufferings of one of those, the gallant Colonel Ponsonby, of the 12th Light Dragoons, while yet the battle raged, and immediately subsequent to its termination, an account has elsewhere been given. Let me not forget to insert the conclusion of the brave man's narrative, because, as he has himself well stated, it tells no solitary tale.

"The battle," he says, after describing how his friend the *tirailleur* officer parted from him, and some Prussian cavalry galloped over him, "was now at an end, or removed to a distance. The shouts, the imprecations, the outcries of '*Vive l'Empereur!*' the discharge of musketry and cannon.

were over; and the groans of the wounded all around me became every instant more and more audible: I thought the night would never end.

"Much about this time I found a soldier of the Royals lying across my legs; he had probably crawled thither in his agony; and his weight, his convulsive motions, and the air issuing through a wound in his side, distressed me greatly; the last circumstance most of all, as I had a wound of the same nature myself.

"It was not a dark night, and the Prussians were wandering about to plunder: the scene in Ferdinand Count Fathom came into my mind, though no women appeared. Several stragglers looked at me, as they passed by, one after another, and at last one of them stopped to examine me. I told him, as well as I could, for I spoke German very imperfectly, that I was a British officer, and had been plundered already; he did not desist, however, and pulled me about roughly.

"An hour before midnight I saw a man in an English uniform walking towards me. He was, I suspect, on the same errand, and he came and looked in my face. I spoke instantly, telling him who I was, and assuring him of a reward if he would remain by me. He said he belonged to the 40th and had missed his regiment: he released me from the dying soldier, and, being unarmed, took up a sword from the ground, and stood over me, pacing backwards and forwards.

"Day broke; and at six o'clock in the morning some English were seen at a distance, and he ran to them. A messenger being sent off to Hervey, a cart came for me, and I was placed in it, and carried to the village of Waterloo, a mile and a half off, and laid in the bed from which, as I understood afterwards, Gordon had been just carried out. I had received seven wounds: a surgeon slept in my room, and I was saved by excessive bleeding."

This is a touching narrative, but it ends well. Many like it could be told, were the sufferers alive to tell them. But out of the thousands who passed that long, long night in the field, multitudes saw no morrow.

Let me not seek either to disturb their rest, or to harrow the feelings, it may be, of relatives, by speaking for them. Better will it be to draw a veil at once over scenes which strip war of all its features except those which, if looked at ere hostilities begin, would go a great way towards curing statesmen of their indifference to human suffering, and suggest some other and more Christian means than battle for settling the quarrels of nations.

Chapter 31

State of Feeling and Condition of things in the Rear

All this while the confusion which reigned in Brussels, Malines, Antwerp, and the other cities nearest to the seat of war sets the power of description at defiance. As one body of fugitives after another escaped from the battle, and the wounded and their attendants began to pour in, Brussels became the scene of a consternation which was far more wild, and, as it seemed, far more reasonable, than that of the 16th.

Who could doubt that the day was lost when they saw whole regiments of Belgian cavalry riding as if for life, and passing clean through the town? Who could refuse credit to the assertions of men in British uniforms, when they protested that their comrades were either killed or taken, and that they alone had escaped the general carnage? Moreover, such as took courage, or had the means of going forth to reconnoitre in the direction of Waterloo, encountered at every step objects which forced upon them the conviction that all was lost.

From an early hour in the morning till late at night every road, track, bridle-path, and avenue that led through the forest of Soignies was crowded. Wagons laden with baggage or stores, sumpter-horses, ammunition-carts, and cars drawn by bullocks, jammed and crushed one against another in the eagerness of their drivers to escape. Many broke down or upset, thus blocking up the way against the crowds that followed, while in innumerable instances the drivers cut the animals loose, and, leaving the baggage to shift for itself, rode off. Then came streams of wounded with their attendants, the latter more numerous than the former, far more numerous than was necessary, of whom many dropped by the way-side, while others, retaining just strength enough to get out of the throng, crept into the wood and there sat down, some of them never to rise again.

But the most hideous crash of all was when the Cumberland Hussars, fine-looking men and well-mounted, came galloping down the great avenue and shouting that the French were at their heels. No mercy was shown by these cowards to the helpless and the prostrate who came in their way. They rode over such as lacked time or strength to escape from them, and cut at the drivers of wagons who either did not or could not draw aside out of their way.

Nor let the humiliating truth be concealed. In the noble army which stopped that day the torrent of violence which had burst upon Europe, were more faint hearts than on any previous occasion had followed England's unconquered general to the field, and these—officers as well as privates—swelled the tide which rolled in, noisy and agitated, towards the capital, and would not be stayed.

The condition of that town during the night between the 16th and 17th, and the eagerness with which both strangers and inhabitants hastened during the course of the latter day to escape from it, have elsewhere been described. As the evening of the 17th drew on, and more certain intelligence from the army arrived, the panic moderated itself a little. They who yet lingered in the place ventured to hope for the best, and withdrew to their chambers, fearful indeed and very anxious, but not despairing.

The dawn of the 18th saw them all afoot, and in spite of the heavy rain which fell the Park was soon crowded. For a while all was still. No sound of firing came over the forest, neither were other signs of war afforded to them, save in the occasional arrival of small bodies of wounded from the field of Quatre Bras, and the hurried visits of the medical attendants to such as already occupied the hospitals. But by and by there was a change.

The roar of cannon burst upon them suddenly; they knew that the battle was begun, and from that moment terror became so predominant in every bosom that the idea of its probably ending in the triumph of the allies seems not to have occurred to anyone. It may not be amiss if we borrow the language of one who, having fled on the 17th to Antwerp, saw and conversed on the evening of the 18th with other fugitives who had succeeded in escaping only in the course of the latter day.

> A hundred Napoleons had been vainly offered for a pair of horses but a few hours after we left Brussels; and the scone of confusion which it presented on Saturday evening surpassed all conception. The certainty of the defeat of the Prussians, of their retreat, and of the retreat of the British army, prepared the people to expect the worst. Aggravated reports of disaster and dismay continually succeeded to each other: the despair and lamentations of the Belgians; the anxiety of the English to learn the fate of their friends; the dreadful spectacle of the wagon-loads of wounded coming in, and the terrified fugitives flying out in momentary expectation of the arrival of the French; the streets, the roads, the canals covered with boats, carriages, wagons, horses, and crowds of unfortunate people flying from this scene of horror and danger, formed altogether a combination of tumult, terror, and misery, which cannot be described. Numbers even of ladies, unable to procure any means of conveyance, set off on foot, and walked in the dark beneath the pelting storm to Malines; and the distress of the crowds who now filled Antwerp it is utterly impossible to conceive.
>
> Thus it was even before the tidings of the commencement of the battle arrived; the sound of firing augmented the terror a hundredfold in the capital, and the feeling soon spread with the intelligence in which it had originated to all the cities near. Malines was abandoned, as Brussels had been, by all who could command the means of further

flight. Even in Antwerp itself many did not feel themselves secure, and therefore escaped as they best could, some to Breda, others to Ostend, Among those who remained there was but one subject of thought that could interest. Every faculty of our minds was absorbed in one feeling, one interest; we seemed like bodies without souls. Our persons and our outward senses were, indeed, present in Antwerp, but our whole hearts and souls were with the army.

In the course of our wanderings (for no one could keep within doors) we met many people whom we knew, and had much conversation with many whom we did not know. At this momentous crisis one feeling actuated every heart, one thought engaged every tongue, one common interest bound together every human being. All ranks were confounded, all distinctions levelled, all common forms neglected. Gentlemen and servants, lords and common soldiers, British and foreigners were all upon an equality, elbowing each other without ceremony, and addressing each other without apology.

Ladies accosted men they had never before seen with eager questions unhesitatingly; strangers conversed together like friends, and English reserve seemed no longer to exist. From morning till night the great Place de Maire was completely filled with people, standing under umbrellas and eagerly watching for news of the battle. So closely packed was this anxious crowd, that when viewed from the hotel windows, nothing could be seen but one compact mass of umbrellas. As the day advanced the consternation became greater. The number of terrified fugitives from Brussels, upon whose faces wore marked the deepest anxiety and distress, and who thronged into the town on horseback and on foot, increased the general dismay; while long rows of carriages lined the streets, tilled with people who could find no place of shelter."

It was not, however, among the timid and the peaceful only

that excitement prevailed in rear of the army to an extent which was positively painful. Every soldier who heard the sound of battle and felt himself so situated as to be incapable of sharing its perils with his comrades, fretted and chafed like a steed which a strong curb restrains; and many such there were.

Not to speak of the continental troops, among some of whom an excellent spirit prevailed, there were English regiments doing garrison duty in the different fortresses; and others, still more distressingly situated, who, having arrived at Ostend on the previous day, were now in full march towards the front. These toiled and strained in the endeavour to reach the scene of action, more than the strength of the less robust members of each corps could endure, and they left in consequence numerous stragglers at most of the villages through which they passed.

But not even the stoutest of them reached the field in time. They had borne the brunt of the American war. They had returned weak in numbers, but unshaken in discipline, from that ill-conducted contest, and burned to wipe out the remembrance of the failure before New Orleans in the encounter of a foe worthy of their renown. But they did not succeed. Night closed upon them just as they passed through the village of Waterloo; and ere they could reach the scene of strife the last shot had been fired.

Meanwhile the Duke returned to the house where, on the previous evening, he had established his headquarters. He arrived at the door silent and thoughtful, and, alighting from his horse, narrowly escaped an injury which might have proved fatal. The gallant animal which had carried his master safely through the fatigues and dangers of the day, as if proud of the part which he had played in the great game, threw up his heels just as the Duke turned from him. and it was by a mere hairbreadth that the life was preserved which, in a battle of ten hours' duration, had been left unscathed.

But the Duke was too much occupied with his own thoughts and feelings to pay much regard to the circumstance. He entered the house. Every apartment was filled with wounded officers and their kind and indefatigable medical attendants: for kind and indefatigable these gentlemen are, as all who in similar circumstances have come under their hands can testify, and greatly is their strength taxed, sometimes till it fails them, even in the British army, remarkable though it be above all other armies for the attention which is paid to this important department.

The Duke's heart bled as he looked round him. There upon one bed lay his long-tried and faithful military secretary, cheerful though mutilated, and anxious only about his chief. Here upon another poor Gordon was stretched, the tide of life ebbing rapidly, though the eye brightened as the tones of a voice never heard except in kindness fell upon his ears. And among them all Dr. Hume, the friend as well as the physician of the headquarters staff, passed to and fro, bringing aid where it was wanted, or else directing others to perform such minor offices as might according to his anxious view of each case, be deputed to them.

Nevertheless, there was one individual within those walls whose habitual *sang-froid* seemed not to have deserted him. The master of the *cuisine* had done his duty. He had kept possession of the kitchen in spite of innumerable endeavours to move him, by alternate threats and entreaties, to the rear; and now sent up for his master's refreshment a meal which would have done no discredit to the most distinguished of the restaurants in Paris.

It was eaten in silence and much sorrow, and then after the fragments were removed the conqueror sat down to write dispatches and private letters, which occupied him the greater part of the night. If the reader should happen never to have seen either the picture by Lady Westmoreland or the engraving taken from it which represents the scene, he is advised to remedy this defect in his researches with as little delay as possible. It will go farther to fill up the void in his imagination than any written record, and doubtless tells the tale with a degree of accuracy which cannot be called in question.

It was not, however, in this quarter alone that sad scenes were enacted. The living tide had rolled onwards, but there was left behind a wreck of human suffering, on which to look back even now over the space which divides it from us is very painful. Wherever the opportunity was afforded the wounded were either carried or crept back from the crest of the position; and the worst cases, if they survived long enough for the proceeding, were removed into the houses. For almost all the buildings along the rear of the line had been converted into temporary hospitals. Straw covered the earthen floors, and coarse but wholesome sheeting was spread over it.

There the wounded and mangled lay down, crowds upon crowds, with scarce an interval between; while the medical men and their assistants gave to each in his turn such attention as it was in their power to bestow. And truly it is in situations like this that men's nerves and hearts are tried. There was no rest, no sleep, all that summer's night—no respite next day, nor for many a day afterwards, to these ministers of health and ease. Indeed, the demand upon their skill was so multitudinous and incessant that the marvel is how they succeeded to any extent in paying heed to it.

So passed the night, and with the first dawn of the morrow parties went forth in every direction to seek for the living among the dead. Many were, of course, found, of whom it was grievous to know, that had it been possible to bring relief but a few hours earlier, their valuable lives might have been saved. It would but awaken griefs which the hand of time has assuaged were the names of individuals thus circumstanced to be placed upon record: yet that a considerable catalogue might be made of them is too certain.

Moreover it was not exclusively to our own countrymen and their allies that the hand of charity was thus held out: wherever a wounded French soldier was found, an English fatigue party carried him where medical aid was afforded; and very grateful most of these veteran warriors seemed to be for the kindness with which they were treated.

It were vain to relate how the intelligence of this great victory affected those who for the last three days had experienced the extreme of terror. Their joy seemed to be well nigh as hard of endurance as the feeling to which it succeeded. At first, indeed, they refused credit to the reports of those who spoke of the triumph of the allied arms; but when actors in the scene came in, bringing with them the same glad tidings, the delight of the listeners vented itself not unfrequently in tears.

"One loud universal buzz of voices filled the streets," writes the authority from which I have already quoted; "one feeling pervaded every heart; one expression beamed in every face; in short, the people were quite wild with joy, and some of them really seemed by no means in possession of their senses. At the door of our hotel the first sight which I beheld among the crowds that encircled it was an English lady, who had apparently attained the full meridian of life, with a nightcap stuck on the top of her head, discovering her hair in *papillotes* beneath, attired in a long white flannel dressing-gown, loosely tied about her waist, with the sleeves tucked up above the elbows.
"She was flying about in a distracted manner, with a paper in her hand, loudly proclaiming the glorious tidings, continually repeating the same thing, and rejoicing, lamenting, wondering, pitying, and exclaiming, all in the same breath. In vain did her maid pursue her with a shawl, which occasionally she succeeded in putting upon her shoulders, but which invariably fell off again the next moment. In vain did another lady, whose dress and mind were a little more composed, endeavour to entice her away. She could not be brought to pay to them the slightest attention, and I left her still talking as fast as ever, and standing in this curious *dishabille* among gentlemen and footmen, and officers and soldiers, and *valets du place,* and in full view of the multitudes who thronged the great Place de Maire."

But it was not thus alone that the inhabitants of the Low Countries, and the visitors who sojourned among them, exhibited their gratitude and gladness for the deliverance which they had experienced. Every door was opened in the capital, and in all the towns and cities near and far away, to receive the wounded. Delicate women waited upon them and dressed their hurts. Ladies of rank and men of property, gave up their rooms or sent their beds and bedding to the hospitals, while wine, brandy, linen, vegetables, fruit, were freely and largely given wherever they appeared to be needed. Nor did the spirit of liberality and kindness fail to be moved largely elsewhere.

England, amid the depth of her sorrows for the fallen, thrilled with gratitude towards the survivors. Subscriptions were set on foot for the purpose of creating a Waterloo fund, out of which immediate relief might be supplied to the families of the dead, or the mutilated soldiers and their widows pensioned. Numbers of medical men at their own expense, and many at the cost of still greater personal inconvenience, hastened from London and elsewhere to lend assistance in providing for the hospitals. In a word, the enthusiasm of Europe seemed never to have been awakened till now, for all nations more or less felt it. But it is time to resume the thread of our narrative.

CHAPTER 32

Battle of Wavre

It has been stated elsewhere that Marshal Blücher, while executing his flank movement in support of the Duke of Wellington, directed General von Thielmann to occupy the position of Wavre; and in the event of an attack in force, to resist and repel it with his whole corps. General von Thielmann was not, however, to abide permanently on the Dyle. Should the enemy either not molest him at all, or show only a portion of his strength, and use it languidly, Von Thielmann was to follow, by brigades, the route of the main army, and, making Contière his pivot on the march, to lend his aid in overwhelming the right and rear of Napoleon.

Von Thielmann attended faithfully to these instructions. He remained on his ground till past three in the afternoon, by which time he had reason to imagine that the corps in advance of him must be well on their way, and then, observing no signs of the enemy, he gave orders for his brigades to stand to their arms, and to form one by one in the routes which it was intended that they should severally follow.

Thielmann's corps consisted of four brigades, the 9th, 10th, 11th, and 12th: of these only the 9th continued at this time, on the farther side of the Dyle; and to a portion of it (to two battalions and the reserve) the occupation of Wavre was to be intrusted. The remaining four were to follow in the track of the brigades which should precede them, and to act as a strong rearguard, on which, in case of a sharp pursuit, the detached battalions might come in.

The order for the march was issued, and the 12th brigade had begun to move, when troops were seen approaching the river, from; the opposite side, and by and by some guns opened. It was Vandamme's corps which thus showed itself; and though their manoeuvring seemed to be cautious, and the cannonade was not very severe, Thielmann judged it expedient to suspend the march of his columns for a while. It was well that he did so.

The attack, feeble at first, grew gradually more earnest. The *tirailleurs* which had approached the further bank of the river were fed continually; and about four o'clock such masses appeared in the distance as satisfied the Prussian general of the work which was cut out for him. He hastened to occupy his position in a soldier-like manner, and prepared to receive the battle.

Wavre stands on the left bank of the Dyle, and is connected with a suburb on the right bank by two stone bridges; one of which falls in upon the principal or central street, while the other spans the stream at the upper part of the town. The river, though at ordinary seasons shallow, had been swollen by the late rains, and this, added to the natural steepness of the banks, rendered it impassable, except by the bridges. Now of these there were four, additional to the stone bridges, within compass of the manoeuvres on a day of battle: one was at Bas Wavre, below the town; the other three at the Mill de Bierge, Lemale, and Lemalette, above it; and though all were of wood, their structure were sufficiently firm to carry whatever weight the march of an army might impose upon it.

Finally, the great road from Namur to Brussels passes through Wavre, and is both broad and well paved; and there is no end to the cross-roads, all of which offer ample facilities for the movement of infantry, while the greater part are practicable for cavalry and artillery likewise.

From the bridge at Bas Wavre to that Lemalette the distance cannot be less than four English miles. Had the course of the Dyle been through open meadows, General Thielmann, with the force which he commanded, would have found himself quite unable to guard its passages; but the nature of the country—though it left him enough to think of—greatly assisted him in these matters. There is much wood on both sides of the river, steep banks, and miry ravines behind them, the combination of which could not fail seriously to impede the movements of troops; and the Prussian General availed himself skilfully of the advantages which they offered in the distribution of his corps.

His first position extended only from Bas Wavre to the Mill of Bierge. In rear of the latter he placed Colonel von Stülpnagel, with the 12th brigade and a battery of cannon; the mill itself being occupied by light troops, and the bridge barricaded. The 10th brigade under Colonel von Kämpfen, formed upon the heights above Wavre; while the 11th. under Colonel von Luck, stood astride of the Brussels road, whence it watched both Wavre itself and Bas Wavre.

The latter village was occupied in force; the suburb of Wavre, lying on the north side of the river, was lightly held by pickets of infantry; the great bridge was barricaded, and all the houses within reasonable distance of the left bank of the stream were loop-holed. Finally, the guns were ranged along the acclivities wherever they could see into the line of the enemy's approach; and the best spirit prevailed everywhere.

Only one mistake was committed on this occasion; but it was a serious one. The 9th brigade, instead of abiding, as Thielmann meant it to do, in support, and becoming applicable to such emergencies as might arise, moved off by Fromont, Bourgeous, and St. Lambert upon Coutière, and left General Thielmann with no more than 15,000 men to maintain the battle as well as he could, against Grouchy with 32,000.

It was about half-past three o'clock when Vandamme's corps began to engage the Prussian light troops which held the woods and houses on the right bank of the Dyle. These were gradually driven in, because it formed no part of Thielmann's plan to maintain a permanent hold even of the suburb; and presently the guns began to open on both sides. The enemy brought up two batteries, one of 12-pounders, with which they cannonaded the town, and endeavoured to keep under the fire of the Prussian artillery; but the attempt was not successful. So judiciously had Thielmann disposed his pieces that, though inferior both in numbers and weight of metal, they maintained a contest not at a disadvantage with the French batteries, and occasioned heavy loss among the columns as often as they showed themselves outside the cover of the woods.

But Grouchy would not, for this, take a denial. He closed up his skirmishers to the edge of the stream; launched his battalions one after another at the bridge; forced his way repeatedly into the openings of the streets, and was repeatedly driven out again. For the tumult of the battle at Waterloo had attracted his attention, while as yet his own light troops, and these only, were engaged; and, riding off to the left that he might the better listen, he soon satisfied himself regarding the true state of the case.

Under these circumstances, and fully believing that the whole Prussian army was in his front, he came to the conclusion that he could not more effectually co-operate with the Emperor than by preventing Blücher from detaching to the assistance of the English. He therefore urged the attack upon Wavre with desperate obstinacy, and suffered, through the resolute defence of the Prussians, enormous loss.

Thielmann had well disposed his troops for this sort of warfare. Only skirmishers lined the bank of the river, and filled the houses which commanded the bridge. The supports wore all concealed among the cross-streets, where they wore sheltered in a great degree even from artillery; and whence, as often as the French columns forced their way beyond the bridge, they rushed out, charged, and overthrew them.

Moreover, reinforcements could be speedily and safely sent down from the heights which overlooked the place whenever the occasion arose, and the guns from the higher platform told heavily. Seeing all this, Grouchy became impatient, and chafed the more that through his own mismanagement a considerable space of time elapsed ere his troops came rightly together: for

Excelmans, with his cavalry, had gone off to reconnoitre along the Louvain road, while Pajol yet lingered about Corbaux, and Milot's division of Gerard's corps was far in the rear, though it made strenuous exertions to come up.

At length the missing brigades arrived, and with more than 30,000 men Grouchy made dispositions to attack, as he imagined, the disheartened remains of Blücher's army. He threw forward an increased number of *tirailleurs* all along his own bank of the Dyle; and the Prussians feeding theirs in like manner, the musketry-fire across the stream became warm and animated. He next directed Milot to march upon the mill of Bierge, and to force at that point the passage of the Dyle. Milot approached the mill, against which one of Vandamme's battalions had vainly wasted its strength, and, covered by the fire of his own cannon, pushed forward.

The ground was wet and swampy, so that his progress was slow, frequent broad drains and ditches checking him continually; but in spite both of these obstacles and of a murderous fire from the Prussian batteries he reached the mill. There then opened upon him such a storm of musketry as no troops could withstand.

From the mill itself, and some houses near it, from the woody bank of the Dyle, and plunging from the high ground that overlooks it, crowds of skirmishers kept up a fire which was both close and deadly; and though the battalions which Milot sent against both the mill and the bridge performed prodigies of valour, they could not effect their object. This attack also was repulsed, and the enemy fell back in some confusion.

It was at this crisis in the battle, about six o'clock in the evening, that Grouchy received the dispatch which Soult had sent off from La Belle Alliance at one o'clock in the day. Grouchy read it—not without chagrin; for the opportunity of acting as was there suggested had passed away; and being now warmly engaged with the Prussians, he could not, without the risk of almost certain destruction, detach largely to his left.

Besides, if he did, what chance was there that his troops, fatigued and footsore, would be able to overtake Bülow, or strike a blow ere darkness should close in? Probably, too, it may have occurred to the French Marshal, that he had not sufficiently kept in view the spirit of the instructions which he had received from his master. He could not assert, even to himself, that he had never lost his touch towards the Prussians; indeed, it was now manifest that Blücher, though worsted in the fight of Ligny, was in full vigour, both mentally and corporeally, still.

The old warrior had so managed his retreat as to out-general the very men who defeated him. With all these reflections about the past awakened, and in exceeding alarm with regard to the future, Grouchy saw or believed that but one course was now open to him: he must, at all hazards, gain possession of the Brussels road, and cut off the troops with which he was engaged from the means of joining the corps in advance of them; and to effect these purposes it was necessary that he should make himself master of Wavre with as little delay as possible.

Exhorting Milot to renew his attempt on the bridge at Bierge, Grouchy galloped back towards Wavre, against which he directed another and more formidable attack to be made. It failed, as all the rest had done; General Gerard, who led, receiving a severe wound in the breast; whereupon a new plan was arranged, and Grouchy himself undertook to superintend its accomplishment. He had already directed Pajol to march upon Lemale; and he now put himself at the head of a portion of Gerard's division, and led it through the miry ravines that run parallel with the river in the same direction.

These movements, as well as the advance of a column from La Baraque, occupied some time, but they led to important results. The bridge at Lemale had not been barricaded, and the dispositions made for its defence by Lieutenant Colonel Von Stengel lacked somewhat of the provident care which General Thielmann in the management of his own people had exhibited. Von Stengel's detachment, consisting of three battalions of infantry, two squadrons of lancers, and one of *landwehr* cavalry, had been left by Zieten to cover the right flank of the 3rd corps; and not reporting to Thielmann or being otherwise formally handed over to him, deserved, in some sort, to be accounted a separate command. Pajol soon observed that the bridge was open. He formed his leading squadrons, dashed at the river, drove back the picket which was in observation, and crossed with the fugitives; presently Milot's infantry came up, and the whole falling furiously upon Stengel compelled him to give ground.

The Prussian position was thus turned, but not on that account did Thielmann withdraw from it. He was keenly alive to the importance of keeping Grouchy in check to the latest moment, and therefore, moved his 12th brigade to the support of Stengel. Indeed, the whole of his little army took ground to the right; the 10th brigade dividing its force so as to supply the gap which the movement of the 12th had occasioned, and the 11th coming boldly to that side of the Brussels road which was in danger; but he could not drive the French across the river.

On the contrary, his columns, missing their way amid the growing darkness, came awkwardly upon points in the enemy's line which it was not intended that they should assail, and were compelled, in consequence, to retire with loss. They accordingly fell back to the rear of a wood which stands midway, or nearly so, between Lemale and the mill of Bierge, and keeping their outposts within a few yards of those of the enemy, lay down.

Meanwhile, in Wavre, and by and by in Bas Wavre, the battle raged with indescribable fury. Vandamme devoted the whole of his corps to the capture of the former place. Mass after mass was thrown upon the bridge, but it passed over only to be driven back again; while the lower part of the street and all the road beyond it were covered with the slain, of whom many fell into the water and were swept away by the strength of the current.

At last, long after darkness had set in, the fire began to slacken. Vandamme saw that he could make no head against men so resolute as those with whom he had to deal; and drawing off the remains of his shattered battalions prepared to pass the night in bivouac.

Accordingly, both bridges remained in the hands of the Prussians, who made use of the first leisure which the enemy afforded them to erect a barricade on the lesser of the two; and then having carefully planted their sentries and otherwise provided against the risk of a surprise, they, in like manner, lay down.

CHAPTER 33

Renewal of the Battle—Retreat of Grouchy

During the greater part of the night of the 18th, Grouchy busied himself in making preparations for a renewal of the battle. No intelligence from the grand army reached him; and as he had by this time assembled the entire strength of his corps, he retained his position astride of the Dyle, and strengthened his left for the operations of the morrow. But it was not so with Thielmann. As soon as the cessation of the enemy's attack left him free to look abroad, he dispatched an intelligent officer to the right, who returned, in due time, with tidings of the complete defeat of Napoleon.

Nothing doubting that Grouchy must have been made acquainted with the catastrophe, Thielmann reckoned, as a matter of course, on the retreat of his own immediate opponent; and he determined to render it as little tranquil to the fugitives as possible. His astonishment may, therefore, be conceived, when, on the first dawn of the 19th, it was reported to him that Lieutenant Colonel Von Stengel had withdrawn his brigade, and was in full march upon St. Lambert for the purpose of rejoining his own corps.

It had been Thielmann's purpose to assume the initiative this day, and to give, instead of waiting to receive, the attack. Indeed, he caused his patrols to be much on the alert, under the persuasion that the enemy would steal away without affording him the opportunity of striking a blow. The departure of Von Stengel (a movement as eccentric as the neglect by this officer of common precautions on the previous day at Lemale) compelled a total change of plan.

Instead of assuming the offensive he was reduced to the necessity of extending his order beyond what it would bear, with a view to show a tolerable front to the enemy; and the results were not fatal only because the courage and constancy of his troops were beyond all praise.

The dawn of the 19th broke, and the two *corps d'armée* continued for some time to face one another. Thielmann naturally concluded that the hesitation of Grouchy arose out of his knowledge of the issues of the great battle of yesterday; and being very unwilling that the latter should escape altogether, he determined to strike the first blow. With this view he pushed forward a body of cavalry towards the high ground above Lemale, which Grouchy had occupied with his left wing, and opened upon the French masses a smart fire from two batteries of cannon.

But the French, instead of falling back, as he had anticipated, replied to the cannonade with a prodigious superiority of force, and forthwith advanced in three columns to attack his position. A furious combat ensued: though outnumbered in a proportion of two to one, the Prussians held their ground with exceeding obstinacy; and when at length compelled to fall back, they did so in excellent order, and very slowly. A wood which had covered the right of their position was lost; they retired, in consequence, to another, slightly in rear of Bierge, where a second and not less defensible position was taken up; and so long as the bridge remained in their keeping they felt that they should be able to maintain themselves.

From the first break of day up to this moment (and it was now eight o'clock in the morning) two battalions of Kurmark *landwehr*, to whom the defence of Bierge was intrusted, had sustained and repulsed repeated assaults from an entire French division. About nine, however, or perhaps a little earlier, numbers began to tell: and the village, and with it the command of the passage of the river, passed into the hands of the enemy. Thielmann, of course, felt that his line was no longer tenable. He began to file off, covering his retreat with such a cloud of skirmishers as checked all endeavour on the part of the French to close with him; and he sent, at the same time, instructions to the officer commanding in Wavre, that both the town and the village of Bas Wavre should be abandoned.

Colonel Von Zepelm, who commanded in the former place, drew off without the smallest molestation; and four regiments of cavalry under the guidance of Colonel Von Marwitz, interposing between him and his pursuers, rendered the remainder of his retreat comparatively secure. Nevertheless, the fighting continued sharply, and with loss to both parties, till past eleven o'clock, when Thielmann, knowing that Brussels was safe, and that whether he kept his touch towards Blücher or lost it could be henceforth of very little moment, struck off in the direction of Louvain.

At a place called Achtenrode, midway between Louvain and Wavre, he once more halted and formed; the French having followed, with their cavalry only, as far as the Brussels road, and placed their infantry *en-potence* along the heights of La Bavette.

It was almost noon on the 19th ere Grouchy received intelligence of the defeat of Napoleon, and the entire destruction of his army. He was completely struck down by the tidings. Nevertheless his presence of mind did not forsake him; for he knew that it had become necessary to act on his own discretion, and to do so promptly.

His first impulse urged him to march towards the late field of battle, and to fall upon the rear of the Allies; but a moment's reflection showed that out of such a rash proceeding no good could arise, and that his only chance of being able to serve the Emperor and his country hereafter lay in extricating his corps by a prompt and well-managed retreat from ' the dangers which encompassed it. He instantly faced about; and covering himself, as well as he could, with a strong rearguard, took the road to Namur. And he did not enter upon it one moment too soon.

So early as the evening of the 18th, General Pirch received orders to push with his corps (the 2nd) of the Prussian army from the field of Waterloo towards Namur. The object of this movement was to interpose between Grouchy and the Sambre, on which it was taken for granted that the French general would direct his retreat. And for a while Pirch moved as men do who are in earnest—traversing Moransal, crossing the Genappe at Bousseval, and passing on, over the Dyle, to Mellery.

This latter place he reached about eleven o'clock on the 19th, the same hour, or nearly the same, at which Grouchy heard of the defeat of the Emperor; but he could not, at least he did not press further. His men and horses began to be much jaded, as well with the exertions of previous days as with the long night march of the 18th; and he halted in order that they might rest for a while, and cook and eat such provisions as the surrounding country could supply.

General Pirch had been directed to feel for General Thielmann as he went on: and now, after a few hours of repose, he sent out a body of cavalry towards Mont St. Guibert, to effect that object. The officer in command, Lieutenant Colonel von Sohr, reached Mont St. Guibert without difficulty, but farther he could not go; for the defile was occupied by French troops, and there were no means of getting round them. He accordingly returned to Mellery, having failed to obtain information of Thielmann; and the repose of the bivouac was prolonged.

Meanwhile Grouchy hastened with rapid strides towards the Sambre. He sent on the mass of his cavalry along the road to Gembloux, causing the reserve artillery and all the wounded to follow in their track; while the infantry he moved in two divisions, in such a line as that it might strike the great Namur road at Sombref.

At the same time he was not unmindful of the necessity of deceiving Thielmann, and even holding him in check. For these purposes he kept a considerable reserve in Wavre and Lemale, with cavalry pickets which were thrown out in the direction of the Prussians; and he neither withdrew the former nor called in the latter till the evening of the 19th was considerably advanced. These dispositions, as well as the isolated nature of his own position, hindered Thielmann from learning till towards midnight on the 19th that Grouchy had actually retreated: and the consequence was, that though he began the pursuit at five o'clock next morning, and continued it with great energy all day, he did not succeed in overtaking the enemy's rear till it had arrived within three English miles of Namur.

It was well for Grouchy that he took time by the forelock, and better still that he had in General Pirch an enemy not quite competent to manage the business which had been intrusted to him. Had this latter officer, as soon as the cavalry brought back their report, got his men under arms, and pushed on, it seems impossible that he could have failed to gain possession of the line of Grouchy's retreat.

For considering that Grouchy did not quit La Bavette till past eleven o'clock, and that he finally evacuated Wavre and Lemale late in the evening, it is clear that the troops whom Colonel von Sohr saw in the defile of Mont St. Guibert could have belonged only to his advanced-guard. Pirch, however, was tired, and so were his men. He therefore preferred abiding where he was, to the risk of overtaxing the energies of his troops, it might be to no purpose; and the consequence was that the whole of Grouchy's corps passed within a few miles of his left flank, which did not make the slightest endeavour to impede or molest the march.

The consequence to Grouchy of this remarkable supineness on Pirch's part was that he had both roads open to him. He eagerly entered upon them, covered each of his columns with a strong rearguard, and was within the intrenchments of Namur with his main body ere a shot could be fired at him. Meanwhile Thielmann pressed after him by way of Gembloux. He threw out all his cavalry, with eight pieces of horse artillery, giving them instructions to bring the enemy to action wheresoever he might be overtaken; and soon after leaving Gembloux behind, it seemed to the officer in command as if the opportunity of fulfilling the wishes of his chief had been afforded.

Some French cavalry were seen in a sweep of the road, which running along a plain, and being very straight, affords more than ordinary facilities of observing remote objects; and the Prussians immediately accelerated their pace, in the hope of coming up with them; but in this they were disappointed. It was not Grouchy's game to fight, if a battle could be avoided, and his rearguard of cavalry broke, in consequence, into a trot, and escaped.

Animated by the hope of overtaking the fugitives, and encouraged to increased exertions by Colonel von Marwitz, the Prussians pushed on. They arrived, in due time, near a village which clusters round the base of the heights behind which, at a distance of three miles, Namur is situated; and beheld a couple of battalions, with three regiments of cavalry and nine guns, formed on the summit in order of battle. The Prussian battery immediately unlimbered and opened its fire, while the two cavalry brigades, diverging to the right and left, endeavoured to turn the enemy's position on both flanks.

One of these movements enabled a regiment of Prussian lancers to charge a body of French horse, which received its opponents with a fire of carbines, and was instantly overthrown. At the same time another lancer regiment attacked the French guns, three of which were taken; but the infantry could not be touched. The battalions threw themselves into the woods, which covered the entire slope of the hill on the further side; and not only made good their own retreat without loss, but restrained and finally repulsed every attempt on the part of the pursuers to overtake their less orderly comrades.

And now, after Thielmann had accomplished his long march, and was fairly in contact with the rear of Grouchy's light column, Pirch made his appearance in full pursuit of twelve French battalions, which, with two batteries, and wholly unsupported by cavalry, followed the route from Sombref to Namur. How it came to pass that Pirch did not succeed in overtaking this column early in the day has never yet been satisfactorily explained. He seems, in spite of his backwardness to break up the bivouac of Mellery, to have caught sight of the mass early in the morning, and he kept it in view during several hours.

But somehow or another the interval between the pursuers and the pursued was never diminished, at least in the direct line of inarch which Pirch, with his infantry, followed. The case was somewhat different as regarded Lieutenant Colonel von Sohr. Having been detached towards Gembloux with his own cavalry brigade, three battalions of infantry, and a battery of horse artillery, this officer soon found out that Thielmann was on that road before him; and struck off in consequence into the *chaussée* which passes through Sombref, making strenuous exertions to head the column in its retreat. At a place called Temploux he came upon two battalions, some cavalry, and four guns. He instantly attacked; and being supported by a cannonade from Thielmann, who was well to the front, and indefatigable in his endeavours to strike home, he carried all before him.

The French fell back in disorder, but their main body was by this time safe; and a strong rearguard—which occupied the fortified suburb of Namur—checked the further progress of the Prussians. Indeed, it is but just towards Grouchy to state, that the whole of his retreat, from the moment that intelligence reached him of Napoleon's overthrow, was conducted with admirable skill. The pursuers, however, were not men to be put off by ordinary hindrances. Pirch soon arrived, with the whole of his corps, and made dispositions for a general attack.

He formed his people into three columns, and about four o'clock in the afternoon let them loose; and such was their ardour, that in less than two hours the French were driven back from the position which they had taken up, and chased into the town. A bold attempt was made to burst open one of the gates, but it failed; and the Prussians, after losing in killed and wounded considerably more than 1500 men, fell back again upon the suburb.

If Pirch had been somewhat negligent in the commencement of his operations, it seemed as if he were determined, now that he had come fairly into collision with the enemy, to give them no rest. He rallied his beaten columns, strengthened them with fresh troops from the reserve, and sent them again to the attack of the town which this time they carried. They did not establish themselves on any of the ramparts, however, till Grouchy had effected the only purpose which he desired to serve by the defence of Namur.

The whole of the French troops, infantry, cavalry, and artillery, filed across the barricaded bridge, and were placed on the further side of the Sambre, while the battalions which fought only to secure this object no sooner became aware that their comrades were safe, than they in like manner escaped. They had taken the precaution strongly to barricade the gates, and to leave the drawbridges raised; and as the Prussians had neither battering-guns nor scaling-ladders with them, some time was necessary, even after resistance had ceased, to carry them over the defences of the place. There is no denying that Grouchy's retreat redounded greatly to his honour, and in some sort atoned for the many and grave blunders which characterized his advance.

CHAPTER 34

Advance of the English Army

While Grouchy was thus occupied in withdrawing his corps by rapid, yet regular marches from the front, the grand army had utterly dissolved itself. Whole brigades throwing away their arms, became a mere helpless throng, and sought no more to put on even the semblance of a compact or disciplined array. Rearguard there was none. One regiment of cavalry, and only one, moved at a slow pace, and, if common report may be credited, it preserved its order as a body-guard to the Emperor. But, except in this instance, the confusion surpassed all that had ever before been witnessed in modern warfare, and there was no power in any one to allay it.

So sudden, indeed, and so deadly came the panic on these tried warriors, that Vivian's cavalry, and the more advanced of the infantry brigades, passed about 10,000 stand of arms, which their owners had left without having fired a shot. And, in truth, this is little to be wondered at. A defeat so decisive as that which the whole French line had sustained, when it befalls just as the twilight has deepened into night, never fails, under the most favourable circumstances, to prove ruinous; for both the physical powers and the vital energies of the defeated are by this time usually overstrained, and darkness gives additional force to whatever obstacles either external objects or their own alarmed imaginations may cast in their way.

But the night of the 18th of June, brought with it sources of trouble to the broken French peculiarly its own. The Prussians were already in the field, and so rapid was their advance along a line perpendicular to that of the English, that the latter, while closing with their adversaries at La Belle-Alliance, suffered from the fire of the former.

Moreover, the Prussians came up comparatively fresh, and eager to avenge the reverses of a former day. When, therefore, it was proposed by the Duke of Wellington that to them should be intrusted the management of the pursuit, their gallant old leader accepted the charge as a privilege. His orders were that neither man nor horse should take rest, and they were faithfully obeyed. The Prussian cavalry, saluting Vivian's brigade with a cheer, were plunged into the heart of the disorderly masses, and giving no quarter, or next to none, soon strewed the wayside with carcasses.

One hundred and fifty pieces of cannon had been taken by the British army in the field; an equal number of guns, with large quantities of baggage, including that of Napoleon himself, as well as his travelling-carriage, fell into the hands of the Prussians in the course of that night and the following day.

It is impossible to state with any degree of accuracy the extent of loss in killed and wounded sustained by the French army in the battle of Waterloo. It is equally out of the question to hazard a conjecture in regard to the numbers who disbanded themselves as soon as the issue of the struggle became apparent. The whole face of the country, to a distance of many leagues, was covered with men in military uniforms, yet destitute of arms, who, through woods and thickets, and by unfrequented paths and difficult cross-roads, made their way as well as they could towards their own homes.

Some thousands, however, still kept together; and in the village of Genappe a portion of them attempted to arrest the progress of their pursuers. But these would not be deterred. They broke through the barriers which the enemy had thrown up, charged and captured a battery of cannon, and chased about 3000 men—all that had regained some show of consistency—pell mell beyond the defile, and over the field of Quatre Bras.

As to Napoleon himself, he never drew bridle till he reached Charleroi. He came into the town just as the dawn of the 19th was breaking, and spoke to his immediate attendants about halting to collect the fugitives: but his own strength was exhausted, and he retired to rest. One hour of broken sleep had not, however, been snatched, ere the alarm spread that the Prussians were approaching, and he instantly mounted his horse again and continued his flight.

His apologists have stated that his great anxiety was to fall in with Grouchy's corps, and that he dreamed even then of staying the tide of war, and gaining time for the formation of a new army—which they seem to think would not have been impossible. It is no easy matter to ascertain the secret thoughts and designs of any one; but this much is certain, that Napoleon did not find, and hardly can be said to have sought, an opportunity of acting upon these plans. He quitted Charleroi within an hour from his entrance into it, and made his next halt at Laon. Though the pursuit of the Prussians was close and rapid, it must not therefore be supposed that there was any lack of order or generalship in their manner of conducting it.

Blücher had had too much experience in war to throw the game out of his own hands after it was won; and hence, though he let loose his cavalry with the comprehensive command that they were to keep up with the enemy and give them no respite, he took care to support his troopers in advance with strong reserves of infantry. The cavalry were in the saddle all night; they rode through Genappe, cut to pieces everything that withstood them, scattered a crowd of fugitives over the face of the country, and halted at last, between Frasne and Mallet, only because their horses could go no further.

The 4th infantry corps marched after them, gathering up stragglers as it went along, and reaching Genappe about an hour before midnight, lay down awhile to rest. But the dawn of the 19th saw them all astir again; and while the cavalry rode straight for Charleroi, the infantry obliqued on the road to Mons. The latter reached Fontaine l'Evêque, where it bivouacked, sending patrols in the direction both of Mons and Thuin; the former held on towards Philippeville, after having detached a brigade towards Wavre for the purpose of observing Grouchy, and communicating with Thielmann, or such troops as he might have thrown out to seek for the main army.

By and by the 1st corps, which had acted hitherto as a reserve to the 4th, came into the line. It kept the high road to Charleroi, passing the Sambre there, and at Chatelet and Marchienne, without falling in with an enemy; for, in truth, with the exception of Grouchy's force, there was no longer an enemy to be encountered, and of him the reconnoitring parties, which penetrated as far to the right as Fleurus, did not succeed in seeing anything.

It would be hard to say what were really the feelings of Napoleon at this crisis. That he halted in Philippeville for four hours, and sent off couriers with dispatches to Generals Rapp, Lecourbe, and Lamarque, directing them to march straight upon Paris, is certain. It is equally true that he expressed great anxiety to reunite himself with Grouchy; and the combination of the circumstances, as well as the general tone of his conversation, led such as were in his confidence to assume that he still meditated a prolongation of the struggle.

But if he did, the idea never had time to mature itself. Fresh alarms constantly overtook him, whereupon he became restless and uneasy. He contented himself, therefore, with issuing orders to the commandants of the various fortresses, that they should defend themselves to the last extremity; and having directed Soult to abide at Philippeville as long as possible, and then to assemble such troops as might arrive and lead them to Laon, he ordered post-horses at two o'clock in the afternoon, and continued his journey towards the latter place.

Meanwhile the Anglo-Belgian army lay on its arms in the field which its valour had won. Long lines of fires marked the bivouac, round which, though the night was not cold, men gladly gathered, most of whom would have been much more contented with their lot had the provisions, of which they stood sorely in need, arrived. But no provisions came, nor were the means at hand to send them forward.

They therefore who had halted on the ridge, slept supperless in the fields or among the houses of La Belle Alliance; others, including portions of the cavalry, having penetrated a good way farther, found whole villages of huts, which the French in the course of the previous night had erected; and scattered over their floors were numerous fragments of meat partly raw, partly half-cooked, which in the hurry of some movement had been thrown away. The British soldiers were very hungry, but they could not bring themselves to taste these viands.

"We found," says a private of one of the cavalry regiments, "raw meat of every description in abundance—beef, pork, and mutton; but it had been so beaten about in the hurry of the strife, and was so vilely dressed—the very hides being in many instances left upon the morsels, and these but indifferently bled—that, faint as we were for lack of food, we could not taste it. We flung it from us in disgust, and refused to dress it."

Hunger, however, had its way—as it always will, even at the close of a ten hours' battle—and if a little marauding ensued, let not the individuals who entered upon it be too severely blamed. The commissaries were scarcely in the campaign of 1815 what they used to be during the three years which preceded it.

At an early hour in the morning of the 19th the allied troops got under arms. No movement in advance was, however, made; for the confusion in the rear had well nigh equalled that which bad prevailed among the broken masses of the enemy. Supplies were, therefore, slow of arriving; but they came at last, and after a hearty but rude meal the columns of march were formed. It was a wild, strange, and melancholy scene that spread itself out beneath the eyes of the victors.

From the ridge above La Belle Alliance each regiment and brigade as it came up obtained a complete view of the whole field of battle. The sun, too, was shining brightly, and a clear blue sky overhung them there; but it hung likewise over the wreck of three great armies, and looked down upon terrible things. Far and near, wherever the battle had raged, the corn was not only trodden down, but beaten into the clay. Long ruts showed where artillery had traversed; deep prints in the soil spoke of the charge of cavalry; and the dead lay in masses.

It was not here, as in other battle-fields, that groups of ten or less, with single carcasses scattered over an extended ground, spoke of the game of war played out. The face of the English position was covered; whole ranks, here and there, as it seemed, entire battalions, having died at their posts; while the slope beneath was strewed with all manner of weapons. There French horsemen lay side by side with their dismounted comrades. There stood guns, some, as it were, yet in position, others upset or faced round, with the brave men who served them four-and-twenty hours earlier lifeless beside them.

Nor did the eye of the gazer fail, amid these many-coloured relics, to discover the remains of those magnificent heavy brigades which had wrought such wonders in the hour of strife. All along the face, of the hill, from its summit down into the valley, and farther on in the ascent towards the French line, the surface of the ground was dotted with soldiers of the Life Guards, the Blues, and, in a greater number, of the Royals, the Greys, and the Inniskillens, who, carried away by their own eagerness, had left all support behind, and died, many of them, in the heart of the enemy's position.

Moreover, the fatigue-parties were out in all directions, and the melancholy spring-wagons were busy in the prosecution of their melancholy work, feeble movements of limbs or attempts to rise to a sitting posture pointed out where the wounded still lay thick among the dead. Nor must we omit, while touching on this ghastly subject, to speak of the wounded horses, which stood or moved about slowly and staggeringly in countless numbers. The reader might suppose that where human suffering is so rife the sufferings of inferior animals, however great, would escape observation; but it is not so.

We defy the most callous to look with indifference upon the horses which have been struck by shot, yet survive the blow. For there is such an air of meek submission about these creatures—they drag their mangled frames about so uncomplainingly, yet with such manifest anguish, that your heart bleeds for them, even while its feelings are given up in the main to deeper griefs.

Such were some of the spectacles that met the gaze of the British troops as they looked back from the heights of La Belle Alliance on the ground which they had maintained throughout the 18th. Neither was the scene much diversified in its nature as they passed beyond it.

Death had been quite as busy here as elsewhere, only it seemed as if he had smitten the men of one nation and no more; for almost all the bodies which they passed were those of French soldiers. Moreover, there were evidences of panic, such as could not be traced on any part of the battle-field, properly so called. Doubtless, the arms both of the dying and the dead lay wherever they had last been wielded, and these were scattered in profusion enough over every foot of ground from the crest of one position to that of the other. But not a musket or sword seemed to have been cast away.

It was different in the fields and along the roads by which the columns now moved. Whole battalions must have thrown down their arms and disencumbered themselves of knapsacks and accoutrements, the better to expedite their flight; while tumbrils and ammunition-carts stood or lay where the drivers, forgetful of all but personal security, had abandoned them. Here and there, too, in front as well as in rear, the curling smoke continued to indicate the spot where, a few days previously, cottage or farmstead had stood. As to Hougomont, it was a mere heap of ruins. La Haye-Sainte also lay in its ashes, and not a few of the houses which had sheltered the French from the storm of the 17th seemed to have shared the same fate.

I have already said that it was late, long past midnight, when the Duke lay down. He had not found time so much as to wash his face or his hands; but overcome with fatigue threw himself, after finishing his dispatches, on his bed. He had seen Dr. Hume, and desired him to come punctually at seven in the morning with his report; and the latter, who took no rest, but spent the night beside the wounded, came at the hour appointed. He knocked at the Duke's door but received no answer. He lifted the latch and looked in, and seeing the field-marshal in a sound sleep, could not find in his heart to awaken him.

By and by, however, reflecting on the importance of time to a man in the Duke's high situation, and being well aware that it formed no article in his Grace's code to prefer personal indulgence of any sort to public duty, he proceeded to the bedside and roused the sleeper. The Duke sat up in his bed; his face unshaven, and covered with the dust and smoke of yesterday's battle, presented a rather strange appearance; yet his senses were collected, and in a moment he desired Hume to make his statement.

The latter produced his list and began to read. But when, as he proceeded, name after name came out—this as of one dead, the other as of one dying—his voice failed him; and looking up he saw that the Duke was in an agony of grief. The tears chased one another from his Grace's eyes, making deep visible furrows in the soldier's cheeks, and at last he threw himself back upon his pillow and groaned aloud. "What glory can pay for all that?" he cried; "what victory is not too dearly purchased at such a cost?"

Hume closed up his paper, unable to reply, and quitting the apartment, left the Duke to make his toilet. This was done in a frame of mind which none except the individual, and not even he, could undertake to describe; yet the storm passed off, and when he appeared that day in public, the leader of the allied armies was as self-possessed as he had ever been. The truth is, that they who speak of the Duke of Wellington as gifted with iron nerves and a heart which is not easily moved, know not what they say.

The difference between him and other men is the same which in all ages has distinguished the hero from one of the crowd. With ordinary men feeling, as often as it is appealed to, controls reason for a while, and is with difficulty subdued. With great men, and surely the Duke is of the greatest, reason exerts itself in the first instance to control feeling and to keep it in its proper place. But feeling is not therefore extinct in them, as was shown in the personal bearing of the Duke on the morning of the 19th of June, and is still apparent in the tone of the letters from which extracts have elsewhere been given.

His whole moral being was shaken and torn by the intensity of his grief for the loss and the sufferings of his friends, yet he never for a moment permitted feeling to cast a shadow over judgment, or ceased to be, to the minutest particular, master of himself. He issued all his orders with the same calmness and deliberation which characterized his proceedings at other times.

The routes which the columns were to follow, the discipline that was to be observed upon the march, the necessary means of preserving this discipline, and the purposes which it was designed to serve, were all explained and set forth in the memoranda which he drew up ere quitting his chamber. And when he rode out of the courtyard of his house, followed by his staff and orderlies, no one could have told from his manner or the expression of his countenance that anything extraordinary had occurred.

The first movement of the allied armies carried them across from the Charleroi to the Nivelles road. Here the corps of Prince Frederick of Prussia had been directed to join, and the whole proceeded by a route divergent from that on which the Prussians were marching, yet having with it an easy communication. They encountered no opposition whatever; not so much as a picket or straggling party of the enemy made its appearance throughout the day, and in proportion as the distance from the scene of the late operations increased the traces of war became less frequent. That night the Duke of Wellington fixed his headquarters in Nivelles; and his army, grievously diminished in numbers, yet full of confidence and flushed with victory, bivouacked round him.

CHAPTER 35

Entrance into France—Abdication of Napoleon

A great battle had been won, but the war was not yet ended; neither could anyone pretend to foretell the effect which might be produced on the public mind of France by tidings of the destruction of the Grand Army. A people so fickle, yet in their own way so deeply imbued with the love of country, might rally round the defeated Emperor, and re-enact the scenes which gave their character to the earlier campaigns of the Revolutionary War.

Or, if they set aside the individual, of whom and of his iron rule the respectable classes were understood to be weary, what reason was there to be assured that, for the sake of some other idol, or under the pretence of maintaining the national independence, they would not arm the whole population of the country, and fight to the last extremity?

It was well known that numbers who objected to Napoleon's return from Elba, ere it took place, had acceded to his cause merely through their abhorrence of foreign dictation. It was equally certain that both these persons, and the more enthusiastic of his partisans, expected nothing from the Allies in the event of a second march to Paris, except the utmost severity of conquest.

The plunder of the capital, with heavy contributions from its inhabitants, were the least of the evils to which they looked forward; for it was whispered timidly, in circles supposed to be well informed, that a plan for the partition of France itself was under consideration. Now the dismemberment of France would never be submitted to till the entire inability of Frenchmen to hinder it had been demonstrated; and though there was nothing to prove that at this period, at least, any such impolitic design had entered into the councils of the Allies, still the least suspicion that such a thing was thought of might drive the French nation to despair.

Wherefore the Duke of Wellington, as prudent as he was enterprising, determined to conduct his future operations as he had done his former invasion of France, by establishing for himself a secure base on which to lean; by preserving among the troops composing his motley army the strictest discipline, and guarding, as far as could be done, the inhabitants of the invaded country from outrage.

Acting in this wise spirit, he issued to the army the General Order of which a copy is subjoined:—

General Order.
Nivelles, 20th June, 1815.

As the army is about to enter the French territory, the troops of the nations which are at present under the command of Field Marshal the Duke of Wellington are desired to recollect that their respective Sovereigns are the allies of His Majesty the King of France, and that France ought therefore to be treated as a friendly country. It is therefore required that nothing should be taken, cither by officers or soldiers, for which payment be not made.

The Commissaries of the army will provide for the wants of the troops in the usual manner; and it is not permitted either to soldiers or officers to extort contributions. The Commissaries will be authorized, either by the Field Marshal or by the Generals who command the troops of the respective nations, in cases where their provisions are not supplied by an English Commissary, to make the proper requisitions, for which, regular receipts will be given; and it must be distinctly understood that they will themselves be held responsible for whatever they obtain, in the way of requisition, from the inhabitants of France, in the same manner in which they would be esteemed accountable for purchases made for their own Government in the several dominions to which they belong.

The better to support his own policy in regard to this matter and as a guard to the property and persons of individuals, the Duke proceeded to organize a military police, which proved itself on various occasions eminently useful, and rarely abused its trust. All British armies are attended in the field by provosts and their guards; and the powers of punishment committed to these functionaries are as summary as they are stern; but a provost, like a magistrate in civil life, cannot be in more than one place at a time; and where he himself is not present, his influence is necessarily in abeyance.

The Duke brought to the aid of this functionary in the Peninsula a body of trustworthy soldiers, who, being formed into troops, became the Staff-corps of cavalry. At the breaking up of the Peninsular army, the cavalry staff-corps was dissolved, and up to the present moment no occasion to re-establish it had arisen; but now that he was about to penetrate across the frontier, it was felt by the commander-in-chief that the system must be revived. Accordingly, the officers in command of the several regiments of cavalry were desired to select from their respective corps three privates on whom they could depend; and the individuals thus chosen were put under the orders of sergeants, at the rate of one for each brigade. It became the duty of these persons to keep the peace on the line of march, and to a wide extent on each side of it.

They were directed to flank the several columns, and to bring up the rear; to protect villages and detached houses; not to punish on their own responsibility marauders, however daring, but to arrest and hand them over to the proper authorities. And the better to insure to them the respect of their comrades, they received each a badge of office—namely, a scarlet belt, which the soldier passed over his right shoulder, and of which the army was by general order made to understand that it protected the wearer against violence, and rendered doubly criminal every attempt to resist or interrupt him in the discharge of his duties.

Having settled this point, the Duke proceeded to draw up a proclamation, which he sent on for general circulation through the frontier towns and villages. It ran thus:—

> I desire the French people to understand that I enter their country at the head of an army heretofore victorious, not as an enemy (except to the usurper, declared to be an enemy to the human race, with whom neither truce nor treaty can be maintained), but to assist them in casting off the iron yoke with which they are oppressed. I have given orders to my army to this effect, and I request that every infraction of them may be reported to me.
>
> The French people are, however, aware that I have a right to require of them that they shall conduct themselves in such a manner as will enable me to protect them from those who may wish to injure them. It is necessary that they furnish the requisitions which shall be made upon them by persons properly authorized so to do, for which regular receipts shall be given; that they behave peaceably, and maintain no correspondence with the usurper or any of his adherents.
>
> All who absent themselves from their homes after I enter France, or shall be found in the service of the usurper, will be considered among the adherents of the common enemy, and their properties seized for the maintenance of the army.

The above proclamation was issued on the 22nd of June, and dated from Malplaquet, to which place the headquarters of the army had then advanced, and thence the same day the Duke proceeded to Cateau. Here a brief halt occurred, of which advantage was taken for the investment of the three important fortresses of Valenciennes, Lequesnoy, and Cambray; the reduction of Maubeuge, Landrecy, Avesnes, and Rocroi being simultaneously undertaken by the Prussians. Moreover, tidings arrived of the approach of 15,000 Saxons, whom the King pressed upon the Duke of Wellington, and whom the Duke, now that these brave men had recovered their senses, readily undertook to command.

He directed them to proceed to Antwerp, and there to wait for further orders, while with his own force he proceeded to clear the way for the advance upon Paris. Lieutenant General Sir Charles Colville was detached with the 4th division to summon Cambray. The commandant refused to open the gates, whereupon the city was attacked on the 24th, and carried by escalade. On the 25th the citadel surrendered; and on the 26th Louis XVIII., for whom the Duke had sent, arrived, and took up his abode in the place. The same day Peronne was attacked by Major General Maitland's brigade of Guards, and after a sharp resistance taken.

Neither were the Prussians backward in the prosecution of that part of the common task which they had engaged to perform. Zieten bombarded Avesnes, and reduced it, making prisoners of three battalions of National Guards and 200 veterans; the castle of Guise was invested; and other places were either carried by assault, or so masked as to insure their speedy fall. Thus a good base was established whence in any events hostilities could be carried on, and the communications with Belgium and Holland, and through them with Prussia and England, were rendered perfectly secure.

Meanwhile the news of Napoleon's overthrow began to circulate in Paris, though no man was bold enough openly to proclaim the fact. There had been great rejoicing on the receipt of his bulletin, which gave an exaggerated account of the success at Ligny; and letters telling of the retreat of the English from Quatre Bras circulated freely. Indeed, from the field of Waterloo itself messages were conveyed full of high hopes regarding the future; and then there came a lull.

For a while the circumstance was attributed to every conceivable cause but the right one. Time for writing dispatches might be wanting, or the Emperor chose to conceal his purposes till they should be ripe for execution; or the courier had met with an accident; or the telegraph had gone wrong. So spake his partisans, including the workmen of the suburbs, and all the refuse of society; while the shopkeepers and wealthier classes, to whom war and its glories had become abhorrent, held a different language.

At last a letter, written by himself, and dated from Charleroi, reached the Minister of War. It made no disguise of the defeat, though it did not allow that the army which fought the previous day had been annihilated, and that the writer, a fugitive, and well nigh alone, was looking in vain for some nucleus round which to gather the fragments of his battalions.

On the contrary, its tone was cheerful and full of confidence, while the minister was exhorted to keep a good heart, and to rouse the people to fresh exertions. The effect of this announcement, when first made public, was to throw all Paris into a state of panic, which, however, gradually gave place to an opposite feeling. The funds rose; as if in a choice of evils the approach of the Allies were considered less intolerable than the continuance of the imperial rule; and though little business was done in the shops, they were neither closed nor wholly deserted.

Napoleon wrote this memorable letter just before he set out for Laon. He then handed over the charge of the army to Soult, and having rested a few hours, hurried forward with post-horses to Paris. He arrived there very early in the morning of the 21st. It soon became bruited about that he was come; indeed, he had scarcely alighted at the palace of the Bourbon Elysée ere he sent for Caulaincourt, and entered with him into a consideration of the state of affairs.

He was much agitated, and began by declaring that the army no longer existed, and that the sole chance of salvation for the country lay in his being invested with the powers of a Dictatorship. But in looking for this he forgot that men's minds were not now as pliable as they had been in 1813. The spirit of party, which scarcely slept while the crisis of the campaign impended, awoke with increased strength now that the battle was lost, and a fierce but brief contest ended in the momentary triumph of the Republicans. A series of resolutions, moved in the Chamber of Deputies by La Fayette, and carried by acclamation, set aside, by omitting to notice it, the authority of the Emperor altogether; while the indignant complaint of Lucien, that the mover was become ungrateful, was repelled with much dignity.

> "You accuse me of ingratitude to Napoleon," exclaimed La Fayette. "Do you forget what we have done for him? Have you forgotten that the bones of our children and of our brothers scattered everywhere—in the sands of Africa—beside the waters of the Guadalquivir and the Tagus—on the banks of the Vistula, and in the deserts of Muscovy, bear testimony to the faithfulness with which he has been served? We have done enough for him. Let us now do our duty to our country."

This speech was heard with deep attention; and at its close the fatal words—"Let him abdicate!" were for the first time spoken.

The idea thus fairly set afloat was taken up by all the more respectable portions of the population of Paris. The National Guard, which had already got under arms, marched to the house where the Chambers sat, and drew up in front of it. The Deputies thus supported, hastened to nominate a committee of five, which was desired to communicate with two other committees—one from the House of Peers, the other from the Ministers of State, on the measures necessary to be adopted.

The committees met the same evening in Napoleon's presence, but no conclusions were arrived at; for when they spoke of abdication and peace, he pressed for men and arms, and a continuance of the struggle. Next morning in the Chambers the subject was resumed, on which occasion General Solignac proposed that the committee should wait upon the Emperor, and inform him at once of the necessity of an immediate com-

pliance with the nation's will.

"Let us wait one hour," cried Lucien.

"One hour be it, then," replied Solignac, "but no more;"

"and if the answer do not come within that space," added La Fayette, "I will move that Napoleon be dethroned."

Thus spoke and thus acted the Democratic or Jacobinical party, which amid the confusion of the hour had acquired a superiority in both Chambers; for the Peers, little influential at the best, took their tone wholly from the Deputies. At the same time Napoleon was not without his adherents, foremost among whom, both in energy and talent, stood his brother Lucien. The latter was clear for making an appeal to force; and had not the Emperor seen too much reason to believe that the National Guard would act against him, it is not impossible but that he might have endeavoured to play over again the game of an earlier period. But the season for such *coups d'état* was past. Napoleon hesitated, wavered, listened to many counsels, and summed up all by affixing his signature to the following document:—

> Frenchmen! In commencing war for maintaining the national independence, I relied on the union of all efforts, of all wills, and the concurrence of all the national authorities. I had reason to hope for success, and I braved all the declarations of the Powers against me. Circumstances appear to be changed. I offer myself as a sacrifice to the hatred of the enemies of France. May they prove sincere in their declarations, and have really directed them only against my person. My political life is terminated, and I proclaim my son, under the title of Napoleon II., Emperor of the French.
>
> The present ministers will provisionally form the council of the Government. The interest which I take in my son induces me to invite the Chambers to form without delay the Regency by law. Unite all for the public safety, in order to remain an independent nation.

At nine o'clock in the morning of the 22nd, just four days

subsequently to the fatal battle of Waterloo, this document was presented by Fouché to the Chamber of Deputies. It was received with every demonstration of respect; and after a few minutes wasted in discussing abstract principles of government, the Chamber resolved to vest, for the present, the powers of the executive in a council of five persons.

Of these two were to be chosen from among the Peers, and three from their own body; but not a word was spoken about a permanent successor to the throne. Indeed, the deputation which waited upon Napoleon to thank him for the sacrifice he had made, carefully avoided all reference to that part of his manifesto; and when directly appealed to, replied only by saying, that the Chamber had given them no instructions on the subject.

"I told you so," exclaimed Napoleon, turning to his brother, who stood near him, "I told you that they would not dare to do it. Say to the Chamber," continued he, addressing himself to the deputies, "that I commit my son to their care, for in his favour I have abdicated."

Meanwhile some strange scenes were enacted in the Chamber of Peers, where Ney and Labedoyère, both escaped from the wreck of the war, had taken their places. The former, smarting under a sense of the wrong done him by the imperial bulletin, sat silent and gloomy, till tidings of Grouchy's successful march in retreat tempted Carnot to rise. The latter spoke of the possibility of still offering successful resistance to the allies. He assured the Chamber that Grouchy could bring with him 60,000 men; that Soult had already collected at Mézières 20,000 of the Old Guard; and that 10,000 fresh levies, with 200 pieces of cannon, could in the space of three days be added to these resources. Ney, instantly starting up, and speaking with a wild vehemence, declared that both the report and the statement founded upon it were false.

> Dare they say to us, who witnessed the disaster of the 18th, that France has yet 60,000 soldiers left? Grouchy cannot have with him more than 20,000, or 25,000 at the most;

if he had had more, he would have been able to cover the retreat, and the Emperor might still be at the head of an army on the frontier. As to the Old Guard, not a man of them will ever rally more. I myself commanded them. I myself beheld their total annihilation before I quitted the field. They are exterminated. The enemy is at Nivelles, with 80,000 men, and may reach Paris in six days if he please.

Upon this Count Flahaut strove to interrupt him, but did not succeed. Ney went on to paint in frightful colours the extent of the national calamity, and then suddenly exclaimed, "Your only hope is in negotiation. You must recall the Bourbons: and for me, I will retire to the United States."

A storm of rebuke burst upon the speaker,, the last announcement especially furnishing his enemies with ample ground of complaint; but Ney listened to it unmoved. He looked round with an expression of bitter contempt in his countenance, and said, "I am not one of those who regard only their own interest. What can I gain from the restoration of Louis—except death for having deserted him? but for the sake of the country I must speak the truth, and I have spoken, and again repeat it."

The question of war or peace being thus settled (for after Ney's declaration no man ventured seriously to speak of resistance), the house proceeded to discuss the merits of the act of abdication, and the point of the succession was taken up. Lucien spoke in favour of Napoleon II., and was interrupted by Count de Pontecoulant, who fiercely demanded by what right an Italian Prince and an alien presumed to offer an Emperor to France.

He objected, likewise, to the condition of the child, a stranger to them all, and residing in a foreign capital; and was making a manifest impression on the house, when Labedoyère rose. The same spirit stirred him then which led him at Grenoble to set an example of defection from the cause of the King; and he poured forth a torrent of invective upon all who exhibited even lukewarmness in the cause of the Emperor.

"The Emperor," said he, "has abdicated in favour of his son. If his son be not instantly proclaimed, the abdication is annulled; for those alone who, caring only for themselves, flattered him in his prosperity, and now turn their eyes towards foreigners, oppose themselves to his wishes. I tell you that it is so. If you refuse to acknowledge the young prince, Napoleon must draw his sword again, and blood will be shed. For we will put ourselves at the head of the brave Frenchmen who are ready to die in his defence; and woe to the base generals who even now, it maybe, are meditating new treasons.

"I demand that they be impeached and punished as deserters from the national standard, that their names be given to infamy, their houses razed, their families proscribed and sent into exile. We will suffer no traitors to abide among us. Napoleon, in resigning his power to save the nation, has done his duty to himself; but the nation is not worthy of him; since after swearing to abide by him in adversity and prosperity, she a second time compels him to abdicate."

A furious tumult immediately arose: Massena, Lameth, and others rebuked the speaker; who, however, continued his wild harangue, till amid the confusion of many voices his was at length drowned.

These scandalous scenes ended, and the question of the succession being evaded in both houses, the Chambers proceeded to name the members of the provisional government, and the choice fell upon Carnot, Fouché, Caulaincourt, Grenier, and Leuriotte. Of these persons four had voted for the execution of Louis XVI., while the fifth was known to be one of the most unscrupulous intriguers of his age; and that they did not command the confidence of the nation soon became apparent. though resolute, one and all, never to acknowledge Napoleon II., they were yet driven, by fears of a military insurrection, to speak of him as their future sovereign; and having done so, they pressed the Emperor to carry his part of the convention into effect. The Emperor saw or imagined that he had no longer an alternative. He therefore retired, at the request of the Chambers, to the palace of Malmaison, near St. Germain, and there issued his farewell address to the army.

And now the question arose, what was permanently to become of him. He himself desired to continue in France, he spoke of discharging the duties of guardian to his son, and renewed from Malmaison the proposal, more than once rejected already, of putting himself at the head of the array as the young Emperor's lieutenant, and falling upon the flank of the allies. But neither the provisional government nor the Chambers would consent to these things. They believed that the invaders would listen to no terms so long as the individual against whom alone they professed to be in arms should pollute the soil of France, and they determined that he should be removed from it.

At the same time their feelings were all abhorrent to such an act of treachery as would be perpetrated were he to be surrendered into the hands of his enemies; they therefore pressed him to follow a course which had been suggested by a private individual, and which, had he pursued it at once, might have saved him many years of mortification.

It was proposed that he should escape to the United States of America, and two frigates were ordered to be placed at his disposal for this purpose. Napoleon is said to have borne himself with much dignity during the few days which he spent at Malmaison previous to his flight. He knew that a spell was upon him, which, for the present, could not be broken, and sustained by some vague hope of better days to come, he yielded to his destiny.

Chapter 36

Advance upon Paris

Meanwhile the advance of the allied armies was not suspended for a moment. The two commanders-in-chief met on the 23rd at Chatillon, where the plan of operations was settled; and it was subsequently carried into effect with all the unanimity and good feeling which prevailed on both sides throughout the campaign. It was arranged that the road by Laon and Soissons should not be followed, except by light corps of cavalry.

The enemy was understood to be there collecting his forces, and as it was not desirable to get entangled in affairs of rear-guards and outposts, the allies determined to turn his left. Accordingly they proposed to march by the right bank of the Oise, to cross the river either at Compiegne or Pont St. Maxence; and interposing between the fugitives and the line of their retreat, to arrive at Paris before them. At the same time their own rear was not neglected.

Prince Frederick of the Netherlands was directed to undertake with his corps the siege of all the strong places on the Scheldt and between that river and the Sambre; while Prince Augustus of Prussia, with Pirch's corps and the corps of Kleist von Nollendorf, just brought into communication with the main army. should reduce the fortresses on the Sambre itself, and between that river and the Moselle.

How Colville, with his portion of Prince Frederick's corps, executed the trust that was committed to him, and with what promptitude and zeal Prince Augustus of Prussia bent himself to his work, has already been stated. It was to no purpose that the Provisional Government of France sent out to request an armistice on the strength of the announcement—which they made with exceeding eagerness—of Napoleon's abdication. Neither the Duke of Wellington nor Prince Blücher conceived that they were bound to listen to such a proposal; and the progress of their columns towards Paris was not suspended.

The Duke having halted his army for a day, permitted the Prussians to gain the start of him. This was desirable on many accounts; for where the same roads are used by the troops of different nations, crowding and confusion are apt to occur; and in order to strike into the contiguous lines which the Allied generals had determined to follow, it was necessary that one should take the lead.

The Prussians, therefore, being upon the left of the French in their retreat, entered with them into many skirmishes, pushed them from the great road which passes by Laon and Soissons, and themselves moved their masses by it. It is not worthwhile to trace their marches day by day, nor yet to tell how indefatigable their detached corps were in cutting in upon the fugitives. That they committed many excesses, and put the inhabitants to great discomfort and uneasiness, cannot, I am afraid, be denied. Let not us, however, whom Providence has saved from the terrible visitation of a victorious enemy, blame them too severely for their conduct.

Their memories were laden with the recollection of bitter wrongs. They were exasperated by the cruelties which the French soldiers had practised on such of their countrymen as fell into their hands, and they acted under the orders of a chief in whom hatred of the French nation had grown into a sort of principle. Moreover, the internal discipline of Prussian regiments was not in 1815 what it seems to be in 1847; but, however this may be, one thing is certain—that the pursuit, as carried on by Blücher, was as untiring as it was close, and that in the course of various affairs from the 20th to the 28th of June he made himself master of 16 pieces of cannon, and took not fewer than

4000 prisoners.

The wreck of the French army was gathered together by Soult at Laon. He led it back as far as Soissons, where Grouchy presented himself with a commission from the Provisional Government, to supersede him. Soult, as might be expected, was exceedingly exasperated, and set off immediately for Paris, while Grouchy did his best to inspire his followers with a confidence which he himself had ceased to entertain. The French are excellent soldiers, but they cannot play a losing game so well as a winning one.

On the present occasion, for example, they were repeatedly brought into situations in which, had their passive courage been equal to the active courage which nobody ventures to deny them, they might have delivered with excellent effect more than one blow upon their pursuers. But their thoughts seemed to be turned absolutely towards Paris; and a cry that their retreat would be cut off, or that their communications were in danger, on no occasion failed to unman them. This was particularly the case on the 28th, when a Prussian detachment, weak in point of numbers, after carrying Longpré, near Villers-Cotterets, by surprise, fell upon a large but somewhat scattered force of French troops at the latter place, and making many prisoners, of whom Grouchy himself narrowly escaped being one, interposed itself between the columns of Vandamme and Grouchy, and blocked up the great road to Paris.

The enemy, though outnumbering their pursuers fivefold, would not venture to attack them. On the contrary they dispersed into the woods right and left of the road, through which they escaped by twos and threes—a grievous blunder, as was proved by the result of the action which about 2,000 of their infantry, with a few guns, were persuaded to accept. These latter beat back the Prussians with loss, and prosecuted their march in good order.

Such were some of the operations of that portion of the Prussian army which Blücher conducted in person to the gates of Paris. Another column—for the army moved in several—proceeded under the orders of Bülow, by the road which conducts from Pont St. Maxence to Maly-la-Ville. Of this force Prince William of Prussia commanded the advanced guard; and in the evening of the same day when the affair last described took place, he found an opportunity of falling upon some detachments from D'Erlon's corps, and upon all that remained of that of Reille.

The fighting was sharp, but it ended in the complete success of the Prussians, who, besides killing many and dispersing more, made 2,000 prisoners. The result of this encounter, and of the operations successfully carried on elsewhere, was, that the French were driven entirely into the cross-roads, while the invaders, making themselves masters of the great roads from Senlis and Soissons, pushed their advanced posts forward, and settled them within five English miles of the capital.

All this while the Anglo-Belgian columns were pressing on by a line of their own, and carrying all before them. The headquarters passed from Nivelles to Cateau, where the halt of a day took place, after which the army again moved forward, and on the 26th arrived at Joncourt. Vermand, Orvillé, Louvres, and Gonesse were reached in succession, at the latter of which places a little incident befell not undeserving of notice.

Prince William of Prussia wrote to the Duke of Wellington, announcing the birth of a daughter on the 18th of June, and begging that his Grace would become her godfather. As may be imagined, the Duke did not decline the responsibility; and the terms in which he accepted it could not but prove gratifying to the illustrious individual who preferred the request.

To H. R. H. Prince William of Prussia.

Gonesse, ce 1 Juillet, 1815.

J'ai reçu la lettre très obligeante que votre Altesse Royale m'a écrite hier, et je suis extrêmement flatté et reconnaissant de l'honneur que votre Altesse Royale me fait par son désir que je sois le parrain de sa fille née le 18 Juin.

Je souhaite avec votre Altesse Royale que l'alliance entre nos deux nations soit aussi permanente qu'elle a déjà été avantageuse à la cause publique, et qu'elle est cordiale.

The result of these movements was, that on the 29th of June the advance of the Anglo-Belgian army passed the Oise, and on the 3rd of July took up a position, with its right on the height of Richebourg, and its left on the wood of Bandy. Here a series of communications took place between the Duke of Wellington and the members of the Provisional Government in Paris, to detail the particulars of which belongs rather to the general historian than to the writer of such a narrative as this.

But of the results I may be permitted to say, that though for a while they proved little satisfactory to either party, in the end the firmness and excellent judgment of the English general brought them to a happy conclusion. He would not listen to any proposition for the suspension of hostilities, so long as Napoleon continued to exercise the smallest influence in the state, or one soldier of the army, which was known to be devoted to him, remained in the capital.

And if, for a brief space, the commissioners suffered themselves to be swayed by motives of mistaken pride, in the end they were glad to give way. They did not yield, however, till such measures had been adopted as left them without a hope to fall back upon; and of these a few words will suffice to give a sufficiently explicit account.

The heights of Montmartre and the town of St. Denis were at this time strongly fortified. By damming up the waters of the little rivers Bouillon and Vieille Mer, an inundation which covered the whole northern face of Paris had been created, while the Canal de l'Ourcq being filled, and its banks converted into parapets and batteries, a very formidable position was made out. There were assembled in the city about 50,000 men, troops of the line and of the Guard, which, with some new levies called *les tirailleurs de la Garde* and about 17,000 veterans, enrolled under the denomination of *fédérés,* might raise the effective force to 70,000, or more.

Besides those, the National Guard, amounting to perhaps 30,000, were under arms; and though the temper of such citizen soldiers might not, perhaps, be such as to promise much, still 100,000 men, with 200 or 300 pieces of cannon, could not, especially in such a situation, be lightly thought of. The more sanguine of Napoleon's adherents insisted upon trying the issues of a battle; and Blücher was at least as eager to play the game of war as they.

But the Duke took a different and a wiser view of the case. He pointed out to his ally that success, even if it were certain, must be purchased at a great expense of life; that under the circumstances in which the adverse parties were placed, success was by no means certain; and that a brief delay—probably not extended beyond a week at the farthest—would render the fall of Paris inevitable, by the arrival of the Austrian and Russian armies, both of which were already across the frontier.

On the other hand, he explained to the French commissioners that the abdication of Napoleon could not be regarded except "as a trick;" and that it was impossible for him, keeping in view the object for which the Allies were in arms, to enter, on account of any such absurdity, into an armistice. They urged him to advise: which, with equal judgment and temper, he declined to do, except as a private individual; and when, as an individual, they besought him to speak out, he recommended that the King should be recalled.

> "I then told them," says he, "that I conceived the best security for Europe was the restoration of the King: and that the establishment of any other Government than the King's in France must inevitably lead to new and endless wars; that Bonaparte and the army having overturned the King's Government, the natural and simple measure, after Bonaparte was a prisoner or out of the way, was to recall the King to his authority; and that it was a much more dignified proceeding to recall him without conditions, and to trust to the energy of their Constitution for any reforms which they wished to make either in the Government or the Constitution, than now to make conditions with the Sovereign; and that above all, it was important

they should recall their King without loss of time, as it would not then appear that the measure had been forced upon them by the Allies."

Meanwhile the military operations on both sides were not suspended. Within the city every effort was made to rouse a spirit of hostility to the invaders, and add to the defences of the place. The heights of Montrouge, as well as Montmartre and St. Denis, were occupied, and the wood of Boulogne swarmed with cavalry. Every approach to the city was barricaded. The old castle of Vincennes was strengthened, and new works were thrown up at La Pirotte.

All the boats on the Seine were seized, and carried to the opposite side from that along which the Allies were stationed—while the bridges were broken down. Still the whole of the south of Paris lay open; and it became an object with the Allies to manoeuvre for the command of the approaches in that direction. Blücher, however, was not willing to give up the hold which he had upon the north face without making trial of the courage and determination of its defenders.

Accordingly on the night of the 29th, just after the commissioners had quitted his colleague, he directed an attack to be made upon the fortified village of Aubervilliers, which General von Sydow carried at the point of the bayonet, making 200 prisoners. A further demonstration on the canal of St. Denis was not, however, attended with a similar result. There the enemy presented a formidable front; and, after a good deal of desultory firing, the assailants withdrew.

Satisfied that it was not from this side that Paris could be successfully assailed, Blücher began to manoeuvre towards the right, while the Duke of Wellington advanced his troops, so as to take up the ground from which the Prussians should remove. Some affairs between the soldiers of the latter nation and the French ensued. In these the French took the initiative by attacking on the 1st of July the village of Aubervilliers; and finding it in a great measure evacuated by Bülow's people, they succeeded in recovering the half of it.

But just at this moment Colville's division, which had been appointed to occupy this part of the line, came up; and his light troops under Sir Neil Campbell soon recovered what the Prussians had been too few in number to retain. Then followed a sharp affair at Versailles, where a brigade of Prussian cavalry, under Lieutenant Colonel von Sohr, got entangled in an ambuscade, and, after performing prodigies of valour, was cut to pieces.

In spite of this loss, however, the movement of the Prussians to the right was not checked. They advanced on the 2nd towards the heights of Meudon and Châtillon; fought a sharp battle for the possession of Sèvres, Moulineaux, and Issy; were again attacked in force on the 3rd, and obtained a signal victory. On this occasion Vandamme led out two strong columns of infantry, supported by cavalry and a formidable train of artillery, and seemed bent on retaking the ground which had been lost on the previous day.

But either the French had by this time become considerably cowed, or the Prussians surpassed themselves in valour; for though the former greatly exceeded the latter in numbers, they did not so much as carry the village of Issy. They fell back, after much firing, in disorder, and were pursued by the Prussian skirmishers up to the very barriers of Paris.

The moral effect of these repulses now began to tell. It was seen, moreover, that the Allies could neither be cajoled nor awed into a suspension of hostilities, for the British troops were not less busy than the Prussians. The whole of the ground opposite Montmartre and St. Denis was taken up by them. They established a bridge over the Seine at Argenteuil, and moved a corps towards the Pont de Neuilly, which entered into immediate communication with Zieten's troops, and threatened Paris on its most vulnerable side.

All further hope of successful resistance hereupon deserted the defenders. They caused their batteries to cease firing; sent out a flag of truce to propose a capitulation; informed the Allied Generals officially of Napoleon's flight, and threw themselves, in some sort, on the mercy of the conquerors. Whereupon, sorely against the will of Prince Blücher, who saw an enemy's capital within his grasp, and expressed the strongest disinclination to relax it, commissioners were appointed to meet in the Palace of St. Cloud; and a military convention was agreed upon:—

Art. 1. There shall be a suspension of arms between the Allied armies commanded by his Highness the Prince Blücher and his Grace the Duke of Wellington, and the French army under the walls of Paris.

2. The French army shall put itself in march tomorrow, to take up a position behind the Loire. Paris shall be completely evacuated in three days; and the movement behind the Loire shall be effected in eight days.

3. The French army shall take with it all its materiel, field artillery, military chest, horses, and property of regiments, without exception. All persons belonging to the depôts shall also be removed, as well as those belonging to the different branches of administration which appertain to the army.

4. The sick and wounded, and the medical officers whom it shall be found necessary to leave with them, are placed under the special protection of the Commanders-in-Chief of the English and Prussian armies.

5. The military, and those holding employments to whom the foregoing articles relate, shall be at liberty, immediately after their recovery, to rejoin the corps to which they belong.

6. The wives and children of all individuals belonging to the French army shall be at liberty to remain in Paris. The wives shall be allowed to quit Paris for the purpose of rejoining the army, and to carry with them their property, or that of their husbands.

7. The officers of the line employed with the *Fédérés,* or with the *tirailleurs* of the National Guard, may either join

the army, or return to their homes or to the places of their birth.

8. Tomorrow, the 4th of July, at midday, St. Denis, St. Omer, Clichy, and Neuilly shall be given up. The day after tomorrow, the 5th, at the same hour, Montmartre shall be given up. The third day, the 6th, all the barriers shall be given up.

9. The duty of the city of Paris shall continue to be done by the National Guard and by the corps of the municipal *gendarmerie*.

10. The Commanders-in-Chief of the English and Prussian armies engage to respect, and to make those under their command respect, the actual authorities so long as they shall exist.

11. Public property, with the exception of that which relates to war, whether it belongs to the Government or depends upon the municipal authority, shall be respected, and the Allied Powers shall not interfere in any manner with its administration and management.

12. Private persons and property shall be equally respected. The inhabitants, and in general all individuals who shall be in the capital, shall continue to enjoy their rights and liberties without being disturbed or called to account, either as to the situations which they hold or may have held, or as to their conduct or political opinions.

13. The foreign troops shall not interpose any obstacles to the provisioning of the capital, and will protect, on the contrary, the arrival and the free circulation of the articles which are destined for it.

14. The present Convention shall be observed, and shall serve to regulate the mutual relations, until the conclusion of peace. In case of rupture it must be denounced in the usual forms, at least ten days beforehand.

15. If any difficulties arise in the execution of any one of

the articles of the present Convention, the interpretation of it shall be made in favour of the French army and of the city of Paris.

16. The present Convention is declared common to all the Allied armies, provided it be ratified by the Powers on which these armies are dependent.

17. The ratifications shall be exchanged tomorrow, the 4th of July, at six o'clock in the morning, at the bridge of Neuilly.

18. Commissioners shall be named by the respective parties, in order to watch the execution of the present Convention.

CHAPTER 37

Occupation of Paris

Thus fell, for the second time, within the space of a year and a half, the capital of France into the hands of foreign troops. On both occasions a degree of mercy was shown to the vanquished, such as they, when victorious, had not been accustomed to exercise; and some there were, among the chiefs of the Allied army, who chafed exceedingly at the circumstance. Prince Blücher especially was indignant at the yielding temper, as he termed it, which the Duke of Wellington displayed. He had made up his mind to take the place by storm. He kept a list of the insults and outrages which had been put upon the inhabitants of Berlin and of Prussia generally, and burned to avenge them.

It was a settled point with him that France should pay the expenses of the war which she had provoked, and he made no secret of his purpose, and began with levying a contribution on the capital. Accordingly his answers to the applications of the Provisional Government for a suspension of arms had breathed throughout a very different spirit from those of his illustrious coadjutor; and when at last Marshal Davoust wrote, in his capacity of commander-in-chief of the French army, to remonstrate, the indignation of Blücher boiled over.

Davoust had been so imprudent as to refer to some verbal arrangement made with officers of the outposts; and to allege that the abdication of Napoleon removed the only ground of war which the Allies had set up. He was answered in these words:—

Marshal,—It is not true that because Napoleon has abdicated, no further motive for war between the Allied Powers and France exists. His abdication is conditional; it is in favour of his son: whereas the decree of the Allies excludes not only Napoleon, but every member of his family, from the throne. If General Frimont has considered himself justified to conclude an armistice with the General opposed to him, that is no reason why we should do the same. We will follow up our victory; and God has given us both the power and the will to do so.

Take care, General, what you do, and avoid devoting another city to destruction; for you know how the exasperated soldiers would disport themselves if your capital were taken by storm. Do you desire to be laden with the curses of Paris, as well as with those of Hamburg?

We shall enter Paris for the purpose of protecting its well-conducted inhabitants from the mobs which threaten them with plunder. There can be no secure armistice concluded anywhere but in Paris. Do not mistake the relative positions of our countries in this respect. Finally, let me observe to you, Marshal, that your desire to treat with us, while contrary to the rules of war, you detain our officers sent to you with cartels, is very surprising. In the usual forms of conventional courtesy, I have the honour to be, Marshal, your obedient servant,

Blücher.

Such an epistle as this, even though addressed to Davoust, whose name abides as a word of bad omen in the north of Germany still, was not calculated to excite the hope of very tender treatment among the Parisians. Neither, indeed, did these unhappy people greatly mistake the purposes of the writer. He had just missed making himself master of Napoleon's person, and the disappointment had no tendency to pour oil upon the waters of his wrath.

Hearing that the ex-Emperor abode at Malmaison, he had dispatched a body of cavalry to surprise the place; and the deed would have been done, had not the French succeeded in breaking down the bridge of Chatou just before the Prussians arrived. Now, as the bridge of Chatou is distant from the palace of Malmaison not more than eight hundred yards, the risk which Napoleon ran could not fail to be imminent, and the disappointment of Blücher was sharp in proportion to the near accomplishment of an object which he had much at heart.

Nevertheless, the Prince Marshal felt himself constrained to yield to the gentler influences which his colleague brought to bear upon him. He, too, affixed his signature to the Convention, and the war came to an end.

There was no attempt, as, indeed, there could be little inducement, to evade the terms of the treaty on either side. Punctually at the hour named the capitulation was ratified; and on the 4th of July the French army, under the command of Marshal Davoust, began its march towards the Loire. The same day the English and Prussians occupied St. Denis, St. Ouen, Clichy, and Neuilly; on the 5th the allies took possession of Montmartre; on the 6th they planted their posts at the barricades—the English on the right of the Seine, the Prussians on the left; and on the 7th both armies marched into Paris.

They were gazed upon by the inhabitants with a strange mixture of terror and curiosity. No crowds gathered in the streets to welcome them, neither were the windows and housetops thronged; but from behind *jalousies* and half-closed blinds multitudes of faces peered out upon the strange spectacle. The troops moved on to the quarters which had severally been allotted to them. The Prussians bivouacked to the south of Paris chiefly; Montmartre remained in the hands of the English, who established, however, a camp in the Champs Elysees; and the bridges as well as all the principal squares, markets, thoroughfares, and public buildings were guarded by patrols furnished from both armies.

In a word, the military occupation of the French capital was complete; and the Chambers of Peers and Deputies, conscious that their functions were ended, dissolved themselves, and the houses were shut up.

It is a matter of history that Louis XVIII. reached his capital amid the shouts of a giddy populace on the 9th of July. The way had been paved for his return by the temper and sagacity of the Duke of Wellington on the one hand, and the duplicity of Fouché and the skill of Talleyrand on the other. But not even the return of Louis and the re-establishment of a legitimate government sufficed to appease the wrath of Blücher or divert him from his purposes. He commanded the municipal authorities of Paris to furnish, for the payment of his army, 100,000,000 of *francs*—a sum equivalent to about 4,000,000*l*. of our money. At the same time he set his pioneers to work upon the bridge of Jena, which he declared himself determined to blow up.

In like manner, when his soldiers clamoured for the destruction of the pillar of Austerlitz, he chimed in readily with their tastes, and had actually gone so far as to make preparations for the accomplishment of the work. It was to no purpose that the leading men in the city implored him to retract these stern decrees, or that the representative of his own sovereign endeavoured to move him.

This gentleman, Count Von der Golz, who, in addition to the high office which he held, seemed to possess some personal claims on the Marshal's friendship, inasmuch as he had formerly served as one of his *aides-de-camp*, wrote to Blücher and entreated him, in the name of Prince Talleyrand, to spare the bridge. The following characteristic answer was dispatched in the handwriting of the marshal himself:

> I have determined on blowing up the bridge, and I cannot conceal from your Excellency how much pleasure it would afford me if M. Talleyrand would previously station himself on it. I beg that you will make my wishes known to him.

In like manner his decision in regard to the forced contribution seemed to be immovable. But here again the genius of the Duke of Wellington prevailed. He, too, wrote to the Prussian marshal, and the admirable tact displayed in the management of a nature so strangely compounded cannot be better shown than by the perusal of the subjoined letters:—

Mein lieber Fürst,   Paris, 9th July, 1815.

The subjects on which Lord Castlereagh and I conversed with your Highness and General Count Gneisenau this morning, *viz.*, the destruction of the bridge of Jena and the levy of the contribution of 100,000,000 of *francs* upon the city of Paris, appear to me to be so important to the allies in general, that I cannot allow myself to omit to draw your Highness's attention to them again in this shape.

The destruction of the bridge of Jena is highly disagreeable to the King and to the people, and may occasion disturbances in the city. It is not merely a military measure, but it is one likely to attach to the character of our operations, and is of political importance. It is adopted solely because the bridge is considered a monument of the battle of Jena, notwithstanding that the Government are willing to change the name of the bridge.

Considering the bridge as a monument, I beg leave to observe that its immediate destruction is inconsistent with the promise made to the Commissioners on the part of the French army during the negotiation of the convention; namely, that the monuments, museums, &c, should be left to the decision of the allied sovereigns. All that I ask is, that the execution of the orders given for the destruction of the bridge may be suspended till the sovereigns shall arrive here, when, if it should be agreed by common accord that the bridge should be destroyed, I shall have no objection.

In regard to the contribution laid on the city of Paris, I am convinced that your Highness will acquit me of any desire to dispute the claims of the Prussian army to any advantages which can be derived from its bravery and exertions and services to the cause; but it appears to me that the allies will contend that one party to a general alliance ought not to derive all the advantages resulting from the operations of the armies. Even supposing the allies should be induced to concede this point to the Prussian army, they will contend for the right of considering the question whether France ought or ought not to be called upon to make this pecuniary sacrifice; and for that of making the concession to the Prussian army, if it should be expedient to make it.

The levy and application of the contribution ought then to be a matter for the consideration and decision of all the allies, and in this point of view it is that I entreat your Highness to defer the measures for the levy of it till the sovereigns shall have arrived.

Since I have had the happiness of acting in concert with your Highness and the brave army under your command, all matters have been carried on by common accord and with a degree of harmony unparalleled in similar circumstances, much to the public advantage. What I now ask is, not the dereliction of your measures, but the delay of them for the day, or at most two days, which will elapse before the sovereigns shall arrive, which cannot be deemed unreasonable, and will, I hope, be granted on account of the motive for making the request.

Believe me, &c.

The second is equally in keeping with the temper and feelings of the writer:—

Mein lieber Fürst,   Paris, 10th July, 1815.
The dinner is to be at Very's today at six o'clock; and I hope we shall have an agreeable day.
I have received news of the expected arrival of the sovereigns today at Bondy, with orders to send guards, &c, which has been done. I believe that they will not stay in Bondy more than a few hours, and they will arrive here this evening.

Believe me, &c.

The combination of remonstrance and hospitable challenge prevailed. Blücher grumbled, but the bridge of Jena was saved.

This account of the Campaign of 1815 is told; if not as pleasantly and with as much accuracy as others might tell it, at all events not without care and anxiety on my part to do justice to so important a subject. For all that followed on the occupation of Paris, including the flight of Napoleon, his endeavours to escape to America, and his final surrender to Captain Maitland of the *Bellerophon*, belong to a wider province than that on which, for the present, I have entered.

The same thing may be said of the condition of France and of its inhabitants during the years of its occupation by a portion of the armies which had conquered it. Doubtless the vanity of a sensitive people received many deep wounds at the period of which we are speaking. The removal of the Car of Victory to Berlin, whence it had been taken, of the Horses of St. Mark, and the rich treasures of the Louvre, could not fail of occasioning much bitterness at the moment. Yet, as the proceeding was dictated by the purest principles of justice, there is probably no right-minded Frenchman living who would now raise his voice against it.

So also in regard to the quartering, throughout a series of years, of foreign troops in the most important of the French fortresses; no measure less stringent seemed to afford a hope of permanent repose to Europe; and that it was as wisely arranged as honourably fulfilled on both sides, the continuance of a thirty years' peace has shown. Moreover, whatever may have been the irregularities of which, on their first arrival in the country, some of the allied troops were guilty, the bitterest enemies of the Restoration will allow that these were soon put a stop to. Indeed, in this as in other respects, the Duke showed himself not less wise in council than gallant in fight.

His letters and dispatches are full of complaints of the lax discipline which prevailed among some of his allies—his orders show that he would permit no such laxity to prevail in the ranks of British regiments; and the consequence was, that till the clemency of the victor produced, as it is apt to do, unbecoming insolence in the vanquished, the French people regarded the soldiers of England as their best protectors against violence from other quarters.

On the 30th of November, 1815, the Duke of Wellington addressed to the allied army, which had fought under him at Waterloo and marched with triumph into Paris, a valedictory order. The several corps that were not required to complete the contingent which England had engaged to furnish, forthwith returned to their respective countries. The Austrians, the Russians, the troops of the minor German states, were already gone; and a large portion of the army of Prussia had departed in like manner.

There now remained only 150,000 men, of which, though composed of the troops of various nations, his Grace assumed the command. These, as is well known, retained a military possession of France till the King's government seemed to have taken root, and the institutions of the country were consolidated; after which they, in their turn, broke up, and peace was restored to Europe.—*Esto perpetua!*

ALSO FROM LEONAUR
AVAILABLE IN SOFTCOVER OR HARDCOVER WITH DUST JACKET

CAPTAIN OF THE 95th (Rifles) *by Jonathan Leach*—An officer of Wellington's Sharpshooters during the Peninsular, South of France and Waterloo Campaigns of the Napoleonic Wars.

BUGLER AND OFFICER OF THE RIFLES *by William Green & Harry Smith* With the 95th (Rifles) during the Peninsular & Waterloo Campaigns of the Napoleonic Wars

BAYONETS, BUGLES AND BONNETS *by James 'Thomas' Todd*—Experiences of hard soldiering with the 71st Foot - the Highland Light Infantry - through many battles of the Napoleonic wars including the Peninsular & Waterloo Campaigns

THE ADVENTURES OF A LIGHT DRAGOON *by George Farmer & G.R. Gleig*—A cavalryman during the Peninsular & Waterloo Campaigns, in captivity & at the siege of Bhurtpore, India

THE COMPLEAT RIFLEMAN HARRIS *by Benjamin Harris as told to & transcribed by Captain Henry Curling*—The adventures of a soldier of the 95th (Rifles) during the Peninsular Campaign of the Napoleonic Wars

WITH WELLINGTON'S LIGHT CAVALRY *by William Tomkinson*—The Experiences of an officer of the 16th Light Dragoons in the Peninsular and Waterloo campaigns of the Napoleonic Wars.

SURTEES OF THE RIFLES *by William Surtees*—A Soldier of the 95th (Rifles) in the Peninsular campaign of the Napoleonic Wars.

ENSIGN BELL IN THE PENINSULAR WAR *by George Bell*—The Experiences of a young British Soldier of the 34th Regiment 'The Cumberland Gentlemen' in the Napoleonic wars.

WITH THE LIGHT DIVISION *by John H. Cooke*—The Experiences of an Officer of the 43rd Light Infantry in the Peninsula and South of France During the Napoleonic Wars

NAPOLEON'S IMPERIAL GUARD: FROM MARENGO TO WATERLOO *by J. T. Headley*—This is the story of Napoleon's Imperial Guard from the bearskin caps of the grenadiers to the flamboyance of their mounted chasseurs, their principal characters and the men who commanded them.

BATTLES & SIEGES OF THE PENINSULAR WAR *by W. H. Fitchett*—Corunna, Busaco, Albuera, Ciudad Rodrigo, Badajos, Salamanca, San Sebastian & Others

AVAILABLE ONLINE AT **www.leonaur.com**
AND OTHER GOOD BOOK STORES

ALSO FROM LEONAUR
AVAILABLE IN SOFTCOVER OR HARDCOVER WITH DUST JACKET

WELLINGTON AND THE PYRENEES CAMPAIGN VOLUME I: FROM VITORIA TO THE BIDASSOA *by F. C. Beatson*—The final phase of the campaign in the Iberian Peninsula.

WELLINGTON AND THE INVASION OF FRANCE VOLUME II: THE BIDASSOA TO THE BATTLE OF THE NIVELLE *by F. C. Beatson*—The second of Beatson's series on the fall of Revolutionary France published by Leonaur, the reader is once again taken into the centre of Wellington's strategic and tactical genius.

WELLINGTON AND THE FALL OF FRANCE VOLUME III: THE GAVES AND THE BATTLE OF ORTHEZ *by F. C. Beatson*—This final chapter of F. C. Beatson's brilliant trilogy shows the 'captain of the age' at his most inspired and makes all three books essential additions to any Peninsular War library.

NAVAL BATTLES OF THE NAPOLEONIC WARS *by W. H. Fitchett*—Cape St. Vincent, the Nile, Cadiz, Copenhagen, Trafalgar & Others

SERGEANT GUILLEMARD: THE MAN WHO SHOT NELSON? *by Robert Guillemard*—A Soldier of the Infantry of the French Army of Napoleon on Campaign Throughout Europe

WITH THE GUARDS ACROSS THE PYRENEES *by Robert Batty*—The Experiences of a British Officer of Wellington's Army During the Battles for the Fall of Napoleonic France, 1813.

A STAFF OFFICER IN THE PENINSULA *by E. W. Buckham*—An Officer of the British Staff Corps Cavalry During the Peninsula Campaign of the Napoleonic Wars

THE LEIPZIG CAMPAIGN: 1813—NAPOLEON AND THE "BATTLE OF THE NATIONS" *by F. N. Maude*—Colonel Maude's analysis of Napoleon's campaign of 1813.

BUGEAUD: A PACK WITH A BATON by *Thomas Robert Bugeaud*—The Early Campaigns of a Soldier of Napoleon's Army Who Would Become a Marshal of France.

TWO LEONAUR ORIGINALS

SERGEANT NICOL by *Daniel Nicol*—The Experiences of a Gordon Highlander During the Napoleonic Wars in Egypt, the Peninsula and France.

WATERLOO RECOLLECTIONS by *Frederick Llewellyn*—Rare First Hand Accounts, Letters, Reports and Retellings from the Campaign of 1815.

AVAILABLE ONLINE AT **www.leonaur.com**
AND OTHER GOOD BOOK STORES

ALSO FROM LEONAUR
AVAILABLE IN SOFTCOVER OR HARDCOVER WITH DUST JACKET

THE JENA CAMPAIGN: 1806 by *F. N. Maude*—The Twin Battles of Jena & Auerstadt Between Napoleon's French and the Prussian Army.

PRIVATE O'NEIL by *Charles O'Neil*—The recollections of an Irish Rogue of H. M. 28th Regt.—The Slashers— during the Peninsula & Waterloo campaigns of the Napoleonic wars.

ROYAL HIGHLANDER by *James Anton*—A soldier of H.M 42nd (Royal) Highlanders during the Peninsular, South of France & Waterloo Campaigns of the Napoleonic Wars.

CAPTAIN BLAZE by *Elzéar Blaze*—Elzéar Blaze recounts his life and experiences in Napoleon's army in a well written, articulate and companionable style.

LEJEUNE VOLUME 1 by *Louis-François Lejeune*—The Napoleonic Wars through the Experiences of an Officer on Berthier's Staff.

LEJEUNE VOLUME 2 by *Louis-François Lejeune*—The Napoleonic Wars through the Experiences of an Officer on Berthier's Staff.

FUSILIER COOPER by *John S. Cooper*—Experiences in the 7th (Royal) Fusiliers During the Peninsular Campaign of the Napoleonic Wars and the American Campaign to New Orleans.

CAPTAIN COIGNET by *Jean-Roch Coignet*—A Soldier of Napoleon's Imperial Guard from the Italian Campaign to Russia and Waterloo.

FIGHTING NAPOLEON'S EMPIRE by *Joseph Anderson*—The Campaigns of a British Infantryman in Italy, Egypt, the Peninsular & the West Indies During the Napoleonic Wars.

CHASSEUR BARRES by *Jean-Baptiste Barres*—The experiences of a French Infantryman of the Imperial Guard at Austerlitz, Jena, Eylau, Friedland, in the Peninsular, Lutzen, Bautzen, Zinnwald and Hanau during the Napoleonic Wars.

MARINES TO 95TH (RIFLES) by *Thomas Fernyhough*—The military experiences of Robert Fernyhough during the Napoleonic Wars.

HUSSAR ROCCA by *Albert Jean Michel de Rocca*—A French cavalry officer's experiences of the Napoleonic Wars and his views on the Peninsular Campaigns against the Spanish, British And Guerilla Armies.

SERGEANT BOURGOGNE by *Adrien Bourgogne*—With Napoleon's Imperial Guard in the Russian Campaign and on the Retreat from Moscow 1812 - 13.

AVAILABLE ONLINE AT **www.leonaur.com**
AND OTHER GOOD BOOK STORES

www.ingramcontent.com/pod-product-compliance
Lightning Source LLC
Chambersburg PA
CBHW030217170426
43201CB00006B/119